Group Captain Peter Townsend, DSO, DFC and bar, CVO, was born in 1914 of a military family and served in the RAF from 1939 to 1944 with great distinction. Appointed an equerry to King George VI in 1944, he served in the royal household for eight years, a position which gave him a unique close-up view of the historical events described in *The Last Emperor*. After the end of his much-publicized relationship with Princess Margaret, he toured the world in a Land-Rover and wrote a book about his travels, *Earth, My Friend*. He is also the author of a book about the Battle of Britain, *Duel of Eagles*. His autobiography, *Time and Chance*, was published recently. Now married with three teenage children, Peter Townsend lives in a converted eighteenth-century farmhouse some thirty miles from Paris

Also by Peter Townsend

Earth, My Friend
Duel of Eagles
Time and Chance: An Autobiography

Peter Townsend

The Last Emperor

Decline and Fall of the British Empire

PANTHER
GRANADA PUBLISHING
London Toronto Sydney New York

Published by Granada Publishing Limited
in Panther Books 1978

ISBN 0 586 03804 3

First published in Great Britain by
Weidenfeld and Nicolson 1975
Copyright © Peter Townsend 1975

Granada Publishing Limited
Frogmore, St Albans, Herts AL2 2NF
and
3 Upper James Street, London W1R 4BP
1221 Avenue of the Americas, New York, NY 10020, USA
117 York Street, Sydney, NSW 2000, Australia
100 Skyway Avenue, Toronto, Ontario, Canada M9W 3A6
Trio City, Coventry Street, Johannesburg 2001, South Africa
CML Centre, Queen & Wyndham, Auckland 1, New Zealand

Made and printed in Great Britain by
Richard Clay (The Chaucer Press) Ltd
Bungay, Suffolk
Set in Linotype Baskerville

ACKNOWLEDGEMENT

The author and publisher are grateful to the following
for their kind permission to reproduce the illustrations
in this book: Her Majesty the Queen, Associated Press,
Bassano and Vandyk Studios, Central Zionist Archives,
Jerusalem, Conway Picture Library, India Office Library,
Keystone Press, *Pakistan Quarterly*, Paul Popper, Press
Association, Radio Times Hulton Picture Library.

Contents

Illustrations

King-Emperor George v and Queen Mary (*by gracious permission of Her Majesty the Queen*)

Queen Victoria with the Prince and Princess of Wales (*Bassano & Vandyk Studios*)

Edward VIII (*Radio Times Hulton Picture Library*)

George VI and Queen Elizabeth (*Radio Times Hulton Picture Library*)

Winston Churchill (*Keystone Press*)

Lord Pethwick Lawrence with Mahatma Gandhi, 1946 (*India Office Library*)

Indian leaders Nehru and Jinnah in 1946 (*India Office Library*)

Lord Mountbatten, Viceroy of India, announces to leaders of the Congress and the League in 1947 the British plan to transfer power to two new dominions, India and Pakistan (*Pakistan Quarterly*)

Clement Attlee (*Conway Picture Library*)

Moslem refugees preparing to flee from the New Delhi area after the partition of India and Pakistan (*Associated Press*)

Eamon de Valera as commandant of the Irish Volunteers at Boland's mills

The General Post Office in Dublin after the Rebellion had ended in April 1916 (*Press Association*)

Aung San, Vice President of the Burmese government, with Pandit Nehru (*Keystone Press*)

A boat carrying 'illegal immigrants' into Israel, captured by the British in 1946 (*Central Zionist Archives, Jerusalem*)

The Grand Mufti of Jerusalem (*Paul Popper*)

Ben Gurion with President Weizmann and Dr James MacDonald, US Ambassador, in 1951 (*Weidenfeld and Nicolson Archives*)

Foreword

One day early in December 1936, I landed with the rest of my squadron at the grass-covered field of Singapore's airbase, Seletar. We had just completed a 'colonial development flight', a 9,000-mile odyssey which had taken us, cruising at 100 mph, across Burma and India to the foot of the Himalayas.

I was twenty-one, and the flight to Burma had a special meaning for me: I was returning, for the first time, to the land of my birth. My father (and his father before him) had spent most of his life there and in India, a servant of the Imperial Crown. Born and raised as I was in the imperialist camp, it never occurred to me that there might be anything wrong, least of all (as some objected) immoral or degrading, about the British King-Emperor ruling over a quarter of the globe and the five hundred million people, mostly foreigners, living therein. On the contrary, I was proud to follow the family tradition and leave home to serve the King-Emperor in some far-flung outpost of his empire. Singapore was then ten days' flying from London; Britain was a land of hope and glory, mistress of the seas, and no one seriously believed that the sun would ever set on the British Empire. The griefs and the insults of the 'natives', whom we fondly took for our grateful protégés, had not yet raised any serious doubts – at least in the minds of us young defenders of empire.

Yet now that my squadron's empire-building flight was over and we had time to look at the papers, we read of portentous events at home. The King-Emperor Edward VIII was about to abdicate in favour of his brother, soon to become George VI. Nothing would have seemed less likely to me in far-off Singapore than that I should one day serve the new King-Emperor in a personal capacity, as one of his equerries. I was to become one of his personal aides, a relatively humble job but one which brought me into close attachment with him and his family. The job came to me out of the blue; the King had asked for nominees among the Royal Navy and the RAF to supplement those invariably chosen from the élite regiments of the Household Brigade. I was chosen, I suppose, principally because I had led a fighter squadron in the Battle of Britain and (by several miracles) survived and because my record was otherwise irreproachable.

The term Equerry-in-Waiting is self-explanatory; I was to wait, very willingly but sometimes, it seemed, interminably, upon the pleasure of His Majesty. My immediate colleague was the lady-in-waiting, a distinguished and invariably amiable lady who waited similarly upon the Queen. At a superior level were the King's three private secretaries, who, in a degree varying with their importance, were the personal and political advisers and executives of the monarch. Other top executives were the Master of the Household, who took care of the domestic staff, supply and official entertainment; the Keeper of the Privy Purse, the King's financial director; and the Crown Equerry, responsible for transport, both horse-drawn and motorized.

When in 1944 I joined his household, he wrote his name George VI, *Rex et Imperator*. Three years later, the royal signature was shortened to George R. The King had ceased to be Emperor; the British imperial line, founded in power and splendour by the Queen-Empress Victoria, had been abruptly extinguished.

The story behind this historical phenomenon which I have told here is not meant to be a work of history. I have told it as it appears to me – an immense and moving human drama involving at once the struggle of millions of people for liberty and independence, and the struggle of one man – the last Emperor – with himself and with a crushing load of adversity. The *décor* is full of amazing contrasts, ranging from the splendid imperial parades, the wild rejoicing in the Empire's glory, in its capital, London, to the corpse-strewn streets of Calcutta, its second city; from the steaming Burmese jungle to the misty bogs of Ireland; from Whitehall to Washington; from Hitler's satanic extermination camps to the terror-ridden Holy Land. All sorts and conditions of men are involved: kings and princes, their statesmen and their subjects – loyal, rebellious, prosperous, starving; black and white, Jew and Gentile; Asiatic and Anglo-Saxon; Christian, Buddhist, Hindu and Muslim. We see men at their best and worst in this wordy, bloody battle for freedom.

During the seventy years between Empress Victoria's acclamation and Emperor George vi's demise, four pillars of Empire – Ireland, India, Burma and Palestine – were dismantled. Utterly foreign to the British in tradition and culture, the people of these lands grew more and more to resent their duty of allegiance to the British King-Emperor. Their struggle for independence gathered momentum under the leadership of some of the most enlightened men of our time: de Valera; Gandhi, Jinnah, Nehru; the youthful Aung San of Burma; Weizmann and Ben Gurion. Yet the fact that these men finally prevailed against the might and prestige of the British Empire was due in no small way to Britain herself who, as an old-timer in the freedom business, was anxious to pass on her experience to others. As a one-time girl member of the Jewish resistance group Haganah said to me, 'Britain was the one country against which a struggle for independence had a chance of succeeding.' It was lucky for the last Emperor's recalcitrant subjects that the British, for all their imperial blunders, understood the subject better than most people.

Prologue

'It is a terrible blow to us all and particularly to poor Bertie.' Thus wrote Queen Mary, the Queen Mother, in her diary for 9 December 1936. She had just heard that her eldest son, King Edward VIII, had decided to abdicate in favour of his brother Albert, Duke of York.

The fateful news had been given to her by the Duke himself. Throughout the four-weeks' crisis he had felt 'like the proverbial sheep being led to the slaughter'. In his mother's presence he had broken down and, in his own words, sobbed like a child. Never did a prince covet less a crown.

On Friday 11 December, that dreadful day, he called it, his brother David ceased to be King Edward VIII. In the evening, the two brothers met for a last talk at David's home, Fort Belvedere, near London. As ex-King, David was at a loss as to what to tell his successor, but he was reassuring.

'You are not going to find this a difficult job at all,' he told his brother.

The new King, however, was far from sure of his ability to tackle the 'job'. Earlier that evening, as he paced the terrace of the Fort with his cousin, Lord Louis Mountbatten, he had suddenly blurted out: 'Dickie, this is terrible. I never wanted it to happen. I am quite unprepared.'

The following afternoon, 12 December, while David sped through France on his way to exile, Bertie was proclaimed King: 'His Most Excellent Majesty George the Sixth by the Grace of God of Great Britain and Ireland and of the British Dominions beyond the Seas, King, Defender of the Faith, Emperor of India.'

The new King-Emperor was to be the central figure, and the mutest, of a long and massive struggle in the cause of human freedom. A struggle of which his empire was the vast arena. Of British kings he would be of the bravest and best; of emperors, the last.

1

The First Empress

Exactly sixty years before the accession of George VI as King-Emperor, his great-grandmother, Queen Victoria, was herself involved in a controversy which, although happily not of such a tragic kind, provoked heated and widespread discussion.

By 1876 Benjamin Disraeli had, in his own words, and for the second time, climbed to the top of the greasy pole. He had again become prime minister to Queen Victoria, the only legitimate child of Edward, Duke of Kent. She was then fifty-seven, had reigned for thirty-nine years, and was the ruler of an empire which her prime minister himself called 'peculiar – I know no example of it, either in ancient or modern history'. It was in fact the greatest empire the world had ever known and was still ripe for expansion. Despite this, its undisputed ruler, Victoria, did not boast the title empress, a title which, although certainly her due, was by most Englishmen considered as vulgar, pretentious, and, as personified by Bonaparte, the Tsar and the German emperor, essentially continental and thoroughly repugnant to British tastes.

But Disraeli had serious reasons for deciding in 1876 to invest Queen Victoria with the prestigious title Empress of India. His intention was that it should symbolize India's special status and personalize Her Majesty's relations with her Indian subjects (who accounted for over three-quarters of her entire empire's population). Victoria would become 'Sovereign over Sovereign Princes', a title which would have looked very grand had not the Indian princes in question been put by one authority 'at the utmost on a level with the Duke of Argyll, chiefs of great clans'. Disraeli, however, argued that some of them had ancestors who were independent princes at a time when Britain was a mere colony of Rome.

The Opposition's main objection to the new title was that it ignored the rest of Victoria's colonial territories.

In 1876, Canada, Australia, New Zealand and South
Africa were settled with whites, most of British stock, so
that they had the closest, if not the most ancient, ties with
the mother country. The colonists were sensitive and felt
in no way inferior to a British-born subject. On the contrary, said Mr Simon MP, they gloried in the fact of being
Englishmen, and claimed all the rights and all the consideration of Englishmen at home.

Gladstone, leader of the Opposition, in his deep, sonor-
ous voice, declared that the Government had shown great
indiscretion in ignoring the colonies. Empress was a title
'that went to impair the dignity and lustre of the Crown',
and he hoped that there would be no further attempts
to 'patch and mend, I would almost say tinker, the royal
title'.

Disraeli's sympathies were all for the colonial empire,
which he had always tried to consolidate. But the relations between Britain and the colonies on the one hand
and with India on the other were totally different. India
should have its Empress.

If in Parliament the atmosphere was fairly restrained,
it was far from so among Victoria's loyal subjects, who
aired their opinions freely in the newspapers and in noisy
meetings up and down the country. At a crowded gathering at Horn's Tavern, Kennington, someone asked,
amidst cheers and hisses:

'What is an emperor?'

'Despotism,' answered a voice from the audience; there
was no title superior to queen; it was a symbol of
righteous government and civil liberty.

At a noisy meeting presided over by the Mayor of
Manchester, it was resolved, among loud cheers and hoot-
ing, that the title of empress was 'prejudicial to the dignity of the Crown, repugnant to the national sentiment,
injurious ... to the British Empire'.

The country, both on the platform and in the press,
were certainly more outspoken than their elected representatives in Parliament. And Mr Gladstone, in a
letter to *The Times*, was decidedly more trenchant than

he had ever been on the front bench of the Opposition. Her Majesty, he wrote, was not justified in assuming the title of empress, 'neither does the solid gold of the time-consecrated crown of England's monarchs require the fictitious and tawdry lustre conferred by this modern and shallow gilding'.

In another letter, 'Anglo-Indian' mentioned that some-one had complained to him that the Indians could not pronounce 'queen', and quoted the example of a certain Honourable Colonel Campbell, whose Indian staff called him 'Unrumble-tum-cumble-sahib'. But surely, protested 'Anglo-Indian', a people who could shout 'Qui-hi' could get their tongues round the word queen.

The Times demolished the claim 'that the natives of India are burning with a wild desire' to see the Queen made empress with the comment: 'A non-existent title, referring to a non-existent state, bestowed gratis by an Englishman ... is the quaintest indication of the wishes of the natives of India.'

On behalf of 'the natives', Pandit Chandra Mukerjea Vidyaratna wrote: 'The title must be an Indian one, and not Sultani, Padshahi, Shahi, etc.,' for 'anything savouring of a Mohammedan title would wake in the Hindu mind bitter recollections of Mohammedan misrule from which England, by the kindness of Providence, delivered us.'

However, an Indian Muslim, Mr Hakim, argued that it was the Muslims who had first given a foothold to the British in India. Mr Hakim preferred 'queen', purely and simply. 'The present desire of the Queen', he wrote, 'to compliment and honour the dusky millions of your fellow-subjects in Hindostan, the most ancient country in the world, will go an immense length ... to crowning the fabric of affection and loyalty to the Throne.'

None of these imaginative arguments overcame the basic objection: empress or emperor, the title was ob-noxious to Englishmen. It suggested not good rulers but, as *The Spectator* said, conquering, oppressive voluptu-aries. It had been 'vulgarized by Muscovite and Corsican'.

It would be a pity to spoil the simple grandeur of the title queen by adding a title which, to the British mind, was associated with '*parvenu* personages and with Asiatic modes of expressing reverence'.

In this spate of chauvinistic outpourings it was *The Spectator* which came closest to the heart of the matter. 'We could fain hope that Her Majesty will ponder well. Is she willing to accept a dignity which ... her descendants must admit to be fairly within the right of Parliament to cancel?'

The Queen had pondered, the people had protested and Parliament had voted. And so Victoria, by act of Parliament (not by the grace of God) became the first Empress of India. No one could honestly deny her right to the title, since she was the head of the greatest empire in history. It was just that the homely Englishman who loved his queen was embarrassed by so foreign and high-sounding a title. And there was not a soul who regretted the new title more than Monsieur Lemoinne, of Paris. He remarked: 'The Queen was undisputed, indisputable Queen; she becomes a *parvenue* Empress.'

The accession of the Empress Victoria to the throne of the Moguls was proclaimed at Delhi, their ancient capital, on 1 January 1877. During the week which preceded the great day, the Viceroy, Lord Lytton – better known as a poet than as a public figure – had been working overtime receiving and returning the visits of some sixty Indian princes, who were condescendingly referred to as 'native chiefs'.

The top-ranking chiefs, with their magnificent carriages and escorts, contrasted with the petty hill rajahs with their shabby vehicles and ragged following, some dressed in cast-off British uniform, others jingling in mediæval chain armour. All the splendour and squalor of the East were present in this visitation.

Of all the Viceroy's visitors, the Khan of Kalat was the most impressive, with his tall and powerful sirdars, wild-looking men from Baluchistan. They were at first persuaded with difficulty from purloining forks and knives from their place at table and from drawing their swords when politely asked to respect camp rules.

In the exchange of presents, the Khan came off better than anyone: a gold medal from the Empress, a jewelled sword from the Viceroy, and – a last-minute surprise – a magnificent elephant.

The 'chiefs of higher rank' were appointed 'Counsellors to the Empress', but this, as *The Times* blandly remarked, meant practically nothing. The Maharajahs of Kashmir and Scindiah were made generals in the British army (with the careful proviso that they would never command British troops). The crowning gift to all the 'greater chiefs' was a beautifully worked banner. Above it gleamed the imperial crown and the Star of India, the latter with its legend 'Heaven's light my guide', which was supposed to epitomize the spirit of British imperial rule. Each of these magnificent memorial standards was inscribed 'From Victoria, Empress of India. 1st January 1877'. The great ceremony was timed for 12.30 pm on that date.

It took place near Delhi. The dirt roads which led to the amphitheatre were that morning jammed with a motley assortment of camel carriages, tongas and palanquins, gorgeously caparisoned elephants with their gilded howdahs, and a vast multitude on foot, clad in every colour. Across the hot dry plain came marching regiments of British infantry, weapons glistening and bands playing, while in the same long cortège could be seen, superbly mounted, a squadron of Punjab cavalry prancing alongside the shabby retinue of some minor chief as it shambled along, bearing a weird assortment of blunderbusses, halberds and swords. To an English observer there came a faint reminder of Epsom Downs on Derby Day.

An amphitheatre had been erected for the ceremony north of the Viceroy's camp. In the centre of the amphitheatre rose a dais emblazoned with the royal arms and the imperial crown. Above stretched a red, white and gold canopy, on top of which was perched, on a small cushion, the imperial crown. The lower part of the canopy was embroidered with the arms of England, Scotland and Ireland – far-away countries lost in the mists of winter.

The 'native chiefs' were also protected by a canopy, but distinctly more sombre in tone. Outside the arena were arrayed the princely troops, infantry, cavalry, and a hundred elephants, their howdahs and trappings glittering with gold, their tusks ringed with brass and their foreheads daubed with paint. The British regiments of foot and their massed bands, flanked by artillery, completed the superb spectacle.

At last the Viceroy arrived, wearing the light blue and silver robes of the order of the Star of India. The Chief Herald, Mr Barnes, who in his many-coloured tabard was 'far the most gorgeous person present', read the proclamation, and this part of the proceedings ended with a somewhat ineffective flourish of trumpets.

As the royal standard was unfurled, artillery began firing the hundred and one crashing salvoes of the imperial salute and a *feu de joie* crackled down the first long line of infantry and back along the rear rank. It was a relief that the guns failed to go off all at once. As it was, their rolling thunder spread panic among the mounted contingents. Elephants and camels stampeded, horses reared and bolted, and several onlookers were trampled beneath the wild rush of terrified animals. When they had been coaxed back to their places, the Viceroy rose to speak. It was the calm after the storm: his voice was scarely audible.

The poet-Viceroy did – on Victoria's behalf – convey some warm truths to the great gathering of princes, potentates and people. They were secure in the protection of the imperial power. The Empress gave a solemn promise to use her great power for the good of the people and to respect the rights of her feudatory princes. This was why the title Empress of India seemed fitting as a symbol unifying the Crown with India. But, she told them, as a price for this gracious gift, she claimed the loyal allegiance of the Indian people – all two hundred and fifty million of them.

It would be too hasty a judgement to say that Victoria had by far the best of the bargain. Her suzerainty was by no means a worthless gift. While the great Tamerlane's dynasty, sapped by bloodshed and and intestine broils (as the Viceroy said), had crumbled to decay, while strife and anarchy had hitherto denied internal peace to India, under the law-giving Victoria, successor to the decadent Moguls, all races and creeds and every subject of Her Majesty could live in peace.

Victoria's 'native subjects' were told that it was in India's own interest that her affairs were run by Englishmen. It was, after all, to English statesmen that India owed her progress towards civilization. Englishmen must for a long time form the channel through which the arts and the influence of the West must flow towards the East 'for the benefit of its children'.

And so with superb self-assurance Victoria proposed herself in the role of Lady Bountiful to her millions of Indian subjects. But she would be only too pleased to have their help in running the country. 'You natives of India ...' said her Viceroy, 'have a recognized claim to share largely with your English fellow-subjects in the administration of the country you inhabit', [to have said 'your country' would having been admitting too much]. Loyalty, incorruptibility, impartiality, truth and courage were the qualities needed. Wherever Victoria ruled, she trusted less to force than to the allegiance of a contented and united people.

With the enunciation of these lofty principles, the reign of the first Empress began.

The next landmark in the Empress's rise to the summit of her imperial power was her Golden Jubilee in 1887. The British, while not entirely sure of their strength – immense though it was – nor of their imperial mission, bolstered up their feelings to the tune of a popular music-hall ditty:

'We don't want to fight, but by Jingo if we do,
We've got the ships, we've got the men, we've
    got the money too.'

In this spirit, the aggrandizement of Victoria's empire continued steadily, although not always smoothly.

With the Khan of Kalat, she had made a new treaty. In neighbouring Afghanistan – where the Empress had no business at all, were it not that the Russians were darkly intriguing there against her empire. and her envoy and his escort had just been murdered – she quite simply occupied the capital, Kabul. The British army then discreetly withdrew within the borders of the Indian empire, a move which infuriated Victoria, who took a bellicose view of the Afghan affair. 'The Queen', she complained, 'has never before been treated with such want of respect.'

In South Africa, beneath the towering *kopje* of Isandhlwana, nearly a thousand of her soldiers had been surprised and massacred before breakfast by ten times that number of Cetywayo's fierce Zulus (one of the reasons for the disaster was that the British could not find the screwdrivers needed to open the ammunition boxes). Cetywayo's Zulu impis were duly defeated and this erring people who had so brashly defied Britannia were then clasped to her broad bosom with the object of staying them from further outrages against the land-hungry but apprehensive Boers.

With the same end in view, the land of the Bechuanas (now Botswana) was added to Victoria's territories – this time without a shot being fired. A few years earlier, Victoria's men (thirty-three of them) had marched into the Boer republic of the Transvaal and made it hers. But the rugged Boers turned, and in a brief but bloody campaign ousted the *rooi-neks*, as they chaffingly called Victoria's pink-faced soldiers, and regained their freedom. Victoria had commented bitterly on 'this cruel civil war ... the Boers being my subjects'. But this was not exactly how the Boer *Oudstryders* saw things.

At the other end of Africa, Victoria had a firm grip on Egypt. Her soldiers, under General Wolseley, had crushed the rebel Arabi Pasha at Tel-el-Kebir, her businessmen had, at the expense of the French, strengthened their hold on the Suez Canal Company; and her statesmen had put an end to the dual Anglo-French control of the country. These high-handed and low-dealing moves had naturally left the French feeling sulky. But Victoria's new pro-consul, Evelyn Baring (like Disraeli, a Jew), had already begun an enlightened rule which was to create in Egypt the foundations of a modern state.

Down south in the Sudan there occurred a disaster which saddened, and maddened, the Empress. The fanatical hordes of the Mahdi Abdullah had closed in on Khartoum where General 'Chinese' Gordon and his men were holding out against hopeless odds. Despite Victoria's urgent warnings, Gordon and his men suffered a heroic but ghastly fate. Glad as the soldiers of the Queen-Empress were to die for her in the far-flung out-posts of her empire, she herself was sad and indignant that they should do so on account of a bunch of bungling bureaucrats at home. She openly rebuked those responsible.

East of Suez, the Indian Empire had gained a fair province. While the Russians intrigued with the Afghan amirs, in Burma – the Golden Land – the French sought to frustrate British trade by scheming with the weakling King Thibaw and his cruel, ambitious wife, Supayalet. The crisis came when Thibaw levied a hefty fine on the Bombay Burmah Corporation for poaching timber from the king's reserves. Wrathful, Britannia sent an ulti-matum, followed by ten thousand soldiers. General Harry Prendergast led them to Mandalay, where he informed Thibaw that Victoria would in future rule Burma.

So Burma became part of Her Majesty's dominions. Soon the Golden Land would become part, also, of India – an error of judgement by the British, for the freedom-loving Burmese strongly objected to being part of any other country, most of all India. Britain was already bad

enough. As a Burmese minister put it, the Burmese
wrote on black paper, the British on white; as a token
of respect the British took off their hats, the Burmese
took off their shoes; the British stood up, the Burmese
knelt down in deference to another. How could Britain
ever hit it off with a people so different?

Much in the news as Victoria's Golden Jubilee approached was Ireland, the pitiable fief of English kings
since their French-born ancestor, Henry II, conquered it
and bequeathed it and its so far insoluble problems to his
successors. Ireland was no place for the heroics and self-
sacrifice that Englishmen were prepared for elsewhere in
the empire. It was a festering sore in the imperial body.
An observer remarked that Ireland was 'not only the most
distressful country in Europe, but in the whole wide
world'.

However a star, as yet unnoticed, had just risen on Ireland's troubled horizon. In the year of Victoria's Golden
Jubilee, there lived at Buree, County Limerick, in a
labourer's cottage rented for ten pence a week, a little
boy, Eamon de Valera. Born in New York, the son of an
Irish mother and a Spanish father, Eamon had been sent
to live with his uncle, Pat Coll, in Ireland. One day
Eamon fell down a ladder and lay stunned on the floor
until discovered by his grandmother. He faintly heard her
ask: 'Is he dead?' Fortunately, for Ireland, he was not.

Other stars, too, were rising, although not all had yet
moved into conjunction with the star of British imperialism. In 1885, two years before Queen Victoria's Golden
Jubilee, a Jewish boy of eleven had written a letter in
which he said that England alone might one day help that
persecuted race to return to its ancient land, Palestine.
The boy's name was Chaim Weizmann, then an excep-
tionally bright pupil in the high school at Pinsk, in
western Russia. The nationlist feeling expressed by the
youthful Chaim had been growing ever since the terrible
pogroms, initiated by Tsar Alexander III, had begun four
years earlier in the town of Elizabethgrad.

As in Ireland, mass emigration to America provided the

Jews with one means of escape from death and ruin. Another solution was that sought by Hibbath Zion, the Lovers of Zion, who believed that in Palestine, the spiritual home of the Jews, a Jewish nation should be created. A year after young Chaim Weizmann had written his letter about England helping the Jews, a son was born, in the Polish town of Plonsk, to Sheindal, wife of Avigdor Green. Avigdor lived in the Jewish pale of settlement and was a fervent missionary of the Lovers of Zion. Of her little boy, Sheindal said: 'The whole world will call him great.'

Chaim and David (who would later change his surname to Ben Gurion), those sons of Pinsk and Plonsk – towns whose names if ever pronounced, would have sounded strangely in London, hub of the British Empire – were destined one day to be the leading figures in a sad chapter of that empire's history.

In far-away Karachi, during the year of Victoria's Golden Jubilee, one of the pupils at the Sind Madrasah High School (its motto was 'Enter to learn, go forth to serve') was an eleven-year-old boy, Mohammed Ali Jinnah. Already, it was said, an astrologer had told him: 'You will grow up to be a king.' He was a studious boy, and learned English in school; in fact he never learned to speak any other language.

Not more than a few hundred miles from Jinnah's home in Karachi, there lived, in Porbandar, in the golden year 1887, an eighteen-year-old Hindu boy. His name was Mohandas Karamchand Gandhi. Although his father had been prime minister in Porbandar, Gandhi's people had long ago been grocers.* Mohandas was already a father, having been married at thirteen to a girl, Kasturbai, of the same age. Because of his 'devouring passion' for Kasturbai, young Mohandas lost a good year's work at school.

But Mohandas had another devouring passion – for truth. One of his school friends told him: 'We are a weak people because we don't eat meat,' and he recited a Gujerati rhyme:

* Gandhi means 'grocer'.

Behold the mighty Englishman
He rules the Indian small
Because being a meat-eater
He is five cubits tall.

So, surreptitiously, Gandhi became a meat-eater. But the thought that this meant deceiving his parents was too much for him and he soon gave it up.

At one stage Mohandas took to stealing cigarettes. Then he wrote a confession to his father, who forgave him – this was for Mohandas an object-lesson in *ahimsa*, non-violence. 'Only he who is smitten with the arrows of love, knows its power.'

Gandhi sailed for England in 1888, the year following Victoria's Golden Jubilee. No one could then foretell that this eighteen-year-old law student, so prone to fantasy and self-indulgence, would one day cause 'the mighty Englishman' to surrender the great and glorious empire over which Empress Victoria now so securely reigned.

Yet already an instrument was being fashioned – by a British civil servant – which would prove decisive in expelling the British from India and achieving her freedom. Allan Octavian Hume, after his retirement, stayed on in India. Conscious of the rising tide of Indian nationalism, he determined, in the best English liberal tradition, to found an organization which could give it official expression. Hume wrote to the graduates of Calcutta University asking for fifty founder members. The response to his letter led to the founding of the first Indian National Congress in 1885. It declared 'the continual affiliation of India to Great Britain ... to be absolutely essential to the interests of our own National Development.'

By 20 June 1887, Victoria had reigned over Britain and the British Empire for fifty years. The British public could rejoice at the phenomenal expansion of the Empire during this time. The population of British North America had quadrupled; Australia's had increased twenty-five times. British territories in South Africa had doubled. Trade with the colonies had increased from

£55,000,000 at Victoria's coronation to over £400,000,000 at her Jubilee, and India's external trade had risen from £21,000,000 to eight times that figure.

It all looked formidable – on the surface. But the purring and preening covered up some alarming truths. Imports had been exceeding exports for years and as long ago as 1877 – ten years before the Jubilee – the trade deficit was £145,000,000. Worse, Britain was losing her lead in steel production.

Rivals were appearing, too, in the political field. Russia's armed power was growing; Germany's too, thanks to Bismarck, who moreover had colonial ambitions, embarrassing to the British, in Africa and the Pacific. And the French, still sulking over Egypt, were manœuvring uncomfortably close to Victoria's territory along the Niger and the Nile. Briefly, as it was so succinctly put,* Britain was no longer the world's workman, policeman and governess.

It was against this background that Britain, on 22 June 1887, celebrated Victoria's Golden Jubilee. But the Empire was less well represented by its tribal chiefs and its statesmen than were the states of Europe by their extravagantly plumed and decorated potentates, even though the latter were crammed into closed carriages and were almost invisible to the public.

One of the thousands of children who waved a flag that day was a four-year-old boy called Clement Attlee. He lived in a roomy house in Putney. Sixty years later, as Prime Minister to the last Emperor, he would hand India back to the Indians.

Six-year-old Ernie Bevin was probably not even aware of all these goings on in London. He was living in the direst poverty with his widowed mother, Mercy, at Winsford, a village on Exmoor, in Somerset. Mercy lay grievously ill. Soon after, she died, and orphaned Ernest Bevin set out alone on the long road which would lead him to the post of Foreign Minister under the last emperor.

* By Edward Grierson, in *The Imperial Dream* (London, 1972).

No one would have dared prophesy, amidst all these effusions of loyalty for the first Empress, that one of her descendants would relinquish the imperial crown within sixty years.

Victoria's favourite grandson was Prince 'Georgie'. His mother, the Princess of Wales, now wrote to him that the Queen was 'in a terrible fuss about your marrying'. In fact Prince George was showing more concern about the marriage prospects of his brother Eddy, to whom he was devoted, than about his own. He hoped that 'dear Eddy will not marry a German ... it would be so much nicer if he married an English person'. In the event, Eddy had fallen in love with the beautiful Hélène, daughter of the Comte de Paris. But the Pope, with the uncharitable outlook of the time, refused Hélène a dispensation to marry the Protestant prince. Eddy eventually became engaged to Princess Mary of Teck, who although British by birth could hardly by blood have been more German.

There then occurred one of those strokes of fate which was to determine the destiny of the Last Emperor. Prince Eddy contracted pneumonia and died. Thus, by a tragic accident, Prince George became the eventual heir to the imperial crown, a fact which would have dramatic consequences for two of his sons – as yet unborn, for their father was still a bachelor. But Victoria's anxiety on this score was soon to be allayed. One 'lovely day, as hot as summer', in May 1893, sixteen months after Prince Eddy's death, Prince George proposed to the lady who had been his brother's fiancée. Princess Mary and Prince George (now the Duke of York) were married two months later.

Among the guests at the royal wedding was Nicholas, heir to Tsar Alexander III of Russia, Nicholas was to prove a despot, crushing, by means of the Black Hundreds (prototype of Hitler's SS), all opposition to his rule. Their policy was simple – to massacre the Jews. Eighteen-year-old Chaim Weizmann disliked Russia intensely – 'not Russia proper, but Tsarist Russia'. So he decided to

go west, to Germany. Too poor to buy a passport, he
floated down the river on a raft bound for Danzig. Once
across the German border, he made for Pfungstadt,
where he got a seventy-five dollars a year teaching job.
He found himself in a 'marvellous new world ... with a
beating heart'. Sadly, though, he found, too, signs of Jew
hatred everywhere. Disappointed, homesick and over-
worked, he returned to Pinsk. The raft had not proved
an auspicious craft on which to begin his arduous journey towards the first presidency of the State of Israel.

It was in an ocean liner that Mohandas Gandhi set out
full of zest across the waters of the Indian Ocean to
South Africa, towards the first milestone on his way to
fame. The time was April 1893.

Gandhi had spent three years in London, experiment-
ing in the art of living and in the search for truth. Some
time after his arrival, he bought, in a Farringdon Street
restaurant, a copy of Salt's *A Plea for Vegetarianism*.
He then went straight into the dining-room and had his
first hearty meal since arriving. Despite his craving for
meat, he managed to find the will-power to keep the
vow he had made to his mother and stick to a vegetarian
diet. Then he took what he considered to be the necessary
steps to become an English gentleman. He bought new
clothes, a chimney-pot hat and evening dress. He acquired
a gold watch-chain. He took dancing lessons, but 'it was
beyond me to achieve anything like rhythmic motion'.
So, to improve his ear for Western music, he bought a
violin and engaged a teacher. Finally, to perfect his
speech, he purchased Bell's *Standard Elocutionist*. Then,
as he said, Mr Bell rang the bell of alarm. Gandhi suddenly woke up to the fact that he was in London to
study law.

While in London he began to read the Bible. The
Book of Genesis sent him to sleep, but he plodded on.
The Sermon on the Mount went straight to his heart,
especially the verse: 'But I say unto you, that ye resist
not evil ...'

In June 1891 Gandhi was called to the Bar. Two days later he sailed for India. His brother warned him, however, that 'only influence counts here', and Gandhi, like Chaim Weizmann, felt sick, frustrated and longed to leave India. Suddenly the chance came. A Moslem firm, Dada Abdullah, offered him a job in their South African subsidiary.

Gandhi arrived in Durban in 1893. He was immediately dubbed a 'coolie barrister' and repeatedly humiliated. He wondered whether to go back to India or to stay and fight for his and the other Indians' rights. He decided to stay. Overcoming his shyness, he made speeches, wrote pamphlets, held forth in the law courts. He helped to found the Natal Indian Congress, feeling, like Hume, that Indian opinion needed official expression.

In 1896 he sailed back to Calcutta. On the way by train to Rajkot, his home town, he stopped off at Allahabad to call on the editor of the local newspaper, the *Pioneer*. He little dreamed that in a prosperous quarter of that teeming town there lived a Kashmiri boy who would grow up to be his closest disciple and the first prime minister of India, Jawarharlal Nehru. Nehru was then seven.

More articles and pamphlets pleading for the South African Indians flowed from Gandhi's impassioned pen. He threw himself with zest into every activity, whether as inspector of latrines, or as a male nurse, or as a member of the Rajkot committee formed to organize the Queen-Empress's Diamond Jubilee celebrations. 'I vied with Englishmen in loyalty to the throne,' he said later. He learned the National Anthem and taught it to the youngsters of Rajkot. But the second verse jarred badly with his conception of *ahimsa*, non-violence:

> 'Scatter her enemies,
> And make them fall ...

Gandhi was long before his time. Years later, the English themselves would change the offending lines.

Gandhi made contact with the great champions of Indian freedom, Lokamanya Tilak and Gokhale. Tilak was as the ocean, Gokhale as the Ganges – 'one could have a refreshing bath in the holy river'.

Suddenly, in the middle of this whirlwind tour, came a cable from Durban: 'Return soon.' When he landed, he was nearly lynched. An English friend, Mrs Alexander, wife of the Police Superintendent, saved him, bravely holding off the crowd with her parasol. Gandhi's assailants were ordered to be prosecuted. But Gandhi replied: 'I do not want to prosecute anyone.' The seeds of *satyagraha*, non-violent resistance, were germinating. Through it, the vegetarian and saintly little Indian would one day break the power in India of the mighty, meat-eating English.

While Gandhi was musing on *satyagraha*, the means by which he would bring an end to the line of Indian emperors, George, Duke of York, was founding a family which, it was hoped, would ensure its continuity. His first son was born in 1894 – 'a sweet little boy', he called him, although father and son were unfortunately not to remain in such tender relationship. Edward (after Prince Eddy) was the first of his seven names, but the little prince would always be known by the last, David.

Eighteen months later, on 14 December 1895, the birth of a second son created a delicate problem. The date was that of the terrible anniversary, as Queen Victoria called it, when each year she recalled the death, in 1861, of her beloved consort Albert, and, in 1878, of her daughter Alice. The boy's father, her beloved Georgie, was deeply upset, but Victoria gladly agreed that his first name should be Albert. The boy's grandfather (later King Edward VII) had chimed in on a more relaxed note with the remark: 'You might like to call him Bertie.' And so it was as Bertie that David's young brother was to be known within the family. No one on that bleak and 'darkly sad' December day would have said that little Prince Albert would ever become emperor, let alone the last.

* * *

Two weeks after the birth of Prince Albert, there occurred
an event which gave a painful prick to the pride of the
British public. The gold rush in the Transvaal, where
the yellow metal had been discovered ten years earlier,
had swamped the little republic with a riff-raff of fortune-
hunters. In time these *Uitlanders* began to hold out for
their rights, but President Kruger ('Does he ever wash'
asked a visitor, 'or do anything but smoke, drink coffee
and spit?') considered the *Uitlanders* as ungodly invaders.

The situation would not have been dangerous, had not
Cecil Rhodes, multi-millionaire and Prime Minister of
Cape Province, wished to exploit it. Rhodes's dream was
to unite South Africa, from the Cape to the Victoria
Falls, under the British. *'Oom Paul'* Kruger frustrated
this dream. But Rhodes had a plan to overthrow him:
the *Uitlanders* in Johannesburg had only to be incited
to the point of rebellion. The British, with an adequate
armed force, would then move into the capital, Pretoria,
and 'restore order' (a technique later perfected by Hitler).

Rhodes named his friend, Dr Leander Starr Jameson,
as leader of the armed force. They were supplied with
ammunition and stores, including thirty-six cases of champagne. The *Uitlanders* in Johannesburg then became so
jittery that it was clear to all (except Dr Jameson) that
there was not going to be a rebellion. Desperate efforts
were then made to stop 'Dr Jim', but to no avail.

> Then over the Transvaal border,
> And gallop for life or death,

wrote the poet laureate later, in a burst of jingoism,
but with little respect for the facts. Most of Dr Jim's
470 men, undisciplined and poorly armed, were anyhow
incapable of galloping: the champagne had done its
work. At Doornkop, just before Johannesburg, Dr Jameson's raid surrendered to the alert Boers. One of them
remarked that he had always thought the British flag was
red, white and blue, but the only time he had seen it,

it was a dirty white rag.

The British public, their pride stung, looked somehow for a show of strength against the uppish Boers. The moment for it would come, but meanwhile another kind of show, more comfortable and convincing, one which would put Doornkop in the shade, was at hand.

In 1897 Queen Victoria had been on the throne for sixty years. Her Diamond Jubilee was celebrated on 22 June. Young Clement Attlee, now fourteen, was once again there with his flag. He drily described this momentous event in British history as 'an expression of the British Empire at the height of its power and prosperity'. The new poet laureate was more lyrical:

> And panoplied alike for War or Peace
> Victoria's England furroweth yet the foam,
> To harvest Empire, wiser than was Greece,
> Wider than Rome.

The Empire that Britain had harvested during Victoria's sixty years' reign was indeed impressive. India, at the Queen's coronation, was governed by the East India Company, a private trading concern; its ruler now was the august Queen-Empress. On the Dark Continent, chartered companies had been active. The East Africa Company had planted the British flag around the source of the Nile; the British South Africa Company was administering territories about the size of central Europe; the Royal Niger Company, with an area not much less, had brought peace and freedom for the first time to its suffering millions, as a London newspaper called them.

In Canada, the Hudson Bay Company's enormous expanse of territory had now become, within the Canadian Dominion, the provinces of Saskatchewan, Alberta and British Columbia.

Australasia, sixty years before, counted four small colonies and a few scattered settlements. But in the year of Victoria's Diamond Jubilee, Australasia contributed seven colonies to the Empire, whose trade was now worth £13,000,000.

The main celebrations were set for Tuesday, 22 June.

The previous Sunday had been devoted to thanksgiving. Throughout the Empire, the thanks of Victoria's millions of subjects went up to heaven. And not only were thanks given in Christian cathedrals and churches throughout the Empire, but in Moslem mosques, Hindu and Buddhist temples, and pagan shrines. For so great was the adoration of the 'Great White Queen' that many took her for a deity.

Britain and the Empire rejoiced as one. In Malta the bells rang out, in Gibraltar there was a military tattoo and the poor were given a free dinner. In Aden, too, the poor were feasted. Bermuda was brightly decorated and British warships fired a sixty-gun salute.

Even President Kruger rose to the occasion and released two of the Jameson raid men from prison. In Zanzibar the Sultan attended a fête to which Indian residents were invited. On the other side of Africa, Lagos was *en fête* and the 'native rulers' held a durbar. 'Extraordinary enthusiasm' was the keynote. In bilingual Port Louis, Mauritius, a statue of the Queen-Empress was unveiled and Catholics and Protestants together gave thanks.

The Senate in Ottawa, Canada, was decorated with two electric signs: God Save The Queen and *Dieu sauve la Reine*. A hundred local and national societies paraded in Quebec – all but eight of them were French. In Montreal, enthusiasm reached a pitch when, at a military parade, three cheers were called for the Queen. Everywhere old scores were forgotten. In Toronto, two discordant elements, the Orangemen and the Ribbonmen, united to honour the Queen.

In the cities of Australasia, functions in Queen Victoria's honour were mingled with good works. Melbourne gave aborigines special rations and clothing; Adelaide raised funds for a home for children, Brisbane a convalescent home, Perth an industrial school for the blind. In Sydney there were special dinners for destitute people, including lunatics. Somewhat primly, New Zealand voted for a statue of the Queen.

In Rangoon, prayers were offered for the Queen in Christian churches and Buddhist pagodas. But, in neighbouring Bengal and Assam, famine and a disastrous earthquake brought only sorrow to thousands, as the rest of the Empire rejoiced.

Elsewhere in India, in Madras, Lucknow and Hyderabad, in Simla, Patiala and Bombay, the poor were fed and clothed, the children given treats. And in Happy Valley, in far-off Hong Kong, an immense choir of Chinese sang 'God Save the Queen'.

From everywhere outside the Empire came greetings and praise. William McKinley, President of the United States, addressed Victoria as 'great and good friend'. The *New York Times* went further – a bit too far, as it turned out – in these expressions of mutual admiration: 'We are a part', it said, 'of the greater Britain which seems so plainly destined to dominate this planet.'

Homage was done in Paris to 'the Queen who has restored virtue and founded liberty'. The Russian *Official Gazette* complimented the British on taking the lead in statecraft and colonial development. And the *Pester Lloyd* of Vienna marvelled that a nation of forty million were able to rule a scattered empire of three hundred million.

Victoria was first and foremost Queen of the United Kingdom. From its furthest corners, from the far-off Orkneys and the fells of Cumberland to breezy Barnstaple and Babbacombe in the West Country, from Dublin and 'rebel' Cork to Cambridge and Ely in the Fens, Victoria's United Kingdom celebrated with one heart and voice.

The eyes of the whole world were on London, the greatest city on earth. Forty-six thousand troops lined the route which was lavishly decorated with bunting, flags and flowers, and hung with draperies.

The Imperial Service Troops, men from the furthest ends of the Empire, with their bronzed and ebony faces, their multi-coloured uniforms and different races, put the crowd in a state of frenzied enthusiasm. It was as if before their very eyes there passed the might of the Empire – their Empire – and it gave them an immense feeling of pride and and power.

As the seventy-eight-year-old Queen-Empress left the Grand Entrance at Buckingham Palace – that august portal through which pass so many of the great – she pressed a special button and lo! a telegraphed message immediately went forth to her three hundred million subjects: 'From my heart I thank my beloved people. May God bless them.' Then she set off in her state landau, drawn by eight cream horses in spanking new harness of gold and morocco, escorted by a squadron of Indian cavalry, lance-pennants waving. Before the Great White Queen (she was but five feet and four inches in height) there lay a three-hour drive down a ten-mile lane of waving and wildly cheering crowds.

A stately cortège preceded the Queen: the royal and diplomatic guests rode in sixteen carriages, in one of which the Papal Nuncio was seated next to the Emperor of China's envoy, who carried a fan. Next came a glittering cavalcade of forty princes, with plumes nodding and uniforms of every colour under the sun, splayed with decorations.

As the procession passed down St James's Street, through London's clubland, Victoria glanced up to read a sign: Thou art alone the Queen of earthly queens.

On the arrival of the Queen at St Paul's Cathedral, the five-hundred-voice choir burst into the *Te Deum*. The Archbishop of Canterbury intoned a prayer, 'O Lord, we give thee hearty thanks for the many blessings ... during the reign of our Gracious Queen Victoria ...'; and, as the service closed, the Archbishop, throwing etiquette to the winds, called for three cheers for the Queen.

Back at Buckingham Palace this brave and beloved old lady was reported as not having suffered in any way from the fatigue of the day's pageant'.

That night, while 2,500 bonfires blazed on hill tops throughout Britain, London itself was ablaze with illuminations. The Bank of England had contrived a 'gorgeous display' – with the pound supreme it could afford it. Loyal illuminated addresses varied in tone from the sporting, '60 not out – well played!', to the assertive, 'Thy sceptre shows the force of all temporal things.'

At her home at Buckingham Palace that evening, the Queen-Empress presided at a family dinner. The great day was over.

> The echoes of this memorable day,
> Not wholly dumb or fled away,
> Shall still go widening, widening on,
> Till Britain with new fires of Union glow.

All that memorable day, the eighteen-month-old Prince Albert slept and played in his nursery. Forty-nine years later, on 8 June 1946, he was to be the central figure of another great pageant in the streets of London. The occasion was one of deeper significance – the Empire, with its allies, was celebrating the greatest victory ever won by men. Then, in bomb-shattered London, where 'grass is growing to hide the scars where houses stood', the scene was drab and austere. And the rain-soaked flags hung limply down as if to emphasize the fact. Where forty princes on prancing steeds had accompanied the first Empress, only a meagre half-dozen royalties stood at the King-Emperor's side. Gone was the glittering magnificence of the Diamond Jubilee.

'What did we get out of winning? Why this Victory Parade?' mused the poet. 'We've got England, shabby, hungry, but England with a future still ...'

Shabby, hungry? What had happened to that once mighty and prosperous mother country? And to the people who, to the *New York Times*, had seemed so plainly destined to dominate this planet! How did that infant who had slept through the Diamond Jubilee come to be where he now stood, King-Emperor of a yet vaster empire, but one that was already disintegrating about him?

Only a few thoughtful observers saw in the Diamond Jubilee more than a show of the might and majesty of the British Empire, and discerned in it a dreadful warning of the responsibilities and dangers it entailed. Rudyard Kipling was one of them:

> Far-called, our navies melt away;
> On dune and headland sinks the fire:
> Lo, all our pomp of yesterday
> Is one with Nineveh and Tyre ...
> For frantic boast and foolish word –
> They mercy on Thy People, Lord.

But while Kipling was warning the British against 'such boastings as the Gentiles use', the Jews were busy laying the foundations of Zionism, which would one day make British rule in the Holy Land 'one with Nineveh and Tyre'.

In August 1897, two months after London had fêted the Queen-Empress, the first Zionist Congress met in Basle, Switzerland. There, Theodore Herzl, Zionism's prophet, loudly proclaimed the need for a universal settlement of the Jewish problem. Congress resolved that 'the aim of Zionism is to create for the Jewish people a home in Palestine secured by public law'.

The struggle for Zion between Jew and Briton was for later. As the nineteenth century ended, the British were more concerned with paying off old scores. First, for the Mahdi's murder of 'Chinese' Gordon. Outside the capital, in September 1898, General Kitchener wreaked a terrible vengeance on the Mahdi's successor, Khalifa Abdullahi. Young Lieutenant Winston Churhill, of the 21st Lancers, was there, thundering along in the last, devastating cavalry charge in British history. 'At last he is avenged,' screamed a placard at the foot of Gordon's statue in Trafalgar Square.

Hardly had Kitchener achieved his bloody work than he was steaming up the Nile to investigate a report of unidentified foreigners at Fashoda (now Kodok). When it was learned that they were French, with Commandant Marchand in charge, *The Times* observed icily: 'We have interests to protect ... We have not shed British and Egyptian blood in smashing the Khalifa only to be robbed of the fruits by a promenade of eight or nine Frenchmen ...' And the public raised the cry: '*Marchez*, Marchand.' Which is exactly what the commandant did. Warned by Kitchener that he was trespassing, he struck camp and withdrew.

Another score which the British had yet to settle was with the truculent Transvaal Boers, who obstinately objected to being the Queen-Empress's subjects. Both sides prepared for the inevitable showdown. When, on 9 October 1899, Kruger demanded the immediate withdrawal of Her Majesty's forces from the Transvaal borders, the British were indignant. The *Standard* called the Boers 'presumptuous little foes', and *The Times* warned as frigidly as ever: 'They have declared war on the Empire. They must pay the penalty.'

But during 'Black Week', in December 1899, it was the British armies who paid in a swift series of disasters. In the middle of that grim week, Prince Albert blew out the four candles of his birthday cake.

Later, on the grassy slopes of Spion Kop, the British again suffered defeat. The morning after the battle, while the Tommies were swearing damnation on all and sundry, there sat at the side of the road, cheerfully munching an army biscuit, a wiry little Indian with a Red Cross badge on his arm. It was Mohandas Gandhi. Believing that India could only win freedom through and within the British Empire, he felt it was his duty to do his bit for the Empire.

Early in 1900, General 'Bobs' Roberts, the veteran of Kabul, wrested from the Boers the beleaguered towns of

Kimberley and Ladysmith. The British could at last rejoice. The boys of Haileybury College, where Clement Attlee was a pupil, demanded a holiday. When it was refused, they marched off to the local town, Hertford, and joined in the celebrations. Young Attlee was once again there to wave the flag, but he and seventy others were caned for their excess of patriotism.

In May 1900, Bobs relieved Mafeking, and the whole of Britain went wild with joy. In London the crowds were reported as 'delirious with delight' and the heart of the city was 'one dense, strident, jubilant mass'. But this explosion of joy and relief hardly touched Victoria, nor would she live to see her rebellious Boer subjects brought to heel. At the beginning of 1901, the venerable Queen-Empress died, to be succeeded by her son, Edward VII. On 2 February 1901, the six-year-old Prince Albert attended Victoria's funeral in St George's Chapel, Windsor. It was the final parting between the first Empress and the boy who would be the last Emperor.

2

'Mr Johnson'

Shortly after Queen Victoria's funeral, it was proposed that the Duke of York, Prince Albert's father, should visit Australia, New Zealand, South Africa and Canada. King Edward VII objected; he disliked being parted from his son and heir. But Arthur Balfour, First Lord of the Treasury, talked him round with the argument that the King-Emperor and his family had a vital role to play in the Empire of the future. 'The King', he wrote, 'is no longer merely King of Great Britain and Ireland and of a few dependencies ... He is now the greatest constitutional bond in a single Empire of free men separated by half the circumference of the Globe.' He should 'visually associate' his family with the Empire.

So the Duke and Duchess of York sailed away on their imperial mission. During the leave-taking the poor Duke was so affected that he broke down. Four days out from Portsmouth he received these cheery lines: 'We hope you are quite well and not sea-sick.' They were signed: 'From your loving Bertie.'

With their duty done in Australia and New Zealand, the royal globe-trotters forged on to Cape Town. The Duke wrote to his father that Kitchener (who had relieved Bobs Roberts as Commander-in-Chief) had 'acacounted for 839 Boers last week'. He had also put on weight (a frequent tendency with victorious generals).

The Duke's long tour left him deeply impressed. In Australia and New Zealand, in Natal and Cape Colony, Canada and Newfoundland, he had found colonies which, sprung from the womb of England, had become vigorous young nations, as loyal to their own land as to the mother-country. Only one thing worried the Duke. On his return at the end of 1901 he alluded, in his speech at London's Guildhall, to 'the impression ... among our brethren overseas, that the old country must wake up'. The press took up the cry: 'Wake up England!' The South African

War over, Joseph Chamberlain, Colonial Secretary, visited South Africa, with the object of reconciling Boers and British. There he met Gandhi. 'You must try and placate the Europeans, if you wish to live in their midst,' he told him – advice which cast a chill over Gandhi.

Gandhi had been hastily summoned to South Africa from Bombay where he finally (he thought) settled with the not uncomfortable prospect of becoming a prosperous, if mediocre, lawyer. Unknown to him, Mohammed Ali Jinnah was living in the same city. Since returning from England, where, like Gandhi, he had been called to the Bar, young Jinnah had for three years walked disconsolately to the office and back, an impecunious lawyer without a brief. But Jinnah who now wore a monocle (inspired, some said, by Joseph Chamberlain's) was at last becoming known. Jinnah stayed on in Bombay to make his name; Gandhi quit Bombay to make his in South Africa.

Gandhi set up his law office in Johannesburg and prepared to intensify the struggle for Indians' rights. His life grew more simple. He bought a book on washing and became an expert laundryman. And when a white barber refused to cut his hair, he turned barber himself and cut his own. While cleaning his teeth (it took him fifteen minutes) he memorized verses of the *Bhagavad Gita* which he had stuck up on the bathroom wall. Naïve as his habits seemed, they all had their place in the armoury with which he would one day fight the mighty Englishman.

At Allahabad, India, young Jawaharlal Nehru, at the tender age of thirteen, was also reading the *Gita* and the *Upanishads*. Soon Jawaharlal would leave the sheltered atmosphere of his home and his British tutor, for the rigours of an English public school. 'In my heart', he said, 'I rather admired the English.'

In 1903, Jinnah, Gandhi and Nehru, unknown to one another, were each steering a separate course which led them to meet in the struggle for India's independence. At the beginning of that year, the Viceroy of India, Lord

Curzon, staged a Grand Durbar at Delhi, in honour of the King-Emperor's coronation, in order to impress Indians with the benefits of British rule. They had enjoyed a half-century of internal peace, political freedom and freedom of the press; justice was dispensed by a benevolent if imperfect administration. On the material side, the country possessed communications and public services which, while far from adequate, were the best in Asia.

Curzon personally checked the smallest details. For instance, he turned down that rousing hymn 'Onward Christian Soldiers' – not because most of those present were Hindus and Moslems, but because the line 'Crowns and thrones may perish' might be taken too literally by the King-Emperor's Indian subjects.

Curzon himself rode – no doubt in acute discomfort, for he had spinal trouble and wore a steel corset – on a splendid elephant covered with silver and gold. Behind the Viceroy's elephant came forty or fifty more, decked and painted and bedizened with cloth of gold and frontlet pieces. Then, after the cavalry, there followed, unbelievably, 120 more elephants.

In the amphitheatre near the Kashmir Gate, where Shan chiefs from Burma, looking like walking pagodas, jostled with fierce Pathans and bejewelled princes, the hit of the parade was the surviving veterans, British and Indian, of the Mutiny, 'old tottering fellows ...' said a spectator; 'the people shouted till they were hoarse'. Those veterans symbolized the cost of Empire – two million British graves lay scattered throughout India.

If the pomp and dignity of the Grand Durbar impressed Curzon and the eight thousand spectators within the amphitheatre, it had failed to stir the patriotism of the hundred million outside. What had really kindled the patriotic feelings of at least some Indians (like Gokhale) was the liberalism they had learned from the British. They were preaching that India's salvation lay not with the British Raj, but in her own hands.

* * *

Soon after Curzon's display of 'pomp and dignity', Von Plehve, Tsar Nicholas's unspeakable Minister of the Interior, set his dreaded Black Hundreds loose on the Jewish population of Kishinev, in south-west Russia. Forty-five Jews were murdered. Joseph Chamberlain, who had been so conciliatory to the Boers (though less so to the Indians), now offered a refuge to the Jews – in Uganda. It was the first public recognition of the Zionist movement, but it split Congress. Chaim Weizmann, anti-Ugandist to the core, told the delegates: 'If the British Government and people are what I think they are, they will make a better offer.'

A year later, on 4 July 1904, Herzl, worn out by the struggle, died. Chaim Weizmann, depressed by the failure of his own struggle for Zionism, set out for England. He believed that there a Jew might work unhindered and be judged on his merits. Moreover, England seemed to be the one country likely to sympathize with Zionism. Weizmann rented a basement laboratory at the Manchester Chemical School. Foreign gentlemen, he was told, always began in the basement.

Early in 1906 came a memorable encounter, as he put it – with no less a personage than Arthur Balfour, who had not long ago put to King Edward VII his visionary ideas of a new-style Empire and the role of its emperor. Balfour asked why some Jews were so bitterly opposed to the Uganda offer. 'Mr Balfour', replied Weizmann, 'supposing I were to offer you London instead of Paris?' Balfour looked surprised. 'But Dr Weizmann, we *have* London.' 'True', replied Weizmann, 'but we had Jerusalem when London was a marsh.'

When George, Prince of Wales, disembarked at Bombay in November 1905, a new viceroy, Lord Minto, had succeeded the great Curzon. Minto's character was more suited to the times. A crack amateur jockey (he broke his neck during his fourth Grand National), he had forsaken the turf for journalism and soldiering, later to become a distinguished public servant. Minto felt (and later wrote to the Prince) that 'we are at the commencement of a great change in India'.

After a succession of durbars, tiger shoots and elephant hunts, of drives in the searing heat across dusty plains and through the teeming, fetid streets of great towns, the Prince's comment on the 'ruling chiefs' was that they 'ought to be treated ... more as equals than inferiors'. It was timely advice. Many of them, as Disraeli had once observed, were already princes when Britain was a Roman colony.

The Prince told Gokhale: 'I have never seen a happier-looking people.' He had not seen – for princes are seldom shown the seamy side – what a journalist in the royal entourage had described as 'the shameless abandon, the ineffable filth and sickening misery' which lay behind the vast crowds of cheering Indians.

Back in England the Prince made his point; he appealed for a wider sympathy on the part of the British administrators.

The Prince and Princess of Wales had been separated from their young family for six months. When they returned from their world tour in 1901, they found that their sons, Prince Edward and Prince Albert, had become a couple of spoiled brats – thanks to their adored and doting grandparents, the King-Emperor and Queen Alexandra. So a tutor, Mr Hansell, was called in to stiffen up their discipline. A year later, Prince Bertie was having trouble with his maths: 'division by 2 seems to be quite beyond him'. The problem would still plague him in his latter days, with the division into two of India, Palestine and Ireland.

His German tutor, Professor Oswald, reported: 'It isn't only that Prince Albert is inattentive, but when I scold him he just pulls my beard.' Prince Bertie was on such occasions summoned to the study of his sea-dog father for a taste of naval discipline. Those interviews were a terrible experience for Bertie, a frail, over-excitable and super-sensitive little boy, not yet ten years old. He quailed before his irascible father (so sympathetic to the fears and failings of all save his own sons). Bertie had already begun to stammer; he stood tongue-tied and defenceless before his father and his tutors. Neither they nor his father could understand the agonies of a stammerer – the humiliation, always before others, and the shame and self-reproach which follows; the ensuing despair and the desire to withdraw into one's lonely world of hurting frustration and impotence. The affliction had hit Bertie very young. Master it as he later would – almost – it would always be the most poignant and personal of the last Emperor's many problems.

A happier young man at this time was Shlomo Zemach. 'We exist almost entirely on bread and olives ... It is a great joy to live by the labour of one's own hands.' So he wrote from Palestine to his friend David Green. David, now nineteen, was brooding one day by the river in Plonsk when he decided to go to Palestine. He managed to get a Turkish visa for a three months' stay, but intended to stay for ever. At Odessa, recently the scene of one of the Black Hundreds' most frightful pogroms, he boarded a dilapidated cargo boat. Two weeks later he reached Jaffa.

David spent his first night in the Jewish village of Petach Tikvah, Gate of Hope, two hours' tramp from Jaffa. But he lay awake. 'Who could sleep through his first night in the Land?' he wrote. 'My soul was in tumult, one emotion drowned my very being: lo! I am in the land of Israel.'

After Petach Tikvah, David joined the isolated settlement at Sejera in the Galilee highlands, there to live the life of a frontiersman. 'No shopkeepers or speculators, no non-Jewish hirelings or idlers ... you follow and guide the plough ... the grain ripens ... you feel yourself a partner in creation.'

But the romantic frontier life had its dangers. At night marauding Arab bands roamed the countryside. So the Jewish settlers organized a night watch system, Hashomer

(Watchman). Out of it would grow Haganah, the Jews' secret defence force.

Some of the Sejera Jews moved on to land bought from the Arabs by the National Jewish Foundation at Um-Juni, near the Sea of Galilee. They called the settlement Daganya. It was the first kibbutz.

It was a time for founding new enterprises. In October 1906, a deputation of Moslems, headed by the twenty-nine-year-old Aga Khan, titular leader of the Moslems in India (who totalled about one quarter of the population), asked Viceroy Minto for safeguards against a Hindu majority. They wanted the Moslems to be represented as a community. Three months later, the All-India Moslem League was founded. Unlike Congress, which, though Hindu-dominated, claimed to represent all sects and beliefs, the Moslem League stood for the rights of Moslems alone.

The upshot of these events was to be separate constituencies for Moslems and lasting opprobrium for the well-meaning Minto, who was accused of trying to divide Moslems from Hindus and so perpetuate British rule.

Jinnah, now thirty, was not involved in these Moslem manœuvres. As private secretary to Dadabhai Naorji, the grand old man of India, he attended that year's meeting of Congress. Dadabhai had once been a British MP. He told the House of Commons that British rule in India had infused new life into a land which had been decaying for centuries. 'The British endowed it with all their own most important privileges ... including freedom of speech.'

Now, fourteen years later, while the privilege of free speech had not changed, Dadabhai's tune most definitely had. Before Congress he declared passionately: 'All our sufferings demand reparation ... We only want *swaraj* ('self-government').' *Swaraj* was inscribed on the Congress banner, behind which marched Jinnah and other fervent reformers.

* * *

In Burma, India's golden but unwilling province, there were also political stirrings. In 1906, Ledi Sayadaw, a Buddhist monk, set the nationalist ball rolling with a religious campaign. In that same year, the Young Men's Buddhist Association – inspired, nicely, by the Young Men's Christian Association – was founded. Not so nicely (for the British), its president, U May Oung, would soon be talking of 'the not unmixed blessing of a Western education, the ebb-less tide of foreign civilization and learning'. He urged Burmans to resist, otherwise their existence as a distinct nationality would be irretrievably lost.

The YMBA soon shed its Buddhist and Christian ideals for strictly political ones, preaching that the Orient had no further reason to debase itself before the West. The proud Burmese, out to embarrass and humiliate Europeans, started the 'foot-wear controversy'. Burmese custom requires shoes to be removed on entering a building. Outside pagodas, 'No Footwear' notices now appeared. The British, with more concern for hygiene than protocol, were turned away by the yellow-robed monks. It was a pinprick, one of many, against British prestige.

Viceroy Minto had already given a fillip to Moslem aspirations. 'Honest' John Morley, Secretary of State for India, had acted on the Prince of Wales's appeal for a 'wider sympathy' for Indians. Their joint efforts led India a step nearer independence. Hitherto, an executive council of six, presided over by the Viceroy, exercised almost arbitrary rule over three hundred million Indians. The Viceroy's council was now enlarged into the Imperial Legislative Council, a debating body with elected representatives of the Indian people. And the Moslems, in their separate constituencies, could now vote for their co-religionists.

One of those elected – by the Bombay Moslems – was Mohammed Ali Jinnah. At the Council's first meeting in January 1910, Jinnah took up the cause of a Hindu –

none other than Gandhi, who would one day be his adversary.

Jinnah's anger was roused by the harsh treatment of Indians in South Africa. Jan Christian Smuts's view was: 'The Asiatic cancer ought to be resolutely eradicated.' Lional Curtis, Assistant Colonial Secretary of the Transvaal, was less harsh but more explicit: 'Mr Gandhi,' he told the Indian leader, 'it is not the vices of Indians that Europeans in this country fear, but their virtues ...'

Gandhi had added more weapons to his armoury of virtue and self-abnegation. He had studied a book on childbirth. His first act as midwife was when he delivered his son, Devadas. Then, during a punitive expedition against the Zulus, he served as a male nurse because, as he said, 'the British Empire existed for the good of the world'. Gandhi was awarded a medal for his services.

Returning from the Zulu affair, Gandhi announced to his wife Kasturbai that he had resolved to end their sexual relationship and become a *brahmachari*; this also meant mastering greed, hatred, violence and untruth. Gandhi had taken the decisive step towards becoming a *mahatma*, a holy man.

He now faced a stern fight against the Transvaal government's anti-Indian laws. Looking for a word to define his non-violent resistance, Gandhi hit on *satyagraha*, a combination of *saty*, truth, and *agraha*, force: truth-force. 'It was the vindication of truth, not by inflicting suffering on the opponent, but on oneself.'

Satyagraha landed Gandhi in gaol three times in quick succession. 'The real road to happiness', he said, 'lies in going to gaol and undergoing sufferings and privations there [for] one's country and religion.' Freed, he went to London, there to plead for the South African Indians. Lord Crewe, Secretary of State for the Colonies, told him: 'It is not possible for Asiatics to have equality with Europeans.'

While in London, Gandhi began to think seriously for the first time about Indian independence. A wave of anti-

British violence was sweeping India. Behind the campaign of hatred loomed the giant figure of Bal Gangadhar Tilak – Lokamanya, beloved of the people. Tilak raised the war-cry: 'Home Rule is my birthright and I will have it.' A series of assassinations of British officials followed. Gandhi commented: 'I share the nationalist spirit, but I totally dissent from the methods.'

Two years later, in December 1911, the ruler of India arrived in Delhi: the High and Mighty George the Fifth, by the Grace of God Emperor of India. He had suceeded his father, King Edward VII.

Shortly after his coronation, King George decided to hold a coronation durbar at Delhi, hoping thereby to allay the unrest and sedition abroad in India. The King-Emperor, accompanied by Queen Mary, left England – and his young family – in November 1911.

Since their last visit to India, Prince Albert had been sent to the Royal Naval College at Osborne, Isle of Wight. His tutor Mr Hansell, was anxious about him, calling him a scatter-brain. Not that there was anything radically wrong with the Prince. On the contrary, he was known as a very straight and honourable boy, kind-hearted and generous – characteristics which would never change. A report stated: 'Prince Albert shows grit and a "never say I'm beaten spirit".' But his work was terrible. 'My dear boy, this will not do,' his father complained, 'if you go on like this you will be bottom of your term ... It will be a great bore.'

The Prince moved on to the Naval College at Dartmouth, where he managed to advance one place during his first term. His father lectured him and followed up with a letter: 'You must really work hard ... as it does look so bad that you are practically last in your term.'

With this paternal rebuke, the King-Emperor sailed for India. His state entry into Delhi was marred by an error of showmanship. The crowds of Indians, who expected the Emperor to be riding not on a horse, but an elephant, were, in the Emperor's words, not particularly demonstrative. The crowds had failed to recognize him. At the royal durbar, Indian princes, lieges of the Emperor, did obeisance – all save one, the Gaekwar of Baroda, who advanced towards the Emperor swinging a walking-stick. He struck a jarring note which in some way was symbolic of the changing times. This royal durbar, for all its fantastic pomp, seemed, too, to strike a faintly anachronistic note. There was something final about it. Indeed, there would never be another. It was held on 12 December 1911. Twenty-five years hence to the day, Cadet Prince Albert (now sweating at his exams) would be proclaimed King and Emperor – the last Emperor to rule over India.

Eamon de Valera, the boy from Buree, near Limerick, had spent an uneventful youth. So far he had not taken part in politics, but events were now to change his outlook.

In April 1912, Prime Minister Asquith introduced the Irish Home Rule Bill into the Commons. But the Protestants of Ulster, led by Edward Carson (a Protestant from Dublin), supported by the Unionist party, had sworn never to submit to a Catholic Parliament ruling in Dublin. Carson threatened that if Britain gave Home Rule to Ireland, Ulstermen would form a separate government in Belfast. He was the first of half a million Ulstermen to sign the Ulster Covenant; Home Rule, it declared, would be 'subversive to our civil and religious freedom'.

By 1913, civil war threatened Ireland. In the north, the Protestants created the Ulster Volunteers; by September they numbered 84,000. In the south, the Catholics formed the Irish Volunteers. Eamon de Valera, believing that Irish independence would be won 'not by ballots, but by bullets', enrolled. Soon he was made captain of the Donnybrook company; his first lieutenant was a former British guardsman. Everything looked quite above-board.

Meanwhile, Mr Augustine Birrell, the Irish Secretary, was fervently praying 'that either Heaven, the King or some other agency will bring about a general election and Home Rule be shelved'. The King himself was inundated with letters from Ulstermen whose gist was: 'May the King never hand us over to the Pope.'

The King-Emperor was deeply worried. 'It seems inconceivable to me', he wrote to Prime Minister Asquith, 'that British commonsense will not ultimately find a solution to this terrible prospect of rebellion and bloodshed.' Finally he succeeded in getting the two sides to meet at Buckingham Palace. But three days later the conference had broken down.

In Dublin, Eamon de Valera had bought himself, for £5, a Mauser rifle.

Mohandas Gandhi went unarmed into his struggle for human liberty, as he called it, in South Africa. His 'army of peace' went into action, courting arrest and imprisonment by deliberately breaking the Transvaal immigration laws. Gandhi then announced that he would lead his army – now swollen to thousands – on a protest march into the Transvaal. Gandhi's orders were: 'Submit to police flogging and abuse. Do not resist arrest.' He himself was arrested three times and finally gaoled, with hundreds more of his 'soldiers'.

Then suddenly Gandhi was freed. He was summoned by Smuts. After weeks of negotiation, the two antagonists reached agreement. South African Indians received what Gandhi called their Magna Carta – the Indian Relief Bill. It was the vindication, he said, of the principle of racial equality. He believed that civil resistance would do away with the ever-growing militarism 'under which the nations of the West are groaning'.

With victory in his pocket, Gandhi, in July 1914, left South Africa, never to return. His destination was England. When he arrived there, the First World War had already begun.

It happened that Jinnah also was in London at that time. Jinnah told Indian students in London: 'Learn all you can of the civilization which the British have taken centuries to build up.' The top Indian politicians, he reminded them, were those who had been educated in England. In December 1913, Jinnah joined the Moslem League. But people still called him the best ambassador of Hindu-Moslem unity.

Jinnah visited London again in 1914. This time he accused the Secretary of State of being a greater Mogul than India had ever known, since she was the only civilized country in the world without a representative government. But Jinnah's visit was ill-timed. British politicians were too preoccupied with the Irish conflict and the problems of a world war to listen to him.

The declaration of war by Britain on 4 August 1914 cooled Irish tempers. The Ulster and the Irish Volunteers, until yesterday ready to spring at each others' thoats, now united to defend Ireland. In this heartening atmosphere, the Home Rule Bill, a month later, became law – but a law suspended for the duration of the war.

In the event, the Irish Home Rule Bill pleased no one. Before long, de Valera was sworn as a member of the underground Irish Republican Brotherhood, the controlling force behind the Volunteers. Plans for a rising in Dublin were discussed. From now on de Valera took frequent walks with his little boy, Vivion, between Baggott Street and the Grand Canal. Soon he knew every landmark in his battalion area.

While de Valera and his comrades secretly prepared – with the help of the Germans – to seize Irish independence by fighting the British, Chaim Weizmann believed that his best chance of helping to gain Jewish independence was to fight on the British side. Weizmann sent the Government details of his experiments on fermentation. First to recognize their use was Winston Churchill, First Lord of the Admiralty.

The young Jewish immigrant David Green, as he worked the soil of Palestine, thought exactly opposite to Weizmann; he tried to join the Turkish army, which would soon be fighting the British. He wrote articles supporting the Turkish cause. They were signed 'Ben Gurion'. He was expelled from Palestine, his passport stamped 'Never to return'. In Alexandria, the British packed him off, as an enemy alien, to New York. Ben Gurion would soon be back – as a corporal in the army of the King-Emperor.

When war broke out, Clement Attlee was holidaying with his brother Tom at Seaton, in Devon. He immediately joined up. Ernest Bevin took part in a determined effort to stop the war. The country-bred lad (who would become Foreign Minister) had got himself the congenial job, when he first arrived in Bristol, as driver of a two-horse dray delivering mineral water. Over the years he had come to the fore in the Trades Union movement, although his efforts on behalf of the proletariat had lost him some customers among his capitalist clientele in the beverage trade.

In 1914, Bevin spoke up forcefully for an international strike against war, but to no avail. The German unions backed out and a movement which might have saved millions from death failed. And so, amidst wild scenes of patriotic enthusiasm, the flower of Britain's youth (and France's and Germany's too) marched off to the slaughter. Some, like Prince Edward, were miserable at being left behind. 'What does it matter if I am shot?' he asked. 'I have four brothers.'

At present, it was his brother Bertie who risked being shot. On 29 July, Midshipman Prince Albert had kept the first watch aboard the battleship *Collingwood* as, with the rest of the Grand Fleet, she slipped through the Dover Straits under cover of dark. The crew were at night defence stations; war was imminent.

The previous year, Prince Albert had been launched on a naval career. He had left Dartmouth with the reputation of being 'an honest, clean-minded and excellent mannered boy'. His captain reported laconically: 'I think he will do.'

But the Prince's health was far from robust. Apart from his stammer, he was tortured by gastric disorders. He suffered in silence, but one of those who knew said of him: 'He has tremendous guts.' But his shipmates frankly doubted whether the Prince would ever stand up to the rigours and the diet of life at sea.

However, Prince Albert survived his first sea-job – a voyage in the cruiser *Cumberland*, which gave him a glimpse of the empire as well as of some of the trials of public service. Wherever he went ashore people thronged to see the King-Emperor's youthful son. At Jamaica, as he struggled with a carefully rehearsed speech, the husky voice of one of the dark beauties who crowded the dais intruded: 'Say, have you touched the Prince?' 'Yeah, three times,' the Prince heard the disconcerting reply. In Canada he complained: 'I was hunted ... by photographers and also by the Americans who had no manners at all.' And in a storm off the Canadian coast, a great wave which caught the *Cumberland* nearly swept him from the scene of British history. He was 'as near as a toucher overboard'.

A few months later, Midshipman Prince Albert had sailed off again on another cruise, this time in the *Collingwood*. But everyone aboard now called him 'Mr Johnson'. The cruise took him a short way down the Empire lifeline to India: Gibraltar, Malta, Suez.

But Mr Johnson's thoughts were centred less on the Empire than on the pursuit of a life on the ocean wave. When the *Collingwood* called at Toulon, a French visitor came aboard and asked: 'May I see the Prince?' The officer of the watch replied: 'I'm sorry, he has gone for a walk.' Then, turning to Prince Albert, who was standing two yards away, he snapped: 'Mr Johnson, please show the gentleman around.' A little later, the Frenchman, still curious, asked a rating: 'Isn't the Prince aboard?' 'Why, yes,' replied Jack Tar. 'That's 'im showin' you around.'

His royal status meant nothing to his gun-room mates. In a letter to his father he wrote: 'I fell out of my ham-

mock with the help of someone else, and hit my eye ...';
news to which the King-Emperor reacted with: 'I should
do the same to the other fellow.'

But the time for sky-larking was over. Steaming darkly
through the night with the Grand Fleet (which had
taken six hours to sail past the King at a recent naval
review), *Collingwood* was making for its war rendezvous,
while from her bridge Midshipman Prince Albert scanned
the silent waters for possible enemy action. He was not
yet nineteen. 'Well does Great Britain merit the Empire
of the Seas when the humblest stations in her navy are
supported by princes of the blood,' a Spanish admiral
had written long ago.

Collingwood was still at sea when, at 2 am on the
fourth of August, Britain declared war against Germany.
King George immediately signalled the Royal Navy his
confidence that it would 'prove once again the sure
shield of Britain and the Empire'. And to his teen-age
son he wrote with feeling: 'May God bless and protect
you my dear boy is the earnest prayer of your very
devoted Papa.'

The King-Emperor himself best described how the people
of his Empire rallied to Britain's cause – a cause which
did not directly concern them except in so far as that it
was Britain's. 'The outbreak of war', he said, 'found the
whole Empire one.' He was proud of the 'splendid troops
which eagerly hastened to us from the dominions overseas'. Of India, the King-Emperor said: 'She has fulfilled
my faith in her single-minded devotion to my person and
empire.'

Burma was known as the most placid province in
India. But some six months after the outbreak of war, on
13 February 1915, there occurred in Burma a momen-
tous, though completely unnoticed, event: the birth, at
Natmauk in the Magwe district, of an infant boy, Aung
San. He would one day lead Burma out of the British
Empire.

*   *   *

It was about this time that Chaim Weizmann met Lloyd George, Chancellor of the Exchequer. Present was the Jewish politician Herbert Samuel, to whom Lloyd George whispered: 'When you and I are forgotten, this man will have a monument to him in Palestine.' Samuel favoured British annexation of Palestine and the planting there of three to four million Jews – a scheme which Prime Minister Asquith called a lyrical outburst, adding that Lloyd George, 'the only other partisan, does not care a damn for the Jews or their past or future, but thinks it will be an outrage to let the Holy Places fall into the possession ... of agnostic and atheistic France'. Britain, however, was careful to see to it that Palestine would not fall to the French.

Meanwhile other influences were working to bedevil the future of Palestine. Sir Henry MacMahon, High Commissioner in Egypt, promised Sherif Hussein of Mecca that Britain, in return for a Sherif-backed Arab revolt against the Turks, would recognize the independence of the Arabs. But when the Arabs learnt that Palestine was not included, they felt cheated.

Added to this there would always be Arabs who refuted the Zionist claim to Palestine as the land which God had promised to Abraham and his seed for ever through Isaac, his and Sarah's son. For Abraham, the Arab argument went, had already made a covenant with God through the circumcision of his elder son (by a bondwoman), Ishmael, of whom God had said 'I will make a nation', and whom the Arabs claim as their ancestor. Nor did Abraham's conjugal adventures end there. Through his concubine, Keturah, he fathered the ancestors of many north Arabian tribes.

The projects that the British were dreaming up for Jews and Arabs remained hypothetical as long as Palestine remained a Turkish possession – which, judging by the series of disasters which befel British arms in 1915, it had every likelihood of doing.

Where, as in India, they were the masters, the British

concentrated on getting on with the war. A first contingent of 70,000 Indian soldiers had reached the western front. Well over a million were to follow.

Gandhi, who had returned to India in January 1915, was recruiting for the British Army. He explained his apparent betrayal of non-violence: 'The British Empire had certain ideals with which I had fallen in love ... every subject ... has the freest scope possible ... That government is best which governs least ... it is possible for me to be governed least under the British Empire. Hence my loyalty.'

Gandhi was an unimpressive little figure with his weak, monotonous voice, his head swathed in an outsize turban and his thin body in a loincloth. The hero of *satyagraha* in the Transvaal did not look a likely leader in the fight for India's freedom.

It seemed no more likely that Jinnah would one day become Gandhi's opponent. The 'ambassador of unity' was living up to his name. To the Moslem League he appealed: 'Can we not bury our differences? It will make our Hindu friends ... feel ... that we are worthy of standing shoulder to shoulder with them.' His cry for unity did not go unheeded. When the Moslem League met on 30 December, two leading members of Congress sat with Jinnah on the platform. One was Dr Annie Besant, a fiery English lady who had taken up the cause of Indian freedom. The other was Gandhi.

Jinnah's initiative was to have its sequel a year later. In December 1916, Congress and the League both held their sessions at Lucknow. In a passionate speech to the League, Jinnah said: 'India's real progress can only be achieved by ... harmonious relations between the two great sister communities.' The meetings of Congress and the League culminated in the Lucknow Pact. It confirmed the principle of separate Moslem electorates, and guaranteed the the Moslems more seats than they could hope to win (this was nick-named 'weightage'). Lucknow was the one bright spot in the dismal story of Hindu-Moslem relations.

*   *   *

While Hindus and Moslems sought reconciliation within the British Empire, in Ireland things were shaping very differently. Eamon de Valera and his comrades of the Irish Volunteers had been waiting impatiently for the signal to rise against the British. Much depended on the Germans, who had agreed to send a shipment of arms and ammunition (it never arrived).

On Sunday evening, de Valera received a message that the Rising was fixed for noon on Easter Monday, 24 April. That morning a battalion of Volunteers and a company of Connolly's Citizen Army made a 'route march' through the Dublin streets, watched by the Bank Holiday crowds. But opposite the General Post Office, Connolly's voice rang out: 'Left turn, GPO charge!' Shortly after, the republican tricolour of green, white and orange was floating symbolically above the royal arms over the Post Office's entrance. There, the rebel commander, Patrick Pearse, son of an Englishman, proclaimed the Irish Republic as a sovereign independent state.

British troops were rushed to quell the rebellion. By Friday, they had regained control (it cost them nearly five hundred killed). The following Wednesday, at 3.45 am, Pearse faced a firing squad.

De Valera was one of the last to surrender. Shabby and dirty, but with head erect, he was escorted to the detention cells. People in the streets jeered and he thought bitterly that the people of Ireland did not yet understand the meaning of freedom. It would not be long before they did.

The Easter Rising was over. After Pearse, fourteen others were shot. De Valera was sure that his turn would come. To a friend, Sister Gonzaga, he wrote: 'Pray for my soul and for my poor wife and little children ...' Unknown to him, the children were being cared for by a neighbour – an Englishwoman.

One morning a British officer entered his cell and read to him the court's verdict: sentenced to death. Then the officer read from a second paper: sentence commuted to penal servitude for life. His daughter

Mairin was told: 'Your father is going to be taken away
to a big house with high walls and little windows with
bars.'

While de Valera was detained during His Majesty's plea-
sure in grim Dartmoor Prison, His Majesty's son, Prince
Albert, was at grips with de Valera's allies, the Germans.
Like every man in the Grand Fleet, Midshipman Prince
Albert had waited for 'the day'. He nearly missed it.
Three weeks after the outbreak of war, he reported sick
with violent pain in the stomach; he could hardly breathe.
He was operated on for appendicitis. But recovery was
slow; the King's surgeon thought he should never go
to sea again. This worried the Prince. Boys of his age –
nineteen – were dying in the front line. He went to
work at the Admiralty and felt a little better: 'Now
people cannot say I am doing nothing.' But soon he was
feeling: 'Life here is very dull and I am longing to get
back to *Collingwood*.' In February 1915 he rejoined his
ship. His father, the King-Emperor, missed him, 'especially at breakfast'. Too soon the 'infernal digestion' laid
him low again, and he was back in hospital. Although he
remained poorly for months, his sailor father thought
it better 'to run the risk of Prince Albert's health suffering than that he should endure the bitter and lasting
disappointment of not being in his ship in the battle
line'. Early in May 1916, Prince Albert, now a sub-
lieutenant, returned to *Collingwood*.

At the same time, his elder brother David 'burned with
desire to be in the firing line: 'Oh, to be fighting ... and
not sitting back here doing so little as compared to them
who are sacrificing their lives ...' But it was Bertie who
would have the chance to fight.

At 2.20 pm on 31 May, action stations were sounded.
The Battle of Jutland had begun. 'Out of his bunk
leaps Johnson,' as his turret commander, Lieutenant
Tait, later reported. Sub-Lieutenant Johnson now felt
fighting fit. On duty in A-turret throughout the battle,
he underwent his baptism of fire. *Collingwood*'s firing

was deadly. She sank a German light cruiser, hit another and set a battle-cruiser on fire. She herself came under heavy fire; two torpedoes missed ahead and astern and she was closely straddled by shells. Prince Albert watched other ships go down, among them the *Invincible* (in which he had dined the night before), which was blown in two. The *Defence* blew up in a huge sheet of flame; the *Warrior*, totally disabled, was abandoned.

Overnight he became a hardened mariner. His first thought was 'Thank God I was back in time', and he made surprisingly light of the loss in battle of over six thousand British sailors. 'There is no need for everyone at home to bemoan their loss when they are proud to die for their country.' Of his part in the greatest sea battle of the war he said: 'It was certainly a great experience.' A rare one, too, considering that royalty and rulers usually shun the fighting in the wars they make.

Champaran, in the land of King Janaka, at the foot of the Himalayas, became, early in 1917, the scene of a war in which there was no fighting, only love – dispensed by Mohandas Gandhi. It was here that he first decided 'to urge the departure of the British' from India.

Trouble arose between the Indian peasants and their British landlords. Gandhi arrived to make an enquiry. Politely refusing a police order to leave, he was arraigned before the magistrate the next day. Immediately 'a sort of friendliness' sprang up between Gandhi and the Collector, magistrate and police. The case was soon withdrawn. The Collector, Mr Heycock ('a good man, anxious to do justice'), offered to help Gandhi with his enquiry. Gandhi was surprised at this 'prompt and happy issue'. He had given India its first object lesson in civil disobedience.

Someone else who, like Gandhi, was trying to urge the departure of the English, was in fact English: that fiery and formidable lady, Dr Annie Besant. Having married an English clergyman, she then embraced atheism, was divorced and, after a long flirt with theosophy (during which she met Gandhi for the first time), she finally espoused the cause of Indian independence. Jawaharlal Nehru listened to her speeches 'dazed and as in a dream'.

One of Annie Besant's most ardent admirers was, strangely enough, the man ultimately responsible for law and order in India – the Secretary of State, Edwin Montagu. Montagu intensified what Nehru called the electric atmosphere in India when he declared, on 20 August 1917, that Britain's aim was 'the gradual development of self-governing institutions and responsible government in India within the British Empire'. Thirty years later, almost to the day, this object would be achieved.

Ironically enough, Montagu, a Jew, did not favour Jewish nationalism as he did Indian; he was one of Chaim Weizmann's bitterest opponents.

In February 1917, Weizmann attended a conference of leading British Jews favourable to Zionism. Sir Mark Sykes, of the Foreign Office, was also present. The Zionists wanted a British protectorate over Palestine. Justice Brandeis, the American Zionist leader, was also in favour. But the French were a problem. They wanted a say in Palestine.

Two months later Weizmann learnt that Britain and France had secretly agreed that Palestine was to be internationalized. This, thought Weizmann, would be fatal to Zionism. Palestine *must* be a British protectorate. Weizmann appealed to Arthur Balfour, now Foreign Secretary, for a declaration in favour of the Zionists.

In September 1917, the draft declaration was brought up for discussion by the Cabinet, but Montagu had it withdrawn. It was again on the agenda for a Cabinet meeting a month later. This time Montagu launched a passionate attack against Zionism. He ended in tears. Weizmann was sent for, but could not be found. Unchallenged, Montagu, the Jew, succeeded in swaying the Cabinet against his Jewish brethren. The text was watered down and a condition added 'that nothing shall be done which may prejudice the civil and religious rights of the existing non-Jewish communities in Palestine' – which were almost entirely Arab.

An amended text was before the Cabinet for final discussion on 2 November 1917. Weizmann waited within call. It was Sir Mark Sykes who burst in on him. 'Dr Weizmann, it's a boy!' he cried, and handed him the official text of the Balfour Declaration. It read:

His Majesty's Government view with favour the establishment in Palestine of a National Home for the Jewish people, and will use their best endeavours to facilitate the achievement of this object, it being clearly understood that nothing shall be done which may prejudice the civil and religious rights of the existing non-Jewish communities in Palestine or the rights and political stature enjoyed by Jews in any other country.

Mindful of the clamour and true to their liberal traditions, the British had launched Indians and Israelites on the path to independence. But from Montagu to Mountbatten, from Balfour to Bevin, thirty more years of bitter and bloody struggle were to elapse before the promised goal was achieved.

Immediate problems faced the freedom-seekers. A few months after the Balfour Declaration, Weizmann headed a Zionist mission to Palestine. King George V wished him good luck. He would need it. That very day he had heard the Arabs were already asking uncomfortable questions. And Weizmann found the British military, from Commander-in-Chief Allenby downwards, cool about Zionist dreams for Palestine.

Allenby, conqueror of Palestine, was told by Weizmann: 'Yours is one of the greatest victories in history ... largely bound up with the history of my people.' Weizmann visited the Emir Feisal, son of Sherif Hussein (now raised to kingship), at his headquarters on a high plateau in the mountains of Moab. From here Feisal's Arab army, under T. E. Lawrence ('Lawrence of Arabia'), was harrying the Turks. That night, in brilliant moonlight, Weizmann looked down from Moab on the Jordan valley and the Dead Sea, and the Judaean hills beyond. It seemed to him that three thousand years had vanished since his ancestors had passed that way on their journey to the Promised Land. Next day, Weizmann outlined to Feisal the Israelites' plans to return to their homeland. Feisal was comprehensive.

At about the same time that Weizmann was discussing the Balfour Declaration with Feisal, Edwin Montagu was in India explaining his own declaration to Viceroy Chelmsford. About himself Chelmsford said: 'Indians consider me a reactionary.' One of his reactionary, if excusable, acts was to criticize the Indian press which, 'in pursuit of their own ends ... harp upon plague, famine, malaria and poverty and ascribe them all to the curse of an alien government'. Chelmsford was not being reactionary, but merely facing the facts of Indian life, as he was when he told the King-Emperor: 'We have here an educated class, ninety-five per cent of whom are inimical to us.'

In India, as in Palestine, there were to be endless pitfalls on the road to independence.

While the British were trying to help the Indians and Israelites on their way to freedom, the Irish were, in characteristic fashion, helping themselves. When, in March 1917, Prime Minister Lloyd George offered immediate Home Rule to 'that part of Ireland that wants it', Mr Redmond and his Irish Party refused to accept the partition of Ireland.

Lloyd George then proposed an Irish convention of all parties in the hope that it would find a formula for Irish self-government. For good measure, the men of the 1916 Easter Rising were freed.

When, in June 1917, Eamon de Valera and his comrades left Euston station, London, for home, they were given a hearty send-off by the London Irish. In Dublin they were greeted as conquering heroes. A month later, de

Valera, as Sinn Fein candidate for Clare, was elected a member of the British parliament. He would never take his seat there, for Sinn Fein, under de Valera's guidance, was planning a separate Irish government, Dail Eireann.

Lloyd George complained that de Valera's speeches to the Irish were 'plain, deliberate ... cold-blooded incitements to rebellion'. When de Valera was elected President of Sinn Fein, he declared: 'There is no contemplation of having a Monarchy in which the Monarch would be of the House of Windsor.' On 17 May 1918, he was arrested and transferred to Lincoln gaol, England. His stay there would be shorter than either he or his gaolers imagined.

The Monarch, as de Valera called him, had been under fire from his own loyal subjects. After the abdication of his cousin Nicky, Tsar of all the Russias, in March 1917, people talked of an English revolution on Russian lines. Author H. G. Wells wanted Britain to rid herself of 'the ancient trappings of throne and sceptre', and its 'alien and uninspiring Court'. To which the King-Emperor retorted testily: 'I may be uninspiring, but I'll be damned if I'm an alien.'

Not every Briton was quite so sure. Many members of the Royal Family had Teutonic names. The College of Heralds itself could not say exactly what the King's name was. It was high time to decide. Edward III had been called Edward of Windsor (where he was born in 1312). That settled it. A royal proclamation of 17 July 1917 stated that: 'Our House and Family shall be ... known as the House and Family of Windsor.'

It was high time to convince people that the Crown was a living power for good, as Lord Stamfordham, the King's private secretary, put it. Lord Cromer thought that 'no stone should be left unturned ... to consolidate the position of the Crown'. It was the link of Empire.

The war, now ending, would see the Romanovs, the Habsburgs and the Hohenzollerns toppled from their thrones. US President Woodrow Wilson was emerging as the saviour of mankind. Republicanism seemed to many a better solution.

Lord Esher, for one, disagreed. He wrote: 'I see a great future for the King ... with the consolidation of Imperial control ... The King and Queen will have to take risks. The strength of republicanism lies in the *personality* of Wilson ... We can "go one better" if we try.' In the event, the Royal Family went two better. The King-Emperor already enjoyed immense personal popularity – witness the tumultuous welcome he received in the streets of London during Armistice week. Now his two elder sons were each to be assigned a task intended to consolidate the position of the Crown.

With his dazzling good looks and easy manner, the King's eldest son, the Prince of Wales, was already a popular figure. With his brother Bertie it was otherwise. After the thrill of the Jutland battle, Prince Albert's health, and with it his morale, had gone sharply downhill. After a year of physical and mental torture (the latter partly due to criticism about his absence from active service), he was finally operated on for a gastric ulcer. As usual, he suffered bravely.

The operation put an end to his career at sea, and he transferred to His Majesty's Ship *Daedalus*, the Navy's air training establishment high and dry at Cranwell, Lincolnshire. He flew for the first time. 'It was a curious sensation ... I did enjoy it ... but ... I would much sooner be on the ground. It feels safer.' However, he insisted on being trained as a pilot and won his pilot's wings. He would be the first pilot ever to wear an imperial crown.

The 'tremendous guts' which he had shown as a young sailor had conquered his fear of flying. Now he had his wings, he went up to Trinity College, Cambridge, 'to learn everything', as he said, 'that will be useful for the time to come'. His cousin, Dickie Mountbatten, was at Christ's, doing the same thing, though little did either of them realize what the time to come held for them. Meanwhile he wanted to help his elder brother, David. That meant public engagements – and the need for even more guts to overcome his dread of public speaking. He struggled with his speech infirmity. A French specialist failed to produce any improvement. An Italian professor was luckier. 'What a good speech you made ... the other night,' wrote his father, the King. 'You only hesitated once, which shows that yr. Italian friend is doing you good ... if you could only stick to it and persevere now.' Welcome as it was, such heartfelt encouragement failed to allay the anguish that Prince Albert felt each time he rose to say a few well-chosen but unpronounceable words.

But the Crown had need of the Prince. A few months before his brother David, the Prince of Wales, set off in August 1919 on the first of his many empire tours, Prince Albert was asked to accept the presidency of the Boys' Welfare Association (later the Industrial Welfare Society). 'I'll do it', said Prince Albert, 'as long as there's no damned red carpet about it.'

The anti-royalist sentiments of the British Labour Party got them nowhere in the general election of December 1918. The republicans of Sinn Fein, on the contrary, won a sweeping victory. The results were greeted with enthusiasm in Lincoln gaol by de Valera and his friends. A month later, at Dail Eireann's first session in Dublin, a declaration of Ireland's independence was signed. Convict de Valera was envisaged as President of the Irish Republic.

Meanwhile, the President-elect was planning a gaol-break. A devoted server at the prison masses, he noticed that the chaplain always left his key in the sacristy. With wax collected from the altar candles, de Valera made an impression of the key. This was passed on to his friends in Ireland.

On the night of 3 February 1919, de Valera escaped.

The news, when it broke, caused delirious joy in Ireland, in England consternation. The *Daily Express* had its own theory: 'Ireland is full of stories of banshees and leprechauns ... De Valera is just a distillation of these mystic things.' A few weeks later the British released the remaining Irish prisoners, and de Valera came out of hiding. When Dail Eireann met on 1 April 1919, de Valera was elected 'President of the Irish Republic'. Next day he formed a ministry. One of the appointments made was that of Richard Mulcahy as Chief of the Irish Republican Army, IRA for short – the new name of the Volunteers. Said the President, echoing Parnell: 'The people of Ireland are marching on the road to freedom.'

Unlike de Valera, Gandhi believed that India's way to freedom lay in helping the British to win the war. In July 1918 he had returned to Kheda on a recruiting drive. The peasants who had supported his *satyagraha* campaign were nonplussed. 'How can you ask us to take up arms?' they demanded. Gandhi's reply was: 'Partnership in the British Empire is our goal. If the Empire perishes, with it perish our cherished ambitions.'

Jinnah's reaction was similar: 'Let England pledge herself to redeem the promise [of Home Rule] ... and we will work heart and soul to save Britain, India and the Empire.'

In July 1918, while Gandhi was on his recruiting drive, the Montagu-Chelmsford Report on Indian reforms was published. Its basic principle was dyarchy, double government. The Indians were to have a large measure of self-government, while the Viceroy and his British provincial governors held the reins of power. The Report had a mixed reception. But it certainly provided India with what Nehru called 'a large instalment of ... self-government'. And Gandhi and Jinnah were prepared to go along with it.

Then things went sadly wrong. A few days after the Montagu-Chelmsford Report came another, the Rowlatt Report, recommending the continuation of the secret war-time trials without jury for terrorism. It hurt and angered Indians. Gandhi immediately decided to resist it. But how? He could not offer civil disobedience against measures aimed at terrorism. The solution came to him

in a dream: a general *hartal*, set for 6 April. 'Let all the
people of India suspend business on that day.'

Unfortunately, Gandhi had made what he called a
Himalayan miscalculation. The Indian masses were not
conditioned for the rigours and discipline of civil disobedience. In Delhi the crowd ran amok and the police
fired back. In Lahore and Amritsar notices urged the
people to 'kill and die'. Between 10 and 12 April, Amritsar was in the hands of the mob. Buildings were fired,
banks looted, Europeans murdered.

On 13 April, Brigadier General Dyer, the military commander, with ninety Indian soldiers, found himself in the
Jallianwalla Bagh, a square entirely shut in by buildings,
facing an excited crowd of ten to twenty thousand Indian
peasants armed with quarterstaffs, *kirpans*, the short Sikh
sword. Dyer ordered his riflemen to open fire. In ten
minutes they killed 379, wounded over a thousand.

The perpetrator of the 'Amritsar massacre' later explained to the Hunter Commission of Enquiry: 'I thought
I would be doing a jolly lot of good.' Indeed, Dyer was
thought by many people (including himself) to be the
saviour of India. This was not the official view. He was
dismissed from the army. Winston Churchill, Secretary of
State for War, told the Commons: 'Frightfulness is the
inflicting of great slaughter or massacre ... We cannot
admit this doctrine in any form ... Such ideas are absolutely foreign to the British way of doing things.'

A British officer said of the Amritsar massacre: 'Force
is the only thing than an Asiatic has any respect for.'
Asiatic Gandhi disagreed. In penance for the violence of
Indians, he made a three-day fast. To the Viceroy, he
wrote: 'If I could popularize love-force, in place of brute-
force ... I could present you with an India that could
defy the whole world ...'

As a first step, he would present an India which
defied Britain.

The last thing that Chaim Weizmann wanted was to
defy Britain. He depended on her. Yet the leader of

Zionism was embarked on an adventure which would land Britain in more trouble than India and Ireland put together.

Weizmann's friend, the Emir Feisal, said of Palestine: 'The Jews are very close to the Arabs in blood, and there is no conflict of character ... In principle we are absolutely one.' Feisal followed up with more conciliatory words: 'We feel that the Arabs and Jews are cousins in race ... We Arabs look with the deepest sympathy on the Zionist movement.'

But Feisal asked for 'a great trustee' to accept final responsibility. This ticklish job was to be assigned to Britain.

Feisal and Weizmann signed an agreement, for encouraging Jewish immigration into Palestine. Weizmann's conception of a Jewish National Home was: 'Always safeguarding the interests of non-Jews, I hope that by Jewish immigration Palestine will become as Jewish as England is English.'

President Wilson sent the King-Crane Mission to Palestine to investigate. Its opinion was that the creation of a Jewish state would be the 'gravest trespass' upon the (quoting the Balfour Declaration) civil and religious rights of existing non-Jewish communities in Palestine. To subject the inhabitants of Palestine to unlimited Jewish immigration and to steady financial and social pressure to surrender the land, would be a violation of Wilson's principle – that people were not be handed about from one sovereignty to another.

The Palestine question, already a mare's nest, was soon to be deposited in Britannia's back-yard, there to defy all her attempts to clear it up.

Shortly after the Peace Conference of 1919, the King-Emperor spoke optimistically of a new era opening. Entirely devoted to the peoples of his Empire, he and his two elder sons were not sparing themselves in the drive to consolidate the Crown. But in India as in her placid province Burma, in Ireland and in the land which would be Israel,

events were working against them and shaping not to consolidate, but to eliminate, the Crown.

3

The way to hell ...

When the great war ended, the King-Emperor had offered up a heart-felt prayer: 'May the morning star of peace ... be here and everywhere the herald of a better day, in which the storms of strife shall have died down and the rays of an enduring peace be shed upon all nations.' But events in his own empire were to mock his faith in the goodness and the brotherhood of man.

Nearest home, there was Ireland. Refused a hearing at the Peace Conference, the Irish resorted to direct action. Between three thousand guerillas of the IRA, and seventy-five thousand British troops and armed police, the Black and Tans, there now raged a war for Irish independence, a squalid war of murder, looting, ambush, arson and atrocities. 'We shall have murder by the throat!' cried British Prime Minister Lloyd George. De Valera's response was: 'If ever the sword was legitimate, it is in such a case as ours.' At present he was safely out of the way in America, while Michael Collins, the 'Big Fellow', directed the IRA with resource and daring – and with a £10,000 price on his head.

The King, who still felt responsible for his Irish subjects, however rebellious, asked: 'What does my Government intend to do towards further protecting the lives of the unoffending people of Ireland ... ?' The King was sickened by the brutalities commited by men wearing his uniform, and wanted the Black and Tans disbanded.

His Majesty's Government was in fact trying to smooth things out. On 23 December 1920, it submitted for the King's assent a bill dubbed the Partition Act, which established two Irish parliaments, one at Dublin, the other at Belfast. Until further notice, Ireland was severed in two.

While the competition in crime (as an Irish judge called it) dragged on between the IRA and the British army, de Valera lay low. But on a bright summer's evening, 22 June 1921, a squad of the Worcester Regiment raided a house in a Dublin suburb, little expecting to find the President of the Irish Republic, whom they arrested.

At Belfast, that morning of the 22nd, King George had opened the new parliament with a speech which came from his heart – and from the heart also of a one-time rebel against British authority, Jan Christian Smuts. Smuts had told the British: 'The Irish wound is poisoning your whole system.' On 13 June, at Windsor Castle, Smuts asked the King: 'Could not Your Majesty bring a message of peace and hope to Ireland?' 'Please draft me a speech,' was the King's reply. When the King delivered it at Belfast that morning, he spoke with feeling of 'that Empire in which so many nations and races have come together in spite of the ancient feuds, and in which new nations have come to birth ... I speak from a full heart when I pray that my coming to Ireland today may prove to be the first step towards the end of strife amongst her people, whatever their race or creed ...'

Immediate orders were given for de Valera's release. 'Did not know what to make of it,' he noted in his diary. He was enlightened when, two days later, he received a letter from Lloyd George: 'Sir, the British Government are deeply anxious that ... the King's appeal ... shall not have been made in vain.' De Valera was invited to London 'to explore to the utmost the possibility of a settlement', but he demurred. The recent Partition Act infuriated him. Smuts, who went to see him, argued that it was not really partition; it was merely that Ulster, always the stumbling-block, was now out of the way. So de Valera, for all his suspicions, went to London. A truce, signed on 10 July, ended the reign of terror.

There was no sign of the morning star of peace in Palestine, but instead, bloodshed. As the Feast of the Passover in April 1920 approached and pilgrims started arriving in Jerusalem, tension grew. Arabs gathered at the Mosque of Omar and, lashed by agitators into a frenzy of fanaticism, marched through the streets of the Old City, burning, pillaging and raping.

Although no more than five Jews were killed, a Jewish pogrom in British-controlled territory only two years after the Balfour Declaration came as a stunning shock to Zionists, who now eagerly awaited the San Remo conference, which would decide the future of Palestine – the Balfour Declaration and the Mandate – and ensure a stronger government. Weizmann's fervent hope was that the Mandate would go to Britain.

The conference met at the end of April 1920, and Weizmann paced nervously outside the council chamber, waiting impatiently for the delegates to emerge. Suddenly he caught sight of Balfour waving to somebody. Weizmann hurried up to him and asked: 'You're waiting for the delegates too?' 'Oh no', replied the author of the Balfour Declaration, 'I'm waiting for my tennis partners. They're very late.'

At last the delegates appeared. Lloyd George congratulated Weizmann: The Balfour Declaration had been confirmed and Britain awarded the Mandate. From everywhere there came enthusiastic cables and press reports. Even the Arab delegation seemed pleased; that evening they celebrated with the Jewish delegation.

The imminent fate of the defeated ruler of Palestine, Sultan Mohamed VI of Turkey, brought Moslems and Hindus together in India. As Caliph – pope of Islam and 'successor of the Messenger of God' – the Sultan was about to be stripped by the victorious allies of his spiritual as well as of his temporal powers. Indian Moslems, indignant at the fate of their pontiff, formed the Khilafat movement in protest. (A few years later, the Turks themselves, under Mustapha Kemal, abolished the Sultanate.)

Gandhi accepted an invitation to a Moslem-Hindu Khilafat conference in November 1919. It eagerly debated a boycott of British goods, but Gandhi had a better idea. He could not find a word in Hindi or Urdu to describe it, so he used the English word non-cooperation.

He believed that 'it is an inalienable right of the people to withhold cooperation'.

The policy of non-cooperation gained ground. In June 1920 the Khilafat movement adopted it. Gandhi informed the Viceroy: 'I have advised my Moslem friends to withdraw their support from Your Excellency's Government and advised the Hindus to join them.' He fixed the opening of the campaign for 1 August. The night before, Tilak died. Gandhi was now undisputed leader of Congress.

With non-cooperation as yet untried, Gandhi still had his critics, among them Jinnah. When Gandhi proposed complete *swaraj*, freedom outside the Empire (which he had hitherto loved so much), Jinnah protested at Gandhi's programme: 'I am fully convinced that it must lead to disaster ... [It] has ... struck the imagination mostly of the inexperienced youth and the ignorant and illiterate ... What the consequences may be I shudder to contemplate.'

Between the Hindu Gandhi and the Moslem Jinnah, a rift was opening. At Nagpur, in December 1920, Gandhi persuaded Congress to accept *swaraj*, absolute independence through non-cooperation. Jinnah was one of the very few to protest. 'Your way is the wrong way,' he argued; 'my way, the constitutional way, is the right one.' Ambassador of Hindu-Moslem unity he would continue to be, but, with his orderly mind and his immaculate London clothes, he felt out of place among this garrulous gathering of Hindus clad in home-spun.

Gandhi was cresting. He carried his message of *swaraj* through non-cooperation to the masses, telling them to burn their European clothes and to spin cloth for themselves. The spinning-wheel became the emblem of *swaraj*. And he emphasized his message by returning to the Viceroy the precious medals he had won on Empire service with a note: 'I can retain neither respect nor affection for a government which has been moving from wrong to wrong ...'

*   *   *

The day that Gandhi launched non-cooperation, the Young Men's Burma Association held a mass meeting in Rangoon. Not that it had any connection with Gandhi's movement, nor that it was anything like so ambitious, but the YMBA's meeting led to Burma striking her first concerted blow for independence. It took the form of a student strike at Rangoon University.

Burma had been created (despite the Burmese) a province of India. A YMBA delegation (the second in a year) arrived in London in May 1920 to claim for Burma the same reforms as for India. They were successful. Burma would soon be on the long road to freedom. While at Nagpur Gandhi was persuading Conress to accept non-cooperation as the basis for the campaign against the British Imperial Crown, in Rangoon, at the same time, the University students' strike was setting the pattern for a similar struggle, from which Aung San, now a five-year-old, would emerge the national hero.

In May 1921, four months after the Rangoon disturbances, another 'disturbance' – the Colonial Office could find no stronger word for it – brought more bloodshed to Palestine. During May Day demonstrations in Jaffa, a fight started between Jewish and Arab workers.

The Jews fought back desperately against the Arab mob. A hundred Jews and Arabs were killed. The disturbance had been yet another terrible lesson for the Jews: for defence they must rely not on the police, but on themselves. Ben Gurion's party, Achdut Haavodah, had already allocated a fund to provide arms for their own clandestine defence force, Haganah. At present Haganah was just a loose association of voluntary local defence forces, without any central authority. Its arms were secretly imported – Ben Gurion saw to that. Two permanent officers were appointed; one of them, Dov Hos, was a friend of Ernest Bevin.

At this time Bevin, another freedom-fighter and secretary of the dockers' union, was attacking the British government in order to unfold, as he said, 'the great

human tragedy of men and women fighting year in,
year out against the terrible economic conditions ...'.
Following an eleven-hour speech, he became famous overnight as the 'Dockers' KC'. The *Daily Mail* wrote: 'By
his masterly statements Bevin has pegged out for himself
a place in the front rank of men who count in social
politics.' Not so masterly would be his handling, as a
member of the Government, of the Palestine problem
twenty-five years later.

If the London dockers had their champion, the London
Irish had theirs, too. When de Valera arrived there on
12 July 1921, he was greeted at Euston station by a
frenzied crowd of London Irish. Two days later he was
closeted alone with Lloyd George – the 'Welsh Wizard'
– at No. 10 Downing Street. The British Prime Minister,
'never', as Churchill said, 'a greater artist than in the
first five minutes of a fateful interview', went all out
to impress de Valera with the power and glory of the
British Empire. De Valera listened as Lloyd George intoned the names of his illustrious predecessors, Pitt, Pal-
merston, Gladstone – who had helped to build this vast
empire. He smiled at the Prime Minister's idea of a
Celtic camaraderie between himself, a Welshman, and
the Irish leader. He remained unmoved as Lloyd George
pointed to the chairs occupied by the Dominion prime
ministers (then meeting at the Imperial Conference):
Canada, Australia, New Zealand, South Africa. 'One chair
remains vacant', exclaimed Lloyd George, 'waiting for
Ireland.'

On 20 July, Lloyd George's proposals were delivered to
de Valera: Ireland was to be made a Dominion, while
recognizing the existing government of Northern Ireland,
'which cannot be abrogated except by their own consent'.

De Valera turned the proposals down flat. Dominion
status, with its independence, self-government and free
association with the Empire was all very well for the far-
flung Dominions. But it was inconceivable to him that
Ireland, with Britain just across the Irish Sea, could

ever enjoy this freedom to the full. De Valera had another idea: external association. To Lloyd George, he wrote: 'External association of Ireland with the ... British Commonwealth ... would leave us with the Republic ...'

The armies of both sides were now getting restive. Lloyd George warned de Valera that the truce could not be prolonged indefinitely. So the President sent a delegation, headed by Arthur Griffith, accompanied by Michael Collins and three colleagues. Griffith's brief was to conclude with the representatives of His Britannic Majesty a 'treaty of association' between Ireland and the British Commonwealth. De Valera's price for external association was an Ireland in which north and south were united. And 'external association' meant what it said: the 'British King' would not be king of Ireland. The Irish would recognize him merely as head of the association. 'If war is the alternative, we can only face it,' de Valera warned.

The Irish delegates in London soon began to disagree among themselves. Collins seemed to be set on Dominion status (independence, with allegiance to the King) as a first step, the freedom to achieve freedom as he called it. It was an intelligent approach to the problem. Smuts had preached it in vain to de Valera; twenty-six years later, India would adopt it with complete success. But de Valera could not bring himself to accept what the British demanded: allegiance to their king.

Griffith was back from London with a new British proposal: an 'Irish Free State' as a Dominion within the Empire; Ulster would have the right to opt out of an all-Irish parliament; Irishmen would owe allegiance to the King as 'Head of the State and Empire'. During the Irish cabinet's tense discussion, Cathal Brugha, Minister of Defence, suddenly turned on Griffith: 'Don't you realize that if you sign this thing you will split Ireland from top to bottom?' Griffith was instructed to tell Lloyd George that the Irish cabinet, rather than adopt the oath of allegiance to the King, would accept the consequences – which meant war.

Once again Griffith faced Lloyd George and his cabinet. Eloquently he defended the Irish counter-proposals, but the British were not impressed. What was the objection, asked Lloyd George, to the generous British terms? Gavan Duffy now spoke: 'Our difficulty is coming into the Empire.' One of the British Ministers sprang to his feet: 'That ends it!' he snapped. Others followed him. It looked like the final breakdown. Next morning, 5 December, however, Lloyd George had a *tête-à-tête* with the man he had once called the 'Chief of the Murder Gang' – Michael Collins. He warned Collins that Ireland's refusal to come into the Empire would be published to the world that day.

In the afternoon, the Welsh Wizard mesmerized the men from Dublin with an ultimatum. 'Here', he told them, are alternative letters, one enclosing Articles of Agreement reached by His Majesty's Government and yourselves, the other saying that Sinn Fein representatives refuse to come within the Empire. We must know your answer by 10 pm tonight. You have until then to decide whether you will give peace or war to your country.'

Crestfallen, the Irish delegates left. Churchill noticed that Collins 'looked as if he were going to shoot someone, preferably himself'. After two hours of bitter wrangling among themselves, the Irish delegates returned to Downing Street. 'Mr Prime Minister,' Arthur Griffith addressed Lloyd George, 'the Delegation is willing to sign.'

It was by then 1.30 am on 6 December. In the small hours of that morning, Collins wrote: 'When you have sweated, toiled, had mad dreams, hopeless nightmares you find yourself in London streets, cold and dank in the night air ... What have I got for Ireland? Will anyone be satisfied with the bargain? ... early this morning I signed my death warrant.' His premonition was soon to prove correct.

The Anglo-Irish Treaty was acclaimed as a triumph. King George called it 'the happiest and greatest event ... For 700 years the statesmen have failed to find a solution ... The Prime Minister [is] indeed to be congratulated.'

De Valera shared none of the 'British King's' joy. For him the treaty was a disaster. A few days later he announced: 'My friends, Irishmen ... The terms of the Agreement are in violent conflict with the wishes of the majority of the nation.'

The Irish president was not on such firm ground as he supposed. On 14 December 1921, the Dail met; the debate on the Treaty continued for over two tense weeks, at the end of which de Valera wearily resigned the presidency. The Dail voted: sixty-four for the Treaty and fifty-seven against. As Brugha had foreseen, the Treaty had split Ireland from top to bottom.

The British sovereign enjoys the undeniable right to be consulted, to encourage and to warn. He is not, as Sir William Anson observed, 'a mere piece of mechanism, but a human being carefully trained under circumstances which afford exceptional chances of learning the business of politics'. King George v had once written (in a school note-book) his own conclusion, drawn from Walter Bagehot's *English Constitution*, that 'a monarchy of the English type ... offers a splendid career to an able monarch ... he is the only statesman in the country whose political experience is continuous'.

The goodness and wisdom of George v had been a powerful influence in the attempt to heal the 'poisonous wound' of Ireland. If de Valera and his Republicans persisted in refusing their allegiance to the British King, George v's exemplary conduct throughout the Irish tragedy contributed enormously to 'consolidating the Crown' among his millions of loyal subjects.

The heir apparent, the Prince of Wales, was also doing his bit on behalf of the Crown. Lloyd George envisaged him as a kind of royal bagman, travelling the Empire to 'sell' the Imperial Crown, particularly among the more difficult clients such as the French Canadians and the Australian Labour Party. Before he set out in August

1919, for Canada, Australia and New Zealand, the young Prince was given invaluable advice from a veteran courtier. 'Never miss an opportunity to relieve yourself; never miss a chance to sit down and rest your feet.' Sterner counsel was offered by his father: 'Don't think you can act as other people. Remember who you are.'

Canada gave him a delirious reception; in New York the welcome was tumultuous. He was, as he said, half killed by kindness in Australia and New Zealand. Meanwhile India, which he was due to visit in 1921, was preparing a different kind of reception.

While the Prince was so strenuously personifying the Crown as the symbol of Empire unity, his brother Bertie worked diligently (as was his manner) to represent it as 'a living power for good'. His role, if quite as vital, was much less glamorous than his brother David's. David made the headlines, Bertie a paragraph in the Court Circular. But it suited Bertie, serious-minded and idealistic as he was, and possessing the solid virtues of his father. 'So different to dear David,' King George said of him more than once. In June 1920 the King had given him that fine old title (as he called it) of Duke of York. When he himself had once borne it, Queen Victoria had sharply objected: 'A Prince *no one* else can be, whereas a Duke any nobleman can be and many are!' King George differed. To 'Dearest Bertie' he wrote: 'I feel this splendid old title will be safe in your hands' and the Duke replied: 'I hope I shall live up to it in every way.'

As President of the Industrial Workers' Society, he had every opportunity of doing so. The object of the Society, as the Duke said, was to get back to the human side of industry, to treat the worker as a human being first and a working hand afterwards. Soon he was able to claim 'very real and human relations are being built up.'

The Duke of York once defined an idealist as someone who will strive for something which may appear unattainable but which he believes in his heart can one day be reached. He was an idealist himself. He told a meeting of the IWS: 'If we do not lead, no one will follow.' Taking the lead himself, he visited factories and mines up and down the country (averaging one visit every ten days). Following his grandfather Edward VII's precept that class could no longer stand apart from class, he talked informally with captains of industry and their employees, with the object, as he put it, of fostering a spirit of comradeship, patriotism and devotion among all classes. He aimed at encouraging the human side of industry, to help the worker to 'free himself from the grip of the machine', and to create cooperation and understanding between employees and employer. Gradually, he became a top authority on industry. The nation called him the Industrial Prince (his brothers, the Foreman).

In line with his efforts to foster comradeship between all classes, he started a boys' camp in 1921. To the rendezvous at Buckingham Palace came four hundred boys, half of them public schoolboys (complete with bowler hat and umbrella), the other half, in reach-me-downs, from industrial areas. The experiment was highly successful (the camps were held annually for seventeen years). One boy wrote: 'We entered the Camp, like animals in Noah's Ark, two by two, but we came out in clusters. It was quite a wrench to say good-bye.' And a minister who visited the Camp found 'a real vital and spiritual force ... of help, of cooperation – in one word, Love.'

But one cloud hung over the Duke's activities: the ordeal of public speaking. He once recalled in a speech Lord Cardigan's order to the Light Brigade at Balaclava, before that 'well-nigh impossible task': 'The Brigade will advance!' It was in that spirit that the Duke faced up to his own well-nigh impossible task of delivering a speech. The consonant *k* invariably brought him to a standstill, so he never said 'King', but 'His Majesty' or simply 'My father'.

His style was strikingly simple and sincere. Youth and Empire were his recurrent themes. 'There never was a time', he told the boys of the Herts School, 'when the British Empire stood in greater need of good citizens ... to keep the heritage of the greatest Empire the world has ever seen.' He exhorted the boys of Bancroft School 'to try and make our native land and the Empire ... the home of loyalty, righteousness and goodwill'. To the workers of Sheffield he gave encouragement for 'our old Country to maintain her proud position in the eyes of the world'. Nearer to reality, he declared to the Boys' Brigade: 'The Empire in her difficulties has greater need for good citizens ... who will be wanted for the critical times to come.' Another time, he said, little realizing his own involvement: 'I am confident that we shall reach our ultimate goal of greater human happiness for the Empire.'

Inevitably, the idealistic Duke, far removed from the scene of action, took an over-sanguine view of things which his brother David, on the spot, saw in their stark reality. Occasionally the Duke would say: 'I have heard from my brother ...'; but his most cherished ambition was 'to know at first hand the nations which make up the comprehensive brotherhood of the Empire'. He was convinced of the righteousness of Britain's imperial mission: 'Events conspire to make us all Imperialists in no militant sense, but as upholders of ideals which have already exercised a widespread influence on the progress of civilization, and which hold ... the future hope of humanity at large.' It was not exactly the view now held by Mahatma Gandhi.

Early in 1922, the Duke of York confessed: 'There are some aspects of my brother's work which I do not altogether envy.' It was an understandable admission.

As the time for the Prince of Wales's visit to India approached, Gandhi was on the war-path. 'It is sinful for anyone, either soldier or civilian, to serve the government,' he declared. 'Non-cooperation aims at the overthrow of the government.' No one was more surprised than himself when he was not arrested for sedition. Viceroy Reading reacted. 'If India honours the Prince', he told reporters, '*swaraj* is within your grasp.' Gandhi responded by announcing civil disobedience for 17 November, the date of the Prince's arrival.

As the Prince's ship, HMS *Renown*, rounded Steamer Point, a placard greeted him with the message: 'Tell Daddy we are all happy under British rule.' It seriously belied the facts, as the Prince was soon to discover.

From Bombay the Prince set off on a four-month tour of India. Gandhi's *hartals* failed to upset the faultless rhythm of the tour, with its military parades, state drives, addresses of welcome, receptions and polo matches. But it was obvious to the Prince that Gandhi and the government were vying for the loyalty of the masses. The holy city of Benares and Allahabad (Nehru's stronghold) were most successful in ostracizing the Prince. Along the troop-lined, deserted streets, shops were closed and the population remained behind shuttered windows. Jawaharlal Nehru, who had been gaoled for sedition before the royal visit to Allahabad, said: 'It was like a city of the dead'; but generously admitted: 'It was hard on the Prince.'

The political antagonism against him seriously worried the sporting Prince. 'I'm very depressed about my work in British India', he wrote to his father, 'as I don't feel I'm doing a scrap of good.' The Emperor sympathized, regretting that things 'should have changed so rapidly since we were there 10 years ago'. He encouraged his son – 'you are doing good for the Empire'.

From the Prince's point of view, which was admittedly limited to his royal progress from one Government House to another, British power in India seemed 'solid, secure and timeless'. He felt unbounded admiration for the machinery of British rule: the Indian Army and Indian Civil Service were dedicated to an 'unwearying trustee-ship', they guarded frontiers, put down riots, alleviated famine, subdued plague; they brought justice to India's formerly oppressed millions; they taught the Indians to govern.

He left India at Karachi on 17 March 1922, with the band crashing out 'God Save the King'. 'Had anybody tried to persuade me,' he said later, 'that all this would be lost in my lifetime, I would have put the man down as a lunatic.'

The day after the Prince's departure, Gandhi was gaoled. As the Prince toured, the non-cooperation campaign had gathered momentum. Gandhi was attracting the townspeople to his essentially peasant movement, and enticing teen-agers to follow him. This they did, blindly, abandoning their classrooms, sowing dissension among the masses and finishing up in gaol. The intellectuals of the freedom movement became alarmed lest it should end in social upheaval.

On 8 February, at Chauri Chaura, eight hundred miles from Bardoli, demonstrators clashed with the police, who fired back. Their ammunition exhausted, the police barricaded themselves in their police station, to which the mob set fire. Gandhi called the atrocity a bad augury, called off his civil disobedience and fasted for five days in penance for the murderers.

He himself, though, was unrepentant. To a statement from Edwin Montagu that 'India would not challenge with success the most determined people in the world' (i.e. the British), Gandhi retorted: 'No empire intoxicated with the red wine of power ... has lived long in this world, and the British Empire, which is based upon exploitation of physically weaker races ... cannot live if there is a just God ...' Gandhi and the Prince of Wales evidently did not see eye to eye on the British Raj.

On 10 March 1922, Gandhi was arrested and charged with sedition. Judge Broomfield reminded him that the law is no respecter of persons, though he acknowledged that Gandhi was 'a great patriot and a man of high ideals and saintly life'. Bowing to the prisoner (twenty years his senior), the Judge pronounced sentence: six years' gaol. 'No one would be better pleased than I if your term were reduced,' he told Gandhi.

As if her problem in India was not enough, Britain was

to get herself inextricably involved in another family conflict between Jew and Arab. The Palestine Mandate granted to Britain at San Remo in 1920 had yet to be ratified. While draft after draft was being discussed and rejected, opposition mounted against the Mandate. Catholics asked why it had been granted to a Protestant country; the Vatican was concerned about the Holy Places, while both in Rome and Paris it was being said that Zionism was merely a camouflage for British imperialism.

But the British Middle East garrison had to be kept somewhere, and the Zionists were the first to argue that a Jewish Home in Palestine would help secure the country as a British base – an argument they were later to reverse.

The Arabs and the ancient Jewish community were convinced that British imperialism was behind the Mandate. Not even Balfour's passionate plea, in the House of Lords, could defeat the 'imperialist' theory. Balfour denied that his Declaration sprang entirely from material considerations. Essentially, it was an idealistic attempt to solve 'the great and abiding Jewish problems'. The Jews' position in world history, religion and politics was 'absolutely unique'.

But the motion 'that the Mandate for Palestine is unacceptable ...' was carried. In the Commons, a similar motion was heavily defeated. Weizmann, perturbed by the Lords' reaction, was reassured by Balfour: 'What does it matter if a few foolish Lords pass such a motion?'

The Government stated its policy in the 'Churchill White Paper' of June 1922 (Churchill was then Colonial Secretary). It quoted Weizmann's own phrase, 'Palestine is to become as Jewish as England is English', and went on: 'His Majesty's government ... have no such aim ...' On the other hand, the White Paper made it possible for the Jews, through immigration, to dominate in Palestine. It thus typified future British policy – an attempt to please both sides.

The League Council unanimously ratified the appointment of Britain as mandatory power, with the responsibility, among others, of 'securing the establishment of the Jewish Home' and of 'facilitating Jewish immigration'. The word Jew or Zionist was mentioned twelve times. The Arabs, as such, were not mentioned at all.

Britain's attempts to satisfy the aspirations of the Indians, the Israelites and the Irish had anything but the desired effect. Indeed, they were to lead to frightful bitterness and bloodshed in each of the countries concerned – with Britain held to blame.

The Irish were the first to be caught up in a war of brother against brother. Relations between Republicans and Free Staters were worsening daily. De Valera urged Irishmen to join the Republican cause and resist the Anglo-Irish Treaty. He appealed to Sinn Fein 'in God's name not to give a British monarch a democratic title in Ireland'; Irishmen, he maintained, would rather die than acknowledge the British king as their king.

Irishmen were in fact already dying in armed clashes between Free State forces and Republican bands. Meanwhile Collins, for the Provisional Government, and rebel de Valera were trying desperately to avoid civil war. By 20 May they had made a pact, and the Government immediately went to work on a revised draft of the new Constitution, which omitted the hated oath of allegiance to the British Crown. The King of England was 'relegated to exterior darkness'.

Churchill, however, warned in the Commons that if the new Constitution did not agree with the Treaty terms (including allegiance to the King-Emperor), there would be no Treaty, but possibly war instead. And when Ireland went to the polls on 16 June, the result was a sweeping victory for the Treaty. Many voters, however, were ignorant of the final draft of the Constitution – it had been published in the papers only that morning.

Tension between the Free Staters and Republicans was acute and at 4.07 am on 28 June 1922 the Free State artillery opened fire on the IRA established in Dublin's

Four Courts. The Irish Civil War had begun. 'I for one rejoice that this task, painful, costly, bloody as it must prove, is being undertaken by those to whom it properly falls,' was Birkenhead's chilling remark. De Valera accused: 'At the bidding of the English, Irishmen are today shooting down ... brother Irishmen.'

For the next year, de Valera, who had re-enlisted as a private in the Volunteers, was on the run, stealing by dark or in disguise from one hiding place to another. The Republican army retreated south, burning barracks and blowing bridges as they went. Then in August they took to the hills and to guerilla warfare. Michael Collins, the Big Fellow, confided to a friend: 'I'm sick of the whole tragic business. To hell with the British, I'm going to see the Long Fellow.' But Collins and de Valera were never to meet again. The Big Fellow was shot down in an ambush by his own countrymen.

On 6 December, anniversary of the signing of the Treaty, the Irish Free State was officially proclaimed, with Cosgrave its President. In Leinster House, an eighteenth-century mansion before whose sooted, grey-black façade sat Queen Victoria in stone (her sour expression earned for the statue the nick-name 'Ireland's Revenge'), the Free State deputies swore to be 'faithful to His Majesty King George v'.

In the south-west the Republican army was cracking and on 27 April 1923 de Valera announced: 'The war so far was we are concerned is finished.'

President Cosgrave now insisted: 'No truck, no negotiations unless the Republicans surrender their arms.' If they did, they might take part in an election. 'We are ready,' replied de Valera, still in hiding. But he was adamant on one point: 'We will never swear an oath of allegiance to a foreign king.'

The elections were held in August. De Valera was still a wanted man but, declaring that nothing but a bullet would stop him, he turned up at a meeting at Ennis. 'My God, 'tis himself!' people cried in the dense, excited crowd. His appearance was brief. As he was led away under arrest, he turned to say: 'Whatever about me, mind the Republic.'

The Free State Government won sixty-three seats against the Republicans' forty-four. But de Valera, now a prisoner in Arbour Hill Barracks, had been re-elected member for Clare by a large majority.

Britain had paved the way to hell with her good intentions. The Indian reforms, the Irish Treaty, the Balfour Declaration and its sequel, the Palestine Mandate, had all produced internal upheaval, and hatred of Britannia in her role of Lady Bountiful, wedged uncomfortably between Hindu and Moslem, Arab and Jew, Irish Catholic and Protestant.

Gandhi was in prison, de Valera too. Jews and Arabs, Semite half-brothers, were also in a sense captive of an ideal which doomed them to fratricide. Despite all the hopeful predictions of a quarter of a century earlier, at Empress Victoria's Diamond Jubilee, there was now something rotten in the Empire of Britain.

4

'The emperorship must go'

In the Emperor's family, however, there was rejoicing. On 26 April 1923, his second son was married in Westminster Abbey. He had first met his bride, Lady Elizabeth Bowes Lyon, at a children's party. He was ten, she five, and she gave him cherries from her iced cake. Altruism, admiration or simply because she did not like them? All three, perhaps, for Lady Elizabeth was a girl unlike most others and knew what she wanted. They next met when he was twenty-five. 'The more I see of her, the more I like her,' wrote Bertie to his mother, Queen Mary, but there were rivals in the field. Lady Elizabeth was loved by many swains, and it says much for Bertie's tenacity, as well as for his other qualities, that, despite his shyness and his stammer, it was he who won her hand.

In January 1923, the Duke of York telegraphed his mother: 'All right. Bertie.' He had been accepted. Later he told Queen Mary: 'I know I am very lucky to have won her over at last.' And the King-Emperor commented: 'She is pretty charming, and Bertie is a very lucky fellow.' In fact, Lady Elizabeth came like a breath of fresh air into the somewhat stuffy atmosphere of the Imperial Family. The Emperor, so gruff and irascible with his own children, melted like butter in the warmth of his daughter-in-law's charm. When she arrived late for dinner, the King-Emperor, a stickler for punctuality, merely murmured: 'You are not late, my dear. We must have sat down too early.' And he wrote to 'Dearest Bertie': 'You are indeed a lucky man ... I miss you ... you have always been so sensible and easy to work with (very different to dear David) ... I am quite certain that Elizabeth will be a splendid partner in your work.'

I saw an unforgettable example of this partnership when, as a schoolboy at Haileybury, I stood in the front rank of the guard of honour as the Duke spoke at the opening of our new dining-hall, whose architect, as befitted this one-time establishment of the Honourable East India Company, was Sir Herbert Baker, associate of Sir Edward Lutyens, creator of India's modern capital, New Delhi. The Duke, in naval uniform, with frock-coat and sword, looked lean and fit, and as if nothing could trouble his personal horizon. But as soon as he started his speech he was in difficulties. Warned of his stammer, we tensed uncomfortably each time he faltered and came to a standstill. However, the Duchess, standing beside him, only smiled and seemed to whisper to him, willing him over the wall of silence and into the next sentence until, at last, with a smile of sheer relief, he pronounced the final words. Her sense of partnership was sublime.

The following year the Duke began to acquaint himself better with his father's empire. On 19 July 1924 – three days after de Valera's release from prison – he and the Duchess visited Ulster, on whose soil, incidentally, de Valera was forbidden to set foot. The reception, said the Duke, was astounding. 'We were received in the same wonderful way ... even in the poorest parts' – which suggests that Ulster's Catholic minority, spiritual supporters of de Valera, were not above saying hello to the son of the British King whom de Valera so detested.

A few months later, the Duke and Duchess of York visited Kenya and Uganda. Back in England in April 1925, the Duke did not find it easy to adapt himself to the daily round of a royal prince, especially as it involved a speech, as President of the British Empire Exhibition. 'I shall be very frightened,' he warned his father, who afterwards commented: 'Bertie got through his speech all right, but there were some rather long pauses.' Something – the Duke and everybody else agreed – had to be done about the stammer. But eighteen more months of agony were yet to pass before the hour of deliverance arrived.

Well might the British rejoice in their monarchy. It was by far the oldest political institution in the country, older than the Law Courts and Parliament. The British

Royal House goes back to Egbert, who ascended the throne in 809. By that time, however, the descendants of Niall of the Seven Hostages, King of Ireland, had been ruling for four centuries. Which goes some way to explain the aversion of de Valera and his Republicans to the British King.

No sooner released from prison, de Valera took up the familiar refrain: 'The sovereignty of Ireland ... cannot possibly be given away. We can never give allegiance to a foreign power.' Nor did he let up on the issue of Ulster, where recently the son of the British King had been so warmly welcomed. In April 1926 he founded a new party, Fianna Fail. De Valera continued his ranting: 'The oath to the King of England was posed as a political test. Why not end the whole abominable prevarication?' By November he was threatening revolution.

Persuasion, not threats, was the technique employed by Chaim Weizmann, President of World Zionism. His aim was to enlist friends – and funds – for the Jewish Home. He told Louis Marshall, a leading American Jew: 'The money is there, in the pockets of American Jews. It's your business and mine to get some of it.' American Jews, like American Irish, were generous in helping their less fortunate brethren abroad.

At the end of 1924 the British ex-premier, Herbert Asquith, on a visit to Palestine, said: 'The talk of making Palestine a Jewish National Home seems to me just as fantastic as it always has been.'

Another visitor to the country was Arthur Balfour. Now seventy-seven, he had been invited to open the Hebrew University on Mount Scopus, Jerusalem, on 1 April 1925. He received a tremendous ovation. But the Palestine Arabs received the sponsor of the Jewish Home with a display of public mourning. In the old city of Jerusalem he passed through silent streets. Weizmann felt deeply chagrined that Balfour's visit should have gone so badly. 'Oh, I wouldn't worry', replied the aged statesman, 'it was nothing compared to what I went through in Ireland.'

In June 1925 Palestine got a new High Commissioner, Field Marshall Lord Plumer, a choleric little man, with walrus moustache, receding chin and monocle. His appearance was misleading. Plumer hated pomp – he thought it bad taste in a land where Jesus lived in poverty. He liked to wander among the crowds in old Jerusalem in 'plain clothes' – bowler hat, blue suit, stiff collar and rolled umbrella – in the vain hope that he would pass unnoticed. When, shortly after his arrival, he attended a Jewish sports meeting, the Jewish anthem '*Hatikvah*' was played. Lord Plumer stood to attention and removed his hat. 'What are they playing?' whispered his daughter. 'I don't know,' replied the new High Commissioner. 'We'll find out afterwards.' Outraged by his apparent homage to the Jews, an Arab delegation waited on him to protest. 'Suppose', Plumer asked them, 'I remained seated while the Arab anthem was played?' Then he added: 'By the way, have you got an anthem?' and the confused Arabs admitted they had not. 'Then you had better get one,' counselled Plumer. 'If I can help I should be only too pleased. '

The three years of Plumer's office were, through no fault of his, a lean time for the Palestine Jews. Immigration in 1925 had reached a record figure of nearly 34,000 (it was 5,500 in 1920). But the numbers fell sharply to 13,000 in 1926, 3,000 in 1927. In that year, 5,000 Jews left Palestine. Jewish business went bankrupt. In the kibbutzim there were signs of starvation. On the political front Ben Gurion was quarrelling with Weizmann.

These years of Zionist weakness allayed Arab fears. As Weizmann said: 'Our relations with the Arabs were not altogether unsatisfactory.' He firmly believed in Arab–Jew co-existence: 'The Jewish Home will always remain an island in the Arab sea. We have to come to an understanding with this people which is akin to us and with which we have lived in concord in the past.' In 1925, to the Zionist Congress, he said: 'Palestine must be built up without violating the legitimate interests of the Arabs.'

With Arab–Jewish relations apparently so calm, Plumer

believed that the solution to the Palestine problem was at hand. He decided to reduce the police force and the military garrison.

No such policy was contemplated in India, although the new Viceroy, Lord Irwin (later Lord Halifax), who had arrived in April 1926, was hailed as a man of God determined on a settlement with India's holy man, Mahatma Gandhi. Irwin (nicknamed 'the Pope') and Gandhi, apart from their common devoutness (Irwin enlivened his with fox-hunting), were outwardly quite different. The little Mahatma wore sandals and a *dhoti* (loincloth), the Viceroy, towering austerely in his viceregal robes, was reproached for looking more kingly than the King.

A year and a half passed before the two men met. Meanwhile, Gandhi made up for the time – and the initiative – lost in Yeravda Gaol, whence he had been released in January 1924, with less than two of his six years' term completed. (This must have pleased Judge Broomfield who had so reluctantly sentenced him.) Gandhi's object was 'to purge Indian political life of corruption, deceit, terrorism and the incubus of white supremacy', and to prepare her for the future struggle. By now the non-cooperation movement was dead. Gandhi felt that a wave of violence was coming. Hindu-Moslem tension was mounting.

Cows and music were the keys to communal strife. Gandhi regarded cow protection as the 'central fact' of Hinduism, but he berated Hindu cow-worshippers: 'In no part of the world are cattle treated worse than in India.'

Music was the bane of the Muslims when played within earshot of their mosques. It disturbed the sons of the Prophet at prayer (five times a day), and especially at the time of the sunset prayer. This unfortunately coincided with the Hindu *Arti* when, to the tinkle of temple bells and the boom of gongs, Hindus are at worship.

As Hindu-Moslem fighting increased, Gandhi decided to fast in the home of the Moslem leader, Mohamed Ali.

Twenty-one days later, he broke his fast. Alas, the
Mahatma had suffered in vain for Hindu-Moslem
brotherhood. Tension continued unabated.

Gandhi was convinced that the British held India for
the benefit of the Lancashire textile trade, so he led a
national campaign for *khadi*, home-spun cloth. *Khadi*
was coarse and uncomfortable. Nehru, however, called it
'the livery of our freedom'. Gradually *khadi* became
fashionable, even with the intellectuals. No good Congressman would dream of wearing anything else.

Gandhi covered thousands of miles preaching his gospel of caste and communal brotherhood. At meetings he
would squat down with Untouchables, challenging the
high-caste Brahmins to do the same. The people deified
him. 'I am no Mahatma!' he cried, but the people took
him for a reincarnation of God, with miraculous powers.
Once, a passenger fell out of the train in which Gandhi
was travelling. The man, unhurt, claimed that Gandhi's
presence had saved him. 'Then why did you fall out of
the train in the first place?' asked the Mahatma.

Gandhi watched for a chance of civil disobedience. It
came with the arrival of a parliamentary commission,
headed by Lord Simon, to investigate the Indian political
system. Indians were outraged because the Simon Commission was all-white. It had no Indian member. When the
Commission arrived in Bombay on 3 February 1928, it
faced a total boycott. Black flags flew everywhere and
thousands of Indians chanted 'Simon, go back'. They
were the only English words they knew.

If the King-Emperor could no longer command the absolute loyalty of his subjects in Ireland and in India, no
such problems arose in his Australasian dominions, and
only minor ones in the other two, Canada and South
Africa. There was a basic reason for this: Ireland and
India – Burma too – were mother countries in their own
right, with their own traditions and culture. They resented the overlordship of a foreign power and of a
foreign king.

Australia and New Zealand, like Canada and South
Africa, were 'white' dominions, largely peopled and entirely controlled by inhabitants of British stock. There
were of course important nuances. Australia had a semi-
stone-age residue of aborigines. New Zealand's Maoris
were integrated with their white compatriots. The Canadian French were a tight and not altogether contented
minority in an Anglo-Saxon sea. South Africa was a
special case, with its whites of Boer and British stock
and its millions of politically destitute blacks. The King
of Great Britain was king of each of these dominions
which, though the degree varied, were British in tradition and in loyalty to his person. When the prime
ministers of the dominions met at regular imperial conferences in London, it was a family gathering, no matter
whether the Canadian premier happened to be French,
or the South African of Dutch descent.

At the conference of 1926, Arthur Balfour defined the
ground rules of membership of this 'Commonwealth
Club'. 'They are autonomous communities within the
British Empire, equal in status, in no way subordinate
one to another, though united by a common allegiance
to the Crown, and freely associated as members of the
British Commonwealth of Nations.' What irked India
and Ireland, and in an increasing degree Burma, was
allegiance to the Crown. The inhabitants of Palestine,
as a mandated territory, were 'protected persons' – without owing allegiance to the King-Emperor, they benefited
from his protection.

The most intensely British of the dominions were Australia and New Zealand. In 1927 their loyalty was stirred
to new depths by a visit from the Duke of York. Before
leaving, the Duke put the reason for his visit in a nut-
shell: 'The furthering of good feeling between the different portions of the Anglo-Saxon race.'

The King-Emperor hesitated before sending his second
son on this, his first imperial mission. Not that he lacked
confidence in the Duke's performance of his royal tasks.
The problem was his son's stammer. It was solved on 19

October when the Duke met Mr Lionel Logue, himself an Australian. Logue wrote later: 'He entered my consulting room ... a slim, quiet man, with tired eyes and all the symptoms ... of habitual speech defect. When he left you could see there was once more hope in his heart.' Logue had appeared on the scene as if by a miracle. When the Duke heard of him, he was sceptical. So many previous cures had failed. But the Duchess was confident. 'Just one more try,' she urged him. Soon the Duke was writing to his father: 'I have noticed a great improvement in my talking and also in making speeches ... I am sure I am going to get quite all right in time.' Logue's secret was correct breathing. As the Duke said, 'Now that I know the right way to breathe, my fear of talking will vanish.'

Thus greatly reassured, the Duke, accompanied by the Duchess, sailed on 6 January 1927 in HMS *Renown*, via Jamaica, and Fiji, to Auckland, New Zealand. There the mayor recalled that the Empire rested not upon constitutions and legal documents, but upon men and human sympathy. The Duke agreed, but a symbol was needed too. 'The Throne is the great bond of union between all parts of the Empire.' In Tasmania, Australia, the Duke got back to what, after all, was the basic fact of Commonwealth life: 'We are among our kith and kin.' Australia and New Zealand, he thought, would one day be one of the greatest homes of the British race.

Sydney, Australia, hailed him and the Duchess as their 'pride and joy'. In Canberra, the new capital, he opened the first meeting of the Federal Parliament. It was the King's earnest prayer, he said, that the future would see 'development and prosperity of the Empire in all its parts', and a determination 'to support one another ... should the need come' (as in due course it would).

The Duke's mission completed, he sailed for home. He wrote to his father: 'Logue's teaching has really done wonders ... I have so much more confidence in myself now'. The written instructions which he received from his father before meeting him and Queen Mary at Victoria Station, London, were not exactly calculated to increase that confidence. The King-Emperor enjoined his thirty-two-year-old son: 'We will not embrace at the station before so many people. When you embrace Mama, take your hat off.'

His success as a royal ambassador whetted the Duke's enthusiasm to know more of the secrets of the Commonwealth and state affairs. The King-Emperor's advisers were sympathetic. Not so the King-Emperor – he judged it unwise and unnecessary for his sons to meet political leaders or to have access to the red despatch boxes which came from his ministers bearing secrets of state. King George v had no reason to believe that his second son would become King-Emperor. When he did, he was seriously handicapped by his ignorance of state affairs.

The fervent loyalty created by the King-Emperor's son in Australia and New Zealand had no parallel in his fifth dominion, Ireland. There, de Valera was working assiduously for the opposite effect. Notwithstanding one civil war, he was now threatening that the question of allegiance to the King might have to be 'bloodily fought out'.

At the 1927 elections, Fianna Fail campaigned to abolish the oath of allegiance. The Free State President, Cosgrave, responded: 'We believe in honouring our bond' (to the Anglo-Irish Treaty). The results once again proved de Valera over-optimistic about Republican feeling in Ireland. Though the Government lost many seats, there was no outright victory for Fianna Fail.

De Valera and the Republican deputies resolved to take their seats in the Dail without taking the oath. When he presented himself before the clerk of the Dail he told him: 'I want you to understand that I am not taking any oath, nor giving any promise of faithfulness to the King of Ireland ...' Picking up the Bible lying on the clerk's desk, he carried it solemnly to the other end of the room, then returned and signed the clerk's register. De Valera believed that there was neither perjury nor falsehood in his act. Not everyone agreed, but whatever the case, he would in future be able to fight for the Republican cause on the floor of the Dail. De Valera's role as an outlaw was ended.

The all-white, Conservative Simon Commission had two black sheep – Labour MPs Hartshorn and Clement Attlee. Attlee was fortunate to share in this great experience, as he put it. Durga Das, well-known Indian journalist, who met Attlee, was 'hardly impressed either by his personality or his intellect'. Attlee thought Congress was foolish to boycott the Simon Commission. But Gandhi, angered at the exclusion of Indians, decided to act.

Sardar Vallabhabhai Patel, a prosperous lawyer, bald, clean-shaven, his massive body swathed in *khadi*, was mayor of Ahmedabad when Gandhi asked him to lead a civil disobedience campaign in the county of Bardoli, near Bombay, where, in 1922, a similar campaign had been cut short by the Chauri Chaura outrage. At Patel's urging, the villagers refused to pay their taxes, whereupon the authorities confiscated their cattle and farm equipment, arresting thousands. Bardoli continued to resist peaceably until, on 6 August, the Government wisely gave way.

Gandhi had scored a signal victory. Elsewhere, however, non-violence provoked violence. During demonstrations at Lahore, Lajpat Rai, 'Lion of the Punjab', was so severely beaten by a police officer that he died. The police officer in turn was murdered. When the Simon Commission arrived in Lucknow, Jawaharlal Nehru, leading a peaceful procession, was caught in a charge of mounted police armed with *lathis* (sawn-off polo sticks). Nehru (India's future prime minister) was half-blinded by blows from a British police-sergeant's *lathi*. 'I did not raise a hand,' said Gandhi's favourite disciple.

Jawaharlal's father, Motilal Nehru (to whom he was devoted), was the grand old man of Indian politics. He looked more like a Roman senator than a Hindu *pandit*. Motilal decided to answer the challenge made by Birken-

head that Indians should produce a new constitution
instead of merely indulging in destructive criticism. Motilal Nehru's report was published in August 1928. Its
moderate tone displeased the revolutionary young Jawaharlal.

At the All-Parties conference held in Calcutta on 28
December 1928 to discuss the Nehru Report, the Moslem
leader Jinnah pleaded for his people: Moslems formed
about one-fifth of India's population. The Nehru Report
gave them proportional representation, but Jinnah demanded that at least one-third of the elected representatives should be Moslems.

When the conference rejected Jinnah's demands he
wept, and turning to a friend murmured: 'This is the
parting of the ways.' Jinnah's cup was not yet full; two
months later, his wife Ruttie died. Sorrowfully, Jinnah
resumed his stern and solitary bachelor's life.

Motilal Nehru's report was accepted by Congress. His
son Jawaharlal's ideas were more revolutionary. He, and
the firebrand Subhas Chandra Bhose, wanted an immediate declaration of independence. Gandhi suggested giving the British until 31 December 1929. If by then India
had not gained freedom as a Dominion, then said Gandhi:
'I shall declare myself an Independence-wallah.'

At this time, communal strife was beginning to disturb
the peace of Palestine. On the eve of the Jewish feast
of Yom Kippur (the Atonement, which falls on the first
moon after the autumnal equinox), an object, exactly
like a bedroom screen, was deposited on the pavement
in front of the Wailing Wall in Jerusalem, that massive
façade of hewn stone blocks, last vestige of Herod's
temple and the sacred shrine of Jewry. In a house above
the Wall lived the Mufti of Jerusalem, Haj Amin El
Husseini, in convenient proximity to the Mosque of
Omar. The Arabs protested that the screen was an outrage to the sanctity of the Wall which, they explained
(quite untruthfully) was as holy to Moslems as to Jews.

The Mufti lost no time in exploiting the situation.

Spiritual leader of the Palestine Arabs, Haj Amin was
handsome, despite his slight build and a somewhat shifty
look in his eyes. The British, who took him for the soul
of charm and sincerity, later discovered that he was a cunning, blood-thirsty rascal.

Haj Amin spread the story that the Jews were intend-
ing to take over the Mosque of Omar. He distributed
forged pictures showing the Jewish flag flying from its
dome. Then, luckily, passions cooled off, to smoulder
until the following year.

In the summer of 1929, Arab crowds, their numbers
swelled by those who had come up to Jerusalem to worship, began rioting near the Wall. The Friday after,
Arabs again flocked into Jerusalem. The Mufti held a
mass meeting. He was careful to avoid any incitement
to violence, but the mob understood. It rushed into the
streets and murdered several Jews. The police force, so
drastically thinned down by Plumer, were unable to cope.
Army reinforcements took three days to arrive. Meanwhile the Administration refused arms to the defenceless
Jews of the kibbutzim, forbade the use of Jewish police.
On 24 August 1929, in the upper room of an inn at Heb-
ron, Arabs armed with knives and axes killed and dismembered twenty-three Jews. Safed, in the north, was the
scene of another frightful pogrom.

Weizmann's blood boiled at the 'indifference, ineffi-
ciency and hostility' of the Palestine administration. He
sped to London to see the new Colonial Secretary, Sidney
Webb (Lord Passfield). Webb, a dapper little bearded
man whose wife Beatrice, in her high cloche hat, seemed
to dominate him, was unsympathetic to the Zionist movement and reluctant to receive its leader. Beatrice Webb,
who deputized for him, was not consoling either. She said
to Weizmann: 'I can't think why the Jews make such a
fuss over a few dozen of their people killed in Palestine.
As many are killed every week in London in traffic acci-
dents and no one pays any attention.'

The brutal methods of Haj Amin, man of God as he professed to be, were anathema to those two men of God, Gandhi and Irwin. It was now that the fox-hunting Viceroy galloped ahead of the field and announced from Delhi that he envisaged a round table conference, and that the natural issue of India's constitutional progress was Dominion status.

The Viceroy, however, riding on a tighter rein, followed up his momentous statement by telling Gandhi that Dominion status for India could not be guaranteed in advance.

A week later, the year of grace that Congress had granted to Britain ended. On 31 December 1929, as the old year yielded to the new, Congress, meeting at Lahore under Jawaharlal Nehru's presidency, unanimously demanded full independence for India, with secession from the Empire. 'We had burned our boats', the forty-year-old president said, 'but the country ahead was a strange and uncharted land.'

26 January was fixed as Independence Day. It revealed in a flash, as Nehru said, the earnest and enthusiastic mood of the country. Great crowds peacefully and solemnly took the oath of independence. Gandhi, ever with his finger on India's pulse, felt that his moment had come. On 2 March 1930, he wrote to the Viceroy. 'Dear Friend', he began, 'while I hold the British rule to be a curse, I do not intend harm to a single Englishman.' He doubted that Britain had any intention of giving India Dominion status in the near future. He charged that land revenue and the salt tax were 'crushing the very life' out of India's peasants. (Hindu money-lenders, Gandhi's co-religionists, were doing so even more). 'My ambition', wrote Gandhi, 'is to convert the British people through non-violence, and thus make them see the wrong they have done to India.' He warned: 'If my letter makes no appeal to your heart, on the eleventh day of this month [March] ... I shall proceed to disregard the Salt Laws.' When no reply came from Irwin, Gandhi, with the words 'Victory or death' on his lips, set out on foot and headed for Dandi, on the coast, 240 miles away. He

covered ten miles a day. The British did not intervene; they thought he would not make it – he was sixty-one.

But on 6 April, Gandhi reached the sea at Dandi. A huge crowd watched as he picked up some salt left by the sea. It was his signal to India to defy the 'nefarious' government salt monopoly. In towns and villages throughout the land, millions of Indians used any expedient they knew to produce home-made salt – mostly unwholesome stuff, but no one cared as long as they broke the Salt Laws.

As too often happened, Gandhi's non-violent campaign provoked widespread violence. Viceroy Irwin was obliged to inform the King-Emperor that one of His Majesty's crack Hindu regiments, the Garwhali Rifles, had refused to fire on Moslem rioters (a rare case of communal solidarity). Irwin, trying to keep order in a non-violent way, gaoled 60,000 Indians, among them his friend Gandhi, and the Nehrus, father and son. (Jawaharlal's lovely but sickly wife, Kamala, was later gaoled, to her intense pride.) Gandhi was extremely happy in gaol. The younger Nehru was philosophic. 'With a wistful eye', he said, 'I looked

> Upon that little tent of blue
> Which prisoners call the sky,
> And at every drifting cloud that went
> With sail of silver by.'

But at night he felt as if he was at the bottom of a well.

With Gandhi in prison, the first Indian Round Table Conference was opened by the King-Emperor in London in November 1930. The British yielded little, but they created an atmosphere of good-will, which would be a help to Gandhi in his next step, a vital one.

But for the sinister designs of the Mufti of Jerusalem, a Palestine round table conference might also have taken place about this time. It was Weizmann's idea. After his depressing encounter with Lady Passfield, he at last got an interview with Passfield himself. Weizmann came away convinced of 'the depth and persistence of Passfield's hostility'. Passfield stated his policy in a White Paper on 21 October 1930. It affirmed that the Zionist inter- pretation of the Mandate – that the Jewish National Home had priority over the rights of the non-Jewish community – was 'a conception which His Majesty's Government had always regarded as totally erroneous'. Passfield offered Palestine a bi-national legislative coun- cil.

The White Paper deeply offended the Jews. But Weiz- mann had many sympathizers.

The Zionist counter-attack on the Passfield White Paper succeeded. A few months later, the Prime Minister read to the Commons a letter he had addressed to Weizmann. 'It rectified the situation,' Weizmann said, and enabled the Zionists 'to make the magnificent gains of the ensuing years'.

The British government's offer of a legislative assembly put Weizmann in a dilemma. The Jewish minority was not strong enough to share the government of Palestine with the Arabs, but Weizmann could not reject the offer without the risk of offending world opinion. So he asked the Government to invite Arab and Jewish leaders to a round table conference in London (where the India Conference was still sitting). The Arabs refused. Haj Amin was counting on a *jehad*, a holy war, to cast the infidels, Jews and British, out of the Holy Land.

The bloodthirsty Mufti, needless to say, envisaged quite a different kind of holy war to the non-violent struggle envisaged by Mahatma Gandhi against the British Raj. He was determined to get his way by non-violence. 'The British are our brothers, too,' he would say.

The Viceroy and the Mahatma met on 17 February 1931. It was a dramatic occasion – ex-convict Gandhi in a *tête-à-tête* with the august Viceroy. Churchill, with his customary verve, protested at 'the nauseating and humili- ating spectacle of this ... seditious *fakir* striding half- naked up the steps of the Viceroy's palace, there to parley on equal terms with the representative of the King-

Emperor'. It could hardly be denied, however, that the spectacle had a singularly human side as well – these two God-fearing men, one white, the other black, one rich, the other poor, with the fate of millions in their hands.

The talks lasted several days. After one particularly late session, Gandhi left after midnight. 'Good night, Mr Gandhi', the Viceroy said, 'and my prayers go with you.'

The Gandhi–Irwin Pact which resulted from the talks was something of an anti-climax. It merely put the clock back where it had stopped. Gandhi agreed to end civil disobedience. Irwin agreed to release passive resisters and to allow salt manufacture on the coast. To the King-Emperor he reported: 'I believe it, Sir, to be definitely untrue that ... he is out to break the unity of your Majesty's Empire.'

By September 1931 Gandhi was in London for the second Round Table Conference. Jinnah had arrived, too. Gandhi was a big hit. In London he stayed in the East End, saying he preferred to live among the poor – who referred to him affectionately as 'Old Gandhi'. His Christ-like utterances and spicy humour appealed to the British. 'I would bend the knee', he once said, 'before the poorest Untouchable of India, but I would not prostrate myself before the King because he represents insolent might.' None the less, he had tea (a drink he hated) with the King. Dressed, as usual, in *dhoti* and sandals, Gandhi was asked afterwards whether he had enough on. 'The King had enough on for both of us,' he cracked.

Broadcasting from London, Gandhi told an American audience that 'the Emperorship must go, but I should love to be an equal partner with Britain, sharing her joys and sorrows'.

Gandhi was obviously bored by the second Round Table Conference. Sometimes he dozed. The conference was a dismal failure. Hindus, Moslems, princes and Untouchables bickered incessantly among themselves. Premier Macdonald admonished them. If they could not agree, then the British government itself would have to draw up a provisional new constitution for India.

When Gandhi landed back at Bombay, he said: 'I have come back empty-handed.' Yet he had won the hearts of the British public. The effect would pay off later.

Jinnah made no impression on the conference. Later he said: 'I began to feel that neither could I help India, nor change the Hindu mentality.' He fet so depressed that he decided to settle in London.

During his exile, Jinnah lived in a three-storeyed villa on Hampstead Heath. He practised at the Privy Council Bar. In the security of his London club, with his lawyer friends, he put his political past behind him. He never dreamed that he would become the creator of a nation.

Gandhi dominated the Indian scene. De Valera was soon to become supreme in Ireland. Since 1927, the converted rebel, at the head of Fianna Fail, had led the Opposition in the Dail, where he doggedly pursued his fight to abolish the oath of allegiance. In the 1932 elections Finana Fail topped the poll and de Valera was elected An Uachtaran, President of the Executive Council. Governor General McNeill, in deference to de Valera's feelings about the British King, had the grace to go down to the Dail to instal the new president, instead of summoning him to Viceregal Lodge. The Imperial Crown was as humbled as when the 'naked fakir' strode up the steps of Viceregal Lodge in Delhi.

Within a few weeks, President de Valera introduced into the Dail a bill to abolish the oath, that 'relic of mediaevalism', as he called it. A year later, the oath was removed for all time from the Irish constitution.

Another imperial appendage still remained: the office of Governor-General. De Valera advised the King-Emperor (as he had a perfect right to do) to remove the courteous McNeill. Domhnall O Buachalla, an obscure shopkeeper (but staunch Republican), was appointed in his stead. He resided, not in Viceregal Lodge, but in a small suburban villa. He attended no functions. He was not, however, above helping himself to a salary of £2,000 a year, more than the President's, but still only one-fifth of the full salary provided.

Thus was the Crown, the unifying symbol of Empire, degraded by the King-Emperor's 'unoffending' (as he had called them) Irish subjects. De Valera became henceforth uncrowned king of Ireland. The Irish were more successful in denigrating the Crown than the Burmese – not that the latter detested foreign rule any less, but their freedom movement lacked coherent leadership. In 1927, U Ottama spread a story among the villages of Burma that the King-Emperor was about to be ousted by the King of France. It mattered little that Louis Philippe, the last French king, had been dead for over seventy years. His arrival in Burma, with four aeroplanes and ten thousand men, was confidently expected. In the meantime, U Ottama raised the standard of revolt at Shwebo. He was quickly arrested and died, a mental case, twelve years later.

At the end of 1930, the Burmese rose again against the British. They were led by Saya San, an ex-monk, who professed to make his men invisible and enable them to fly. Believing themselves invulnerable, Saya San's men advanced fearlessly against the British machine-guns. By 1932 the rebellion was crushed and fifteen years were to pass before Burma rid herself of the hated foreigners. Saya San's rebellion was recalled as 'an epic struggle'. The official records said of it: 'Its object was ... the enthronement of a jungle King ... It had little to do with modern politics.'

What Burma lacked was an inspiring political leader, a national hero. At this moment, unknown to the Burmese, there was one in the making – Aung San. Like his predecessors, whose rebellions came to grief, he had begun as a pupil in a Buddhist monastery, but for a reason of his own he was sent on to Yenangyaung High School. He had a great urge to learn English.

By the early thirties, the Irish, the Indians and the Israelites who dreamed of Zion, found themselves with proven leaders and substantial political gains. De Valera was now to steer Ireland into calmer waters. For Gandhi and Weizmann it would not be such plain sailing.

While Gandhi was away in London, there had been widespread trouble in India, to which the Government had riposted with drastic measures. In the United Provinces (Nehru's country) a slump in prices had left the peasants without enough in hand to pay their rent. The Indian peasant, wrote Nehru, has 'an amazing capacity to bear misfortune ... famine, flood, disease and continuous grinding poverty, and when he would endure no more, he would quietly and almost uncomplainingly lie down in his thousands or millions and die'. In the terrible summer of 1931, however, the peasants decided, with the support of Nehru, on a no-rent campaign. On 26 December 1931, Nehru was arrested.

When Gandhi landed at Bombay two days later and learned the full facts, he immediately telegraphed Viceroy Willingdon (Irwin's successor) asking for an interview. To which the Viceroy replied tartly that the Government of India had no intention of basing its policy on Gandhi's private view. Then, for good measure, on 4 January 1932, Gandhi was arrested. Once again, he found himself the guest of the King-Emperor – this time at Yeravda Gaol. A few months earlier it had been at Buckingham Palace.

The Government now cracked down on Congress with terrible severity. It was outlawed, its records, funds and offices seized. Its president, Vallabhabhai Patel, headed a list of thirty thousand detainees. They filled the gaols and overflowed into temporary prison camps.

At Yeravda Prison, Gandhi, when he was not immersed in the newspapers, washed his clothes, spun *khadi* and watched the stars. And he wrote a little book on God, in which he said: 'You may pluck out my eyes, you may chop off my nose, but that will not kill me. But blast my belief in God, and I am dead.' Truth, he maintained, is identification with God, and from truth non-violence is born.

In Naini Prison, across the Ganges from Allahabad, his

home-town, Jawaharlal Nehru felt 'cut off from the strife outside'. His wife, the beautiful Kamala, was ill in bed (she suffered from a chronic pulmonary condition), but fretting because she could not take part. Nehru's sisters were gaoled for a year. In a charge by mounted police, Mrs Nehru was beaten unconscious by police *lathis*. The thought of his 'frail old mother, lying bleeding in the dusty road' obsessed him.

Yet Nehru, romantic and impulsive, was philosophical too. 'We cannot play at revolution in a dressing-room,' he said.

Stunned by the Government's vigorous action, the civil disobedience movement began to decline. Gandhi himself dealt it a blow when he decided, in September 1932, to 'fast unto death' – not on behalf of the movement, but of the Untouchables, the *Harijans* (Children of God), as he called them.

Gandhi made it clear that his fast unto death was not against the British. His sole aim was 'to sting Hindu conscience into right action'. Three hundred million Indians passionately followed the fast. Only five thousand of them had radio sets, but word of the Mahatma's progress flew from mouth to mouth until it reached the remotest villages. A week later, Gandhi's ordeal was over. In a few days he was back at his spinning wheel, humming 'God is great and merciful'.

In May 1933, Gandhi, still in prison, began another fast – this time a twenty-one days' marathon for self-purification. The Viceroy immediately released him – the last thing he wanted was that Gandhi should die on his hands, especially for a cause which was of no concern of the British. As a gesture of thanks Gandhi suspended civil disobedience for six weeks. Nehru too was freed, three months later. He hurried to Poona to see Gandhi – for the first time in two years.

A few weeks before Gandhi and Nehru were reunited in Poona, Jinnah, in his home on Hampstead Heath, had entertained an old friend to dinner. His name was Liaquat Ali Khan. Educated at Exeter College, Oxford, he had (like Jinnah before him) been called to the Bar of the Inner Temple. Liaquat was now a member of the United Provinces Legislative Council.

The talk the two men had that summer evening in London marked a turn in the destiny of a nation – which did not yet exist. Liaquat pleaded with Jinnah: 'You must come back.' In April 1934 Jinnah was back in India – still reiterating his favourite theme: 'Nothing will give me greater happiness than to bring about complete cooperation between Hindus and Moslems.'

At that moment, Nehru was back in gaol in Alipore, Calcutta purging a new sentence of two years for sedition. He had been arrested early in February. Kamala, usually stoical, was this time overcome. She knew she was fatally ill, Jawaharlal did not. 'Suddenly', he said, 'she clung to me and collapsed.' After five months of freedom Nehru returned to seclusion and loneliness. It was his seventh imprisonment.

In July, Nehru heard that Kamala was critically ill. He was temporarily freed to see her. He thought sadly of their eighteen years of marriage – how many of them she had spent in hospital, he in prison. The thought that she might die obsessed him. After eleven days of freedom he was led back into captivity. It was suggested to him that if he gave an assurance not to take part in politics, he might be released to be with Kamala. But when he next saw her, she asked him: 'What is this about an assurance? Don't give it.'

Kamala was now sent to Bhowali, in the hills, and Nehru transferred to the nearby gaol of Almora, to be near her. Kamala's health worsened. In October she went to Germany for treatment. Almora Gaol seemed to Nehru to be drearier than before.

Nehru found that 'gaol encourages introspection'. Musing on the British and their rule in India, he wrote: 'All my predilections are in favour of English and the English people ...' By unifying India into a single state the British had given Indians a sense of patriotism. They had brought the fruits of western civilization – science, industry, railways, telegraphs, irrigation works, schools and hospitals. The Protestant, individualistic Anglo-Saxon English had, Nehru thought, been good for the Indians – they had shocked them out of their torpor, given them a stable, authoritative government.

Yet despite these material blessings, India was an impoverished servile nation. The viceregal pomp and splendour, the ostentation of the provincial governors, were merely an imperial frontage to the grinding poverty, illiteracy and unemployment of India's millions. The Indian Civil Service, for all the admiration he felt for it, had signally failed. The 'limited, hide-bound education' provided by British public schools (Nehru had been at one himself) had left ICS men ill-equipped, intellectually and emotionally, for the changed dynamic conditions now confronting India.

The ICS, Nehru admitted, had thrown up exceptional men. Sir Harcourt Butler, Governor of the United Provinces, was certainly one of them. Philip Woodruff* says of him: 'He was not particularly concerned about democracy or freedom ... He liked Indians ... He loved Lucknow.' Harcourt Butler's advice to young ICS men was: 'The most important thing is to be accessible to people ... to be not an official only, but a friend. There are few questions which cannot be settled in personal discussion over a cheroot and a cup of tea.'

Sir Malcolm Hailey was another great ICS figure, a man of superior intellect, of humility and humour. As Governor, in Lahore, of the Punjab, he decided one evening to go for a walk with his dog in the pouring rain. Wearing only a shirt and shorts – it was so hot – he was immediately soaked to the skin. When a procession came towards him bearing banners and shouting slogans, he decided to join it, to see for himself how the police would deal with the demonstrators. He smiled on reading in the newspaper next day: 'At one point, the procession was joined by a disreputable European with a dog.'

* In *The Men who Ruled India*, Vol. II (London, 1954).

Such behaviour seemed to Nehru, the rebellious ex-public schoolboy, as somewhat 'old-world, suitable for the Victorian age'. The new India, Nehru felt, must be served by earnest, efficient workers.

A new India had just been conceived – along British lines – in the Government of India Bill. It was introduced into the Commons in February 1935 – just as Nehru, at Almora Gaol, was 'rejoicing at the whisper of spring in the air'. Unfortunately, Nehru's peace was shattered by the new bill. He had already castigated the 'petrifying provisions' of the White Paper, which preceded it. The Bill provided a new constitution for India, with self-government in eleven provinces, but the Viceroy and the provincial Governors were given reserve powers – just in case, Nehru complained, the Indians did not prove fit for self-rule 'by doing just what British policy required'.

Winston Churchill, too, was scathing. He denounced the Bill as a 'monstrous monument of shame built by pygmies'. Clement Attlee, although he stood politically poles apart from Churchill, was also critical; he wanted immediate political independence for India.

Much of the criticism was hasty and ill-judged. When, a decade later, Attlee, as Prime Minister, transferred British power to independent India's Prime Minister Nehru, it was on the basis of the 1935 constitution which both he and Nehru had so maligned.

The India Act (1935) received the royal assent in August.

The King-Emperor, now seventy, had been on the throne for twenty-five years. His Silver Jubilee celebrations took place on 6 May 1935. Never in his life had he seen more people in the streets. Their warmth and enthusiasm touched him so much that he exclaimed: 'I am beginning to think they must really like me for myself.' Not even his most rebellious subjects, not Gandhi, nor de Valera, would have disagreed. The Imperial Crown, the Oath, the Emperorship – these were strictly constitutional

issues which the King-Emperor would never allow to come
between himself and his people. 'My very, very dear
people,' he called his five hundred million subjects, as
most of them listened to his rich, vibrant voice speaking
to them over the air on Jubilee Day. 'I dedicate myself
anew to your service for all the years that may still be
given to me . . .'

It was not, alas, to be given to him to see out as much
as a single year. And already, in the cry that went up
from the crowd as the King-Emperor's second son, Albert,
Duke of York, drove by in the royal procession, 'There
goes the hope of England,' there seemed to be a portent
of things to come.

Another critic of the India Act – though a mild one compared to Nehru – was Mohammed Ali Jinnah. He complained that the Communal Award would not satisfy
Moslems. Jinnah had returned to London in the summer
of 1935 to wind up his affairs. In October he returned to
India for good, to undertake his grand mission as he
called it.

At that time Jawaharlal Nehru also went to Europe.
His mission was a tragic one. He had been released from
gaol in September in order to go to Badenweiler, Germany, to the bedside of his dying wife, Kamala. Early in
1936, Kamala breathed her last. 'That fair body', Nehru
said, 'and that lovely face were reduced to ashes.' Of
Nehru it was said that 'his eyes held a world of agony'.
He now flung himself anew into the struggle for Indian
freedom.

With the passing of the India Act, India lost its fairest
province, Burma. The Golden Land received a new constitution under the Burma Act (1935). The Burmese parliament, like the legislatures of the Indian provinces, was
now to get complete control of its internal affairs. This
led to a grim struggle between the political parties, who
vied for popular support with their demands for the
elimination of British rule. The main contenders were

Dr Ba Maw's Sinyetha (Poor Man's) Party and U Saw's Myochit (Nationalist) Party. But a new group was emerging. It took the name Thakin, 'Master', as a dig at the British who liked Burmese to call them by that title. Young men, mostly recruited among ex-students, they were communistic in outlook, using the hammer and sickle as their emblem.

One of the most truculent students at Rangoon University in 1936 was Aung San, secretary of the Students' Union and editor of the university magazine *Oway*. When *Oway* accused the university's Burmese bursar of 'avuncular intentions' towards some of the girl students, editor Aung San was expelled. Aung San, the boy from Natmauk, had arrived on the Burmese political stage, a Thakin in the making.

A friend, Dagon Taya, described young Aung San as a political animal. Politics were his consuming passion, and they made him 'crude, rude and raw'. But he was scrupulously honest. At first he was a poor speaker, spending hours practising his speeches in his room, which was always in a mess. 'Books on the table, on the bed, on the floor,' as Bo Let Ya, another friend, described it. His bed was always unmade. Dirty towels and clothes dangled from the mosquito net.

The British had given a new constitution to India and Burma. They tried to do the same with Palestine. Sir Arthur Wauchope, appointed High Commissioner in 1931, was determined to give Palestine its own constitution with self-rule through a legislative council. But Weizmann and the Zionists rejected the idea. They informed Wauchope they disapproved of his enthusiasm for self-government.

There had been serious convulsions in the Zionist world. Weizmann, worn out by the struggle, found himself voted out of the presidency at the 1931 Congress. Winston Churchill commented: 'I don't believe the Jewish people are so stupid as to let him leave.' They were not. Although Weizmann returned to his scientific researches, his hand remained on the helm of the Zionist movement.

Ben Gurion was one of those who criticized Weizmann, although he felt deeply for him. The Congress of 1933 was a triumph for Ben Gurion. The Jewish international labour movement backed him solidly. With Weizmann out of office, Ben Gurion now dominated Zionist policy.

Upon the divided Zionist camp, there now fell the dreaded shadow of Nazism. In January 1933, Adolf Hitler had become Chancellor of the German Reich. Hitler was haunted by the Jews: 'There lurks in the background the menacing figure of that Jewish international foe ...' he once screamed to an electrified audience.

The year 1933 saw the first mass immigration of Jews to Palestine – 30,000 poured into the Holy Land, compared with 4,000 in 1931. The figure was to swell to 42,000 in 1934 and to top 61,000 in 1935. The Arabs of Palestine were angry. Why, they asked, should so many thousands of fugitives from an essentially European catastrophe be unloaded on to tiny Palestine, when in the same period a European country like Britain took only 3,000?

The British, whose policy was to limit immigration to the 'absorptive capacity' of the country, were just as worried at the rising tide of immigrants. But they left the immigration laws unchanged – not that it inspired any gratitude among the Jews, who merely complained more loudly that the British had not opened wider the Gates of Zion.

When the Zionist Congress met in Lucerne in 1935, Weizmann was re-elected to the presidency. Ben Gurion called Weizmann the champion of the Jewish people, upon whose shoulders there rested 'a burden not borne by any other Jew for the last two thousand years'. The re-instated president informed Wauchope of Zionism's official boycott of a legislative council. But Weizmann warned the Congress: 'In spite of our differences [with England] the Jewish people must never forget that it is

to England that we owe this opportunity of discharg-
ing a memorable historic function.'

For all Weizmann's qualities and prestige, it was Ben
Gurion, now Chairman of the Executive, who had become Zionism's guiding spirit. His plan was a Jewish
state, its corner-stone: immigration.

Ceaselessly, the immigration ships (both legal and
illegal) disembarked their thousands of European refugees, who cried out in their joy and sang hymns at the
sacred moment when their feet touched the shores of
the land they called home. But in October 1935, a totally
unromantic event sullied this atmosphere of rejoicing. A
barrel labelled 'cement' fell from a crane of the Belgian
ship SS *Leopold II* on to the quay at Jaffa, disgorging its
contents – not cement, but thousands of machine-gun
bullets. Hand in hand with their return to the Holy
Land, the Jews were engaged in gun-running.

The barrel of ammunition touched off the long-
expected explosion. In October 1935, the Arabs declared
a general strike, and the Mufti turned the heat on the
High Commissioner. He demanded that a Palestine parliament with an Arab majority should be created, that the
purchase by Jews of Arab land should cease, that Jewish
immigration be stopped.

He was firmly told that there could be no question
of stopping Jewish immigration. Shortly afterwards, a
debate in the Commons put paid to Wauchope's dream
(the Zionists' nightmare) of a legislative council. British
rule was to remain.

Haj Amin, Mufti of Jerusalem, now took more positive
action. He raised the standard of rebellion. On 15 April
1936, Arabs murdered two Jews in Jaffa. At their funeral
in Tel-Aviv a riot broke out. Twenty more Jews were
massacred. The Arab Higher Committee, formed under
Haj Amin's leadership, then declared a general strike, to
continue until the British put an end to Jewish immigration. Violence and atrocities multiplied. Soon, the Arabs
turned their fury from the Jews to the British. One of
their most brilliant and ruthless leaders was a Syrian,

Fawzi ed Din el Kauwakji, an old friend of the Mufti's. His guerilla bands crippled road, rail and telegraph communications. British policemen were stoned.

In the midst of this disorder the British government announced a royal commission of enquiry, headed by Lord Peel. Its aim was 'to do justice to all sections of the Palestine population'.

But, the rebellion speard. Wauchope, who felt that his sacred mission was to bring peace to the Holy Land, hesitated to shed more blood. The Jews themselves acted likewise. They practised *havlagah*, a policy of self-restraint comparable to Gandhi's *satyagraha*. Their defence force, Haganah, indeed the entire Yishuv, the Jewish community, refrained from all retaliation.

But Haganah was being transformed from a static, defensive force into an offensive *corps d'élite*. Responsible for this was an ascetic, serious-faced Scottish soldier, with penetrating eyes and a shock of untidy dark hair, who had just arrived in Palestine. His name was Orde Wingate. Asked by David Hacohen, Haganah's chief arms procurer, what he had read on Zionism, Wingate replied: 'There is only one important book on the subject, the Bible, and I have read it thoroughly.' Wingate told Haganah trainees: 'We are establishing the foundations for the Army of Zion.'

The Jews, like the Indians and Burmans, were steadily preparing for a struggle with the Imperial Crown – which was now to have a struggle with itself.

Barely seven months after King George v, in his Jubilee speech, had told his people 'I dedicate myself anew to your service,' he spoke to them again – for the last time – in his Christmas broadcast. On 17 January 1936, the King wrote, almost illegibly, in the diary he had kept for fifty years: 'I feel rotten.' On the night of the 20th, as he lay on his death-bed, he asked (so it is said): 'How is the Empire?' Then, 'at 5 to 12', as Queen Mary recorded 'my darling husband passed away'.

'The King is dead. Long live the King.' The traditional formula was hardly appropriate to the reign of King Edward VIII. He had a private problem, as he called it; he was in love, with Mrs Wallis Simpson, ex-wife of a lieutenant in the US Navy, presently married to an Englishman, Mr Ernest Simpson. The King formed the hope 'that one day I might be able to share my life with her'.

But the King was head of the Church of England, which does not recognize divorce. He foresaw that the pursuit of his 'private hopes' might mean that he would have to withdraw from the succession. On this score, however, he comforted himself that 'Bertie, to whom the succession would pass, was in outlook and temperament very much like my father.'

The prospect which was such a comfort to King Edward – that his brother Bertie could replace him – was a ghastly one for Bertie. For a long time he closed his mind to it – he refused to believe that the King would give up the crown for Mrs Simpson. But on 20 October, he had his first inkling that his fate was sealed. He was informed that Prime Minister Stanley Baldwin had shown the King some of the more lurid reports in the foreign press. Baldwin had begged the King to prevail on Mrs Simpson to withdraw her divorce suit to which the King replied, somewhat disingenuously, that this was not his, but Mrs Simpson's, business.

A week later, on 27 October 1936, Mrs Simpson was granted a decree nisi. In six months' time she would be free to marry the King, a fact which brought the King's heir, his brother Bertie, face to face with his destiny – the throne of England.

On 16 November the King informed Stanley Baldwin: 'I intend to marry Mrs Simpson as soon as she is free ...' If the Government objected, then, said the King, 'I am prepared to go.' The following day he told his brother. 'Bertie was so taken aback ... that in his shy way he could not express his innermost feelings ... Next to myself, Bertie had most at stake, it was he who would have to wear the crown if I left and his genuine concern for me was

mixed with the dread of having to assume the responsibilities of kingship.' Indeed, the Duke of York was now
beginning to feel 'like the proverbial sheep being led to
the slaughter'. But he told a friend: 'If the worst happens
and I have to take over, you can be assured that I will
do my best to clean up the inevitable mess ...'

On 3 December, the Duke of York, arriving at Euston
station from Scotland was 'surprised and horrified' to see
posters blaring 'The King's Marriage'. He immediately
went to see his elder brother, 'who was in a great state
of excitement'. Later that day, they met again at Queen
Mary's house, where David said he could not live alone
as King and must marry Mrs Simpson. The King, 'after
making this dreadful announcement', asked his brother
Bertie to come to his home, Fort Belvedere, not far from
Windsor. When next the Duke of York faced his elder
brother alone: 'I found him pacing up and down the
room', he said, 'and he told me his decision that he
would go.' Two days later the Duke again saw his
brother: 'I could see that nothing I said would alter his
decision. His mind was made up.' That evening, as the
Duke told the news to Queen Mary, he felt so distraught
that he broke down and sobbed like a child.

Next morning, 10 December, at Fort Belvedere, the
King sat at his desk, the Instrument of Abdication before
him. 'I Edward the Eighth of Great Britain, Ireland and
the British Dominions beyond the seas, King, Emperor of
India do hereby declare my irrevocable decision to re-
nounce the Throne ...' At his side stood the Duke of
York, who wrote of his last minutes before becoming
King-Emperor: 'I was present at the fateful moment
which made me D's successor to the Throne. Perfectly
calm, D signed ... It was a dreadful moment.' But not
for the King who had just signed away his crown and
his empire: 'Like a swimmer surfacing from a great
depth', he said, 'I left the room and stepped outside, in-
haling the fresh morning air.'

Twenty-four hours later, ex-King Edward sailed away
from England into exile. He thought of his brother: 'He

will make a fine king.'

On 12 December 1936, the people acclaimed their new King-Emperor, George VI.

5

'I am quite unprepared' 1936–9

At his accession council on 12 December, the new King-Emperor addressed his Privy Councillors: 'I meet you today in circumstances which have no parallel in the history of our country ... I declare to you ... my resolve to work before all else for the welfare of the British Commonwealth of Nations.'

The abdication had rudely shaken the British Imperial Throne. The King-Emperor himself feared that it might 'crumble under the shock and strain of it all', but there was some consolation when Mr Maxton, moving in the Commons that 'the people require a more stable and dignified form of government of a republican kind', was defeated by four hundred and three votes to five. Yet to the question murmured by King George v on his deathbed: 'How goes the Empire', it might be answered that, as a symbol of Empire unity, the Throne undeniably commanded less awe and respect than it did in Empress Victoria's day – this despite the energetic efforts made among the King-Emperor's subjects to personalize it.

Gandhi had been preaching to three hundred million Indians – over half the British Empire's population – that the Emperorship must go. In Ireland, de Valera had abolished the oath of allegiance to the King and – only the day before – had practically abolished the King. In Burma and in Palestine there were vigorous anti-imperialist, or more precisely, anti-British movements.

In forty years, Victoria's empire had been transformed. As the British Commonwealth of Nations (a title the diehards rather despised) it had become, broadly speaking, a club over which Britain presided and of which the committee members were the 'white' dominions – Canada, Australia, New Zealand, South Africa and Ireland (impatient to resign). The colonies (like Burma), the protectorates and mandates (like Palestine) were ordinary members, bound by rules made at the club's headquarters in Whitehall, London. For India, an extra-ordinary member by virtue of her size and importance, the rules had been somewhat relaxed. The glory of the Empire was no longer sung by the poets, as in Victoria's day; it tended rather to be the butt of music-hall jokes, not always in the best taste. The Empire's purposeful splendour and idealism had been marred by bloody massacres, by rebellion and sordid civil war. Financially, the cost of running and defending the Empire had brought Britain to the verge of bankruptcy. Before long one of her keenest imperialists, Lord Lothian, would be jauntily telling Americans: 'Well boys, Britain's broke.'

In his resolve to work for the Commonwealth-Empire, the new King-Emperor was to run head on into the dynamic, anti-imperialist forces which had for years been gathering momentum in certain of his possessions, and which were almost entirely ignored by the conservative, insular British. He was to lead his Empire through its finest hour to victory, but suffer the disillusionment of watching the mother-country's plight provide millions of his people with the chance of ridding themselves of his rule. 'Britain's misfortune is our opportunity' was to be their cry. Finally, divested of his imperial crown, he was to see those recalcitrant subjects safely delievered from the womb of his Empire to independent statehood. The lengthy, painful process called for courage, wisdom and humanity on his part – qualities which the last Emperor possessed in high degree.

Eamon de Valera had been quick to see in the Abdication a heaven-sent opportunity of removing once and for all the British King from Irish internal affairs. While the other Dominion leaders were gravely discussing the crisis with Baldwin, de Valera acted. He had two bills drafted. The first eliminated the King from the Irish Free State constitution. However, de Valera was anxious to avoid rupture with foreign states (especially the USA and the Vatican) whose representatives were accredited to the King. So his second bill, the External Relations Bill, authorized His Majesty to act for this purpose on behalf of the Irish Free State. A republican nightmare threatened when it looked as if the British parliament would enact the bills before the Irish Dail did so – which would have left Edward VIII king of an independent Irish monarchy. So the Dail was hastily summoned and, on 11 December, passed the two bills. The Irish Free State, under its new name Eire, was now virtually a republic. Despite its flagrant disrespect for the rules of the Commonwealth club, the other members sportingly acknowledged Eire's continued membership.

On 17 January 1938, there were official talks between de Valera and Neville Chamberlain, the new British prime minister. When de Valera revealed that partition was one of the subjects for discussion, the Ulster prime minister, Lord Craigaivon, immediately called a general election, to get public backing for his policy of giving 'not an inch' to the Catholic south.

Another delicate subject was the British right to the Irish ports, Berehaven, Lough Swilly and Cobh, vital to the British fleet in time of war. De Valera had no wish for Eire to be involved in another English war, and Chamberlain saw his point. He returned the ports to Ireland, only to be trounced later for doing so by Britain's wartime leader, Winston Churchill: 'Many a life and many a ship was soon to be lost as a result of this improvident example of appeasement.'

Partition was the stumbling-block of the talks – de Valera called it unjust; as long as it lasted there could never be friendship between Britain and Ireland. Chamberlain, while refusing to coerce Ulster, was willing to state publicly that he would welcome the end of partition. But Craigaivon would not hear of such a statement, and it was never made.

King George read the reports of the talks 'with great interest and occasional bewilderment'. He was relieved when they ended in agreement and wanted to meet de Valera, the poor boy from Buree, Limerick, who had made His Majesty an undesirable alien, as the King later said, in Ireland. But a meeting between king and ex-rebel did not find approval with the provincially-minded Chamberlain, who none the less had the goodness to return to de Valera the field-glasses taken from him on his arrest during the Easter 1916 rebellion. De Valera responded with an equally charming gesture. Having heard that the Home Secretary, Sir Samuel Hoare, was drafting a bill on British prison reform, the distinguished ex-convict offered to submit his recommendations. Hoare jumped at the offer. A few weeks after his accession, it was announced that the King-Emperor George VI hoped to go to India in the winter of 1937–8. He felt a keen desire to visit the Empire that he had inherited, but never seen, to be crowned in its capital, New Delhi, and to meet his Indian subjects. But reasons of state decreed otherwise: it was thought unwise for him to quit his realm of England before the dust raised by the Abdication had settled; he would need (having been denied the secrets of those red ministerial despatch boxes) time to learn how his government functioned; it was unfortunate, too, that, as the India Act was due to take effect on 1 April 1937, there were no other glad tidings for the Emperor to bear to his Indian people; and lastly, a sad reflection on the stresses of modern emperorship, his doctors feared that he would be so exhausted by the programme connected with his coronation (due in May 1937) that he was unlikely to survive the rigours of another coronation ceremony in India.

The Emperor's Viceroy, Lord Linlithgow (who had succeeded Willingdon in April 1936) and the Secretary for India, Lord Zetland, demurred at these counsels of caution. They argued that Indians would be bitterly disappointed if the Emperor did not appear among them. Zetland insisted, too, that it would be disastrous if, instead of giving priority to India, the King-Emperor visited some other dominion first.

The Emperor, above all else a man of duty, decided that his place was at home. 'I do need time to settle in,' he informed Zetland in February 1937, and the coronation durbar was postponed. Better wait, the Emperor was advised, until India had become a self-governing dominion – which, the Emperor (somewhat frustrated by now) observed, would doubtless mean relegating the visit to his old age.

India was in a state of ferment. Gandhi had withdrawn from the leadership of the Indian National Congress, but its president, Nehru, still regarded him as 'the permanent Super-President'. Nehru had called the India Act (1935) a charter of slavery. He was out to wreck the Constitution. But when, under it, elections were held in 1937, he threw himself into the fray with incredible energy. The masses hailed him as their idol, as he encouraged them to 'fight for freedom, build Congress into a mighty army'. Congress swept the polls, leaving Jinnah's Muslim League nowhere. Modestly, Nehru insisted: 'It was Gandhi's spell that gave us the vote.' Less modestly he boasted: 'There are only two parties in the country, the Congress and the British.' This was too much for Jinnah. 'There is a third party, the Muslims,' he replied. 'We are not going to be dictated to ... to be camp followers of any party. We are ready to work as equal partners.'

Flushed with victory, Congress contemptuously spurned Jinnah's offer. In none of the eight provinces where they had a majority did they need the Muslim League's help to form a ministry. At Lucknow, in October 1937, Jinnah drew his own conclusions. He told the Muslim League conference: 'The majority have clearly shown their hand that Hindustan [India] is for the Hindus.' Congress policy, he warned, would result in class bitterness and communal war. Enthusiastically, Muslims rallied to his cry 'Islam is in danger'. The first shots had been fired in the Hindu-Muslim war which was to end in Pakistan and Partition.

Gandhi, 'out of an anguished heart', reproached Jinnah for his 'declaration of war'. He was right. Jinnah had returned to the front. In a sullen, acrimonious correspondence he duelled with Nehru. 'I must confess that

I do not yet know what the fundamental points of dispute are,' wrote Nehru in February 1938. Jinnah fired back: 'I am only amazed at your ignorance.' Nehru replied condescendingly: 'We [Congress] have to deal with all organizations and individuals ... we do not determine [their] importance ...; this importance does not come from outside recognition but from inherent strength.' Jinnah retorted witheringly: 'Your tone and language again display the same arrogance ... as if the Congress is the sovereign power. Unless the Congress recognizes the Muslim League on a footing of complete equality we shall have to wait and depend on our inherent strength. Having regard to your mentality, it is really difficult for me to make you understand ...'

Jinnah's concern for his Muslim co-religionists was not confined to India. Referring to the Arabs of Palestine, he declared, in October 1938, that the British had 'thrown their friends to the wolves ... broken solemn promises. Only those succeed with the British who ... are in a position to bully them.'

This the Palestine Arabs tried to do when the Peel Commission (a royal commission of enquiry sent to look into recent riots,) reached Palestine in November 1936. They boycotted it until persuaded by sympathizers, both Arab and British alike, not to be so foolish in thus ruining their chances of influencing policy. The first Jewish witness before the Commission was Chaim Weizmann. He spoke of the six million European Jews (a bitter and unconscious prophecy, as he later said), 'pent up in places where they are not wanted, and for whom the world is divided into places ... which they cannot enter'. He called the Jews a disembodied ghost of a race. 'There should be one place in God's wide world where we could live and express ourselves in accordance with our character.' That place could only be Zion, Palestine. The Jews' steadfastness to Zionism was, he concluded, 'perhaps our misfortune. If it had disappeared there would be no Jewish problem, but here we are. It is our destiny.'

Haj Amin, Mufti of Jerusalem, told the Commissioners that the Mandate was inconsistent with the Covenant of the League of Nations. US President Wilson's anti-Zionist King-Crane Commission had supported this view. The Jews' aim, insisted the Mufti, was to rebuild the Temple of Solomon on the ruins of the Dome of the Rock and the El Aqsa mosques. The British, he demanded, must abandon the Jewish National Home project and put a halt to Jewish immigration and the purchase of land. He wanted the Mandate replaced by an Anglo-Arab Treaty for Palestine. The world of Islam, he reminded Lord Peel and his Christian colleagues, had always been the refuge of Jews from Christian persecution.

Four days before Haj Amin had thus spoken, a new current of thought had emanated from the British side. It arose at a session when Weizmann, alone, confronted the commissioners. One of them, Professor Coupland, suddenly asked his views on partition – 'might it not be a final and peaceful settlement – to terminate the Mandate by agreement ... and split Palestine in two halves, the plain being an independent Jewish state ... and the rest of Palestine, plus Trans-Jordania, being an independent Arab State?'

Weizmann asked for time to consider the idea. A Jewish state, however small, he reflected, could be a contribution to mankind. It was Weizmann's own deep conviction that God had always chosen small countries for conveying his messages to humanity. 'It was from Judaea and from Greece ... that the great ideas which form the most precious possessions of mankind emerged.' He might have added that it was from another small country, England, that the idea of a multi-racial Commonwealth of nations emerged and took shape.

Lord Peel's brilliant, forthright report was published on 7 July 1937. It concluded: 'We feel justified in recommending that Your Majesty's Government should take the appropriate steps for the termination of the present Mandate on the basis of Partition.' The British government at first agreed. Later, it changed its mind.

Zionists, in gloom and anguish, debated partition at their 1937 Congress. For the first time since the Dispersion a Jewish state, be it ever so small, had become a reality. Should they grasp it? The religious parties and the American delegation said 'No'. Mrs Golda Meyerson, Ben Gurion's close collaborator, joined the *Neinsagers*. Then Ben Gurion's voice rang out. The British declaration, he cried, was 'one of the greatest acts in history. This is the beginning of redemption for which we have waited 2,000 years.' With the vision of a prophet he described the distant, promised land – ignorant that betrayal was at hand. The Zionist Congress did not share his faith. It declined the offer of a Jewish state, begging Britain for a more generous one.

Haj Amin's Arab Higher Committee rejected Peel's partition plan out of hand, and immediately ordered their terrorist bands to resume their work, which the Mufti was soon to direct from the safety of his retreat across the border in Lebanon. With Arab terror mounting, *havlagah*, or non-violence, put an almost unbearable strain on the Yishuv. Haganah, the Jewish defence force, became more aggressive. Their special Night Squads, led by Orde Wingate, struck dread into the Arab marauders. And now the illicit Revisionist organization, Irgun Zvei Leumi (Etzel for short), begged Ben Gurion for leave to answer terror with terror, to take an Arab life for a Jewish one. Not only that, they wanted to murder British citizens in the hope of pressuring the Mandatory Government. Ben Gurion refused. He gave Irgun an ultimatum – to accept the discipline of Yishuv authorities, or be outlawed. Irgun were soon to choose the latter course, and to harry the British with slaughter and destruction.

At present, the Mufti's men were doing so to such effect that delegates from the Arab states and Palestine, gathered at a conference at Bloudan, near Damascus, in September 1937, saw fit to lecture Britain: 'We must make Great Britain understand', they declared, 'that one must choose between our friendship and the Jews. Britain must change her policy in Palestine or we shall ...

side with other European powers whose policies are ini-mical to Great Britain.' It was a dark threat and one that Britain, with Hitler and Mussolini playing fast and loose on her doorstep, could not ignore.

By the end of 1938, the initial enthusiasm of His Majesty's Government for Palestine partition had van-ished. Jews and Arabs were summoned to a conference at St James's Palace, London, in February 1939. Replying to Prime Minister Chamberlain, Weizmann said: 'The hopes and prayers of millions of Jews scattered through-out the world are now centred, with unshaken confidence in British good faith, on these deliberations.' The British, in return, urged Arabs and Jews to trust them. Yet des-pite Weizmann's wishful words, the only thing that Arabs and Jews were agreed on was that Britain had consist-ently broken her promises. Beyond that, there was dis-cord. The Arab delegates refused to sit with the Jews, or even meet them. Malcolm MacDonald, the Colonial Secretary (who had hitherto been so sympathetic to Weiz-mann), made it clear that, if no solution were reached, the British government would impose its own.

In the impasse which was soon reached, it did. One side had to be appeased, but it was clearly not to be the Jews. Ben Gurion had told MacDonald: 'If Britain has to fight, the Yishuv will stand behind her as one man.' His words, sincere as they were, were superfluous. Mac-Donald knew as well as Ben Gurion that the Jews' only hope of survival lay in a British victory.

The support of the Arabs, on the other hand, was vital. They held the key to British and American oil supplies, and to the security of the British garrison based on Suez.

Yet MacDonald's conscience was troubled. When 'Baffy' Dugdale, Lord Balfour's niece, reproached him for be-traying the Jews and ruining the fair name of Britain, he put his hands to his head and groaned: 'Yes, I have thought of all that.' But the stark fact remained: to fly in the face of the Bloudan and other Arab threats, and jeopardize their relations with the Arabs, might well have cost the British their victory and the Palestine Jews their ultimate survival.

MacDonald had intimated to the Jews early on in the conference the line he was compelled to take, but a little later Weizmann received unexpected confirmation of British policy when he received a letter from the Colonial Office marked 'Confidential'. It contained the outlines of the coming White Paper: an Arab state in five years, limitation of Jewish immigration, etcetera. The letter had been sent in error to him instead of to the head of the Arab delegation.

The St James's conference collapsed on 17 March – the day that Hitler announced from the Hradchin Palace, Prague: 'Czechoslovakia has ceased to exist.' The Second World War was less than six months away.

One day in mid-May, MacDonald invited Weizmann to his country home. Weizmann talked for a long time with MacDonald, while his secretary, Yeheskiel Sacharoff, waited outside. When at last Weizmann reappeared, he was trembling and white with anger. Cursing MacDonald, he cried: 'That he could do this – he who made me believe he was a friend!' Weizmann then outlined to Sacharoff the future British policy as given to him by MacDonald: no partition, no Jewish state and no Arab state either. The aim was to create an independent Palestine state. Jewish immigration – 'at the very moment', as Ben Gurion said, 'when millions of European Jews were facing merciless destruction' – was to be limited to 75,000 during five years. It would then cease, unless the Arabs were prepared to acquiesce in it. Jewish land purchases were to be severely restricted.

The MacDonald White Paper published on 17 May 1939, came under heavy attack in Parliament, notably by Winston Churchill, who called it a plain breach of a solemn obligation. The Balfour Declaration, he said, was a pledge not to the Jews of Palestine but to world Jewry, in return for which Britain received important help in the First World War, as well as the Palestine Mandate. Lloyd George, prime minister at the time of the Balfour Declaration, denied that it was made entirely out of good will. 'We wanted to receive in return the effctive support of the Jews of the world.' The Arabs, he maintained, had benefited from Jewish immigration. 'The Land of Canaan, once flowing with milk and honey, has reappeared.'

These two great men pleaded in vain. The White Paper was adopted, though by only eighty-nine votes. (Government majorities usually ran to four hundred.) The Jews felt betrayed. Ben Gurion called the White Paper an 'infamous document' and qualified his loyalty to Britain: 'We shall fight the war as if there were no White Paper, and the White Paper as if there were no war.'

While not acclaimed by the Arabs either, the White Paper did pacify the extremists. The Arab rebellion subsided, and during six years of war the Arabs, with certain exceptions, rallied to Britain's side. One who did not was Haj Amin, Mufti of Jerusalem. He fought the British from Berlin.

Another who was to go over to the enemy was Aung San. After the 1936 student riots, Aung San had been re-admitted to Rangoon University. In 1938, at the age of twenty-three, he left his law classes in order, as he said, to serve in the cause of Burma's freedom. He joined the Dobama Asi-Ayone, the party of the Thakins, and became its general secretary. He was now Thakin Aung San – the title fitted him to a *t*, as his friend Bo Let Ya said, for the Thakins were blunt, crude and outspoken. They wanted independence, if necessary by force. At party headquarters, Aung San was the one whom visitors asked to see. Dishevelled, absorbed in the newspapers, he would not even look up when they asked for him by name. Some took him for the office boy. Visitors who stayed the night were offered Aung San's room. It pleased them to be sharing the General Secretary's quarters – but not for long. 'No one could share a room with Aung San. Only bugs could,' said Bo Let Ya. Around midnight the visitors would decamp into the corridor.

But the young man who would become the idol of Burma was shaping his destiny. His colleague Thakin Nu (U Nu) was, as a writer (his ambition was to become Burma's Bernard Shaw), the first to appreciate Aung San's sterling qualities: 'He wrote pure and pithy prose, in Burmese or in English; he was precise and hard-working; he was a thinker.' Life at the Dobama Asi-Ayone was hard. Gone was the 'dandy time' the two ex-students had enjoyed at the university, when, with ample pocket-money, they could buy silk clothes and eat the best meals. Now they were poor, and working hard on one meal and a few cups of tea a day. When Aung San was hungry, he would sit tight in a corner with a book. 'He was made of steel,' said U Nu.

The Thakins drew inspiration from the Indian Congress. They went out to the workers and peasants and became their spokesmen, harassing the government with strikes and demands for better working conditions. Like Gandhi, they campaigned for the wearing of national dress; the gaily coloured *longyi** and the clack-clack of wooden slippers became symbols of Burma's fight for freedom. In the House of Representatives, Thakin Mya appealed to Burmans to 'wreck' the new constitution (just as Nehru was doing in India). The *Sangha*, the Buddhist *pongyi* (priest) brotherhood, supported the Thakins, who gained their first martyrs when ten of them, and seven *pongyis*, were shot by police at a mammoth demonstration in Mandalay in 1939. Aung San, accused of leading a conspiracy to overthrow the government, was imprisoned.

The Thakins now joined up with Dr Ba Maw's Poor Man's Party to form the Freedom Bloc. Aung San was its secretary. He publicly proclaimed that the Freedom Bloc's aim was independence. Accused this time of sedition, a warrant was issued for his arrest and a price – not a very big one, five rupees – put on his head. A similar warrant was out for U Nu who said to himself: 'If I am

* Sarong, kind of wrap-round skirt.

guilty of sedition, I should go to gaol.' Not so Aung San.
He decided to go underground, to quit Burma and look
for contacts abroad – in China. Aung San, with a comrade,
Hla Myaing, slipped away in a Chinese ship bound for
Amoy, China. Bo Let Ya saw them off from the Rangoon
docks. In the sampan which carried them out to the waiting ship, Aung San, wearing Chinese clothes, sat motion-
less, looking out to sea. In due course he would return –
in the uniform of a Japanese colonel.

6

War 1939

In August 1939 Europe was basking uneasily in the hot summer, with the feeling that peace could not last much longer. Nostalgically, the King-Emperor returned to the haunts of his youth. He sailed in the royal yacht back to the Naval College at Dartmouth, to the starting-point of his career from cadet to king. He organized his boys' camp at Abergeldie, the fourteenth-century castle on Deeside where he had holidayed himself as a youngster and had first discovered the spell of Balmoral, the highland retreat close by, built by the widowed Queen-Empress Victoria. But this summer his stay at Balmoral was rudely interrupted. On 22 August came the stunning news of the Hitler-Stalin pact.

In the early morning of the 24th, the King was back in London. Prime Minister Chamberlain put him *au courant* with the situation which during the next ten days was to move swiftly to its tragic climax. Japan, Germany's anti-Russian ally, was obviously shaken by Hitler's sudden friendship for Stalin. Might it not help to detach Japan from Germany, the King-Emperor suggested, if he were to send a friendly message, as from one emperor to another, to Hirohito of Japan? No, advised Lord Halifax (now Foreign Secretary), fearing a snub.

King Leopold of the Belgians, Roosevelt and the Pope had all appealed to Hitler to desist from violence. Why not an appeal from the King-Emperor whose people were pledged to resist Hitler if he attacked Poland? But Chamberlain hesitated, and once again the King felt frustrated at not being able to use his personal influence.

Very soon, it was too late. On 29 August, Hitler decided on war. At dawn on 1 September his armies invaded Poland. By the 3rd, the King-Emperor was at war with the maniacal German Fuehrer. 'I had a certain feeling of relief,' he wrote in his diary, 'that those ten anxious days of intensive negotiation with Germany ... were over. Hitler had taken the plunge, with the knowledge that the whole might of the British Empire would be against him.'

More precisely, the whole might of the Empire was not and never would be, available. De Valera had maintained: 'We do not want to get involved,' and declared Ireland neutral. Relations with Britain were conducted through representatives in each capital. But Ireland's man in Berlin raised a problem. Under the External Relations Act he had to be accredited by the King-Emperor. As Anthony Eden, Foreign Secretary, told de Valera, 'You will appreciate the difficulties ... asking the King to sign credentials addressed to Herr Hitler.' A chargé d'affaires solved the problem.

With Britain at war, India was automatically at war, too. The fact was peremptorily announced by the Viceroy. The Punjab backed the allies, the princes 'had thrown themselves at the King-Emperor's feet'. But Congress were outraged. Nehru thought that there was 'something rotten' where 'one man, and he a foreigner and a representative of a hated system, could plunge four hundred millions of human beings into war without the slightest reference to them'. Gandhi did not immediately complain, but called on the Viceroy. 'As I was picturing before him the House of Parliament and Westminster Abbey, and their possible destruction, I broke down.' Gandhi pledged in public not to embarrass the British – a pledge that he, the truth-seeker, was not to keep.

Burma, like India, was conscripted to fight for the Emperor, although her future leader had gone over to the enemy.

It was upon the old faithfuls that the King-Emperor could always rely. The Australian parliament was not even summoned to declare war. 'One King, one flag, one cause' was Australia's battle-cry. In New Zealand, Parliament voted to a man to follow their king. Canada took a little longer, but on 9 September the Canadian parliament voted, without a division, to make the King's cause their own. Marching, too, in the Imperial Army, came the loyal host of colonies.

And so the naval cadet who was always bottom of his class, the delicate, stammering prince who squared up bravely to every ordeal, the 'Foreman' and camp organizer, the country-gentleman, devoted father, and the reluctant heir who had picked up the fallen crown, the man called George, *Rex et Imperator*, now led his empire to war. Would the Empire survive? The world shook its head in doubt. But the Emperor, at the head of his people, was quietly confident. He told them on 3 September, the first day of war: 'We can only do the right as we see the right and reverently commit our cause to God. If one and all we keep resolutely faithful to it ... then, with God's help, we shall prevail.'

One who felt most pessimistic about Britain's future prospects was the American ambassador in London, Mr Joseph P. Kennedy.* A few days after the outbreak of war he put it gloomily to the King that the war would ruin Britain. Was it then worth resisting Hitler's seizure of territory in Eastern Europe which business-wise, was of little value to Britain?

The King-Emperor did not see things in such material terms. 'The ultimate issues,' he had told his five hundred million subjects the day that war was declared, was that, if Hitler's primitive doctrine of Might is Right were allowed to triumph, 'the people of the world would be kept in the bondage of fear, and all hopes of settled peace and the security of justice and liberty among nations would be ended.'

On that score the King-Emperor could claim to speak for all his subjects, including the most recalcitrant ones. To Kennedy he replied: 'The British Empire has once again shown to the world a united front.' Its mind was made up, he affirmed, which was true enough, even admitting that the minds of India, Burma and the rest of the colonial empire had been made up for them.

The King-Emperor was not at this moment among those of whom the psalmist sang: 'Some trust in chariots, and some in horses.' His Majesty's armed forces were too

* Father of John, Robert and Edward Kennedy.

thin on the ground – and in the air – for that. A deeply
religious man, he preferred to 'remember the name of
the Lord our God'. On a note-pad on his desk he had
scribbled a line from Isaiah: 'They helped every one his
neighbour and everyone said to his brother, Be of good
cheer.' In his Christmas Day broadcast he warned his
people of 'the dark times ahead of us' and, quoting a
well-known poem encouraged them: 'Go out into the
darkness and put your hand in the hand of God. That
shall be to you better than a light, and safer than a
known way.'* No one could tell what the year 1940
would bring.

Two days before Christmas, Muslims of India celebrated
– on a rather different note – the Day of Deliverance,
which Jinnah had called for 'as a mark of relief that the
Congress regime has ceased to function'.

On the outbreak of war, Jinnah, like Gandhi, had
conferred with the Viceroy. He hoped, he told Linlithgow, that he would strengthen his hand. 'Does that
mean', asked Linlithgow, 'that in the seven provinces
where Congress are in power, you want me to dismiss
their ministries?' 'Yes', snapped Jinnah, 'turn them out at
once. Their object is to destroy both you British and us
Muslims.'

But the Congress itself was shortly to decide the fate
of its ministries. The war was less than two weeks old
when it issued a manifesto, drafted by Nehru. 'The crisis
that has overtaken Europe', it said, 'is not of Europe
only, but of humanity ... It is likely to re-fashion the
world for good or ill, socially and economically.' India,
it went on, had been the outstanding example of modern
imperialism. 'If the war is to defend the status quo, imperialist possessions, colonies, vested interests, and privilege, then India can have nothing to do with it. If however the issue is a world order ... based on democracy,
then India is intensely interested in it.' Cooperation with

* From 'The Gate of the Year' by Marie-Louise Haskins (published privately, 1908).

Britain was offered as between equals. But first the British government must declare what its war aims were in regard to democracy and imperialism. Gandhi himself presented the manifesto to the Viceroy. He asked him for a declaration on India's future of 'a really satisfying kind'.

Linlithgow next saw Nehru, who said of him: 'Possessing all the qualities and failings of an old-fashioned British aristocrat, he sought with integrity and honesty ... to find a way out of the tangle. But ... his mind worked in the old groove and shrank back from any innovation; his vision was limited by the traditions of the ruling class out of which he came; ... he disliked those who did not show a becoming appreciation of the high mission of the British Empire.'

Nehru was one of those whom the Viceroy disliked. He found him 'doctrinaire to a degree', with a mind closed to every argument. He 'soared above the mundane matters with which I was trying to wrestle ... into the airy heights of his brilliant imagination ...'

On 17 October 1939, the Viceroy made his eagerly awaited declaration which, in the words of his Reforms Commissioner, H. V. Hodson, was as eloquent as it was hazy. There was no mention of immediate independence. His Excellency advised India to tread cautiously along the road to freedom which – it was a promise – would be theirs, in the form of Dominion status, at the end of the war. As for war aims, it was too early yet to define them in detail – the fight was against aggression.

The Viceroy's declaration was hardly of the really satisfying kind requested by Gandhi. For Nehru, it was 'a refusal of all we had asked for'. Congress thereupon called upon its provincial ministries to resign, and by November 1939 the seven Congress-held provinces had retrograded to direct rule by the Governor – or, in Nehru's words, the full-blooded autocracy of the middle nineteenth century. A month later Congress dug its toes in: no help in the war effort without immediate independence.

Jinnah's hour had dawned. On Deliverance Day, 22

December, Muslims flocked to support him, the outcast whom Congress had — and still — refused to recognize as the Muslim leader. And when Congress chose a Muslim president, the revered Maulana Kalam Azad, it was the last straw. Said Jinnah: 'They had now added insult to injury by selecting that showboy.'

Under Azad, Congress returned to the attack at its Ramgarh session in March 1940. Britain, it accused, was carrying on the war 'for the preservation ... of her Empire, which is based on the exploitation of the people of India, as well as of other Asian and African countries'. Complete independence was the cry. 'Dominion status within the imperial structure is wholly inapplicable to India.' Rather than support the British, Congress decided on a civil disobedience campaign against them. Gandhi was to lead it.

Jinnah — Quaid-i-Azzam, the great leader, as his growing army of followers called him — was meanwhile strengthening the Muslim League position. He opened with a broadside at Congress. Its sole aim, he declared, was to annihilate every other organization in the country, and to set itself up as a Fascist authoritarian organization. Ninety million Muslims, sixty million Untouchables, six million Christians, Jews and Parsees were threatened by oppression from a Hindu Raj nearly three hundred million strong.

Jinnah fired more shots in an article in *Times and Life* on 9 March. Democratic government, he argued, was totally unsuitable to India, with its heterogeneous population, of which two-thirds were Hindus and the remainder mainly Muslims. The difference between Hindus and Muslims was not only one of religion, but of law and culture. They were two separate civilizations, Hinduism being based on caste, Isam on the quality of man. 'A constitution must be evolved', Jinnah pleaded, 'that recognizes that there are in India two nations.'

On Jinnah's 'two-nation theory' the Muslim League took its stand at its Lahore conference on 23 May 1940. It adopted a resolution which said in effect that the only constitutional plan acceptable to Muslims would be one which recognized that Muslim-majority areas (as in the north-western and eastern zones of India) should be grouped as sovereign independent states. It was called the Pakistan resolution. Jinnah declared shortly afterwards: 'No power on earth can prevent Pakistan.'

Barely two weeks after the Lahore session, the German army invaded Denmark and Norway. Many Indians were now for striking at the British. But on 27 April, Gandhi declared: 'I have no desire to embarrass the British, especially at a time when it is life or death with them.' By May, the German panzers and stukas had crushed Holland into submission and pinned the Anglo-French armies against the Channel coast. The evacuation from Dunkirk was under way. Britain faced invasion and defeat, but again Gandhi cautioned: 'We do not seek our independence out of Britain's ruin. That is not the way of non-violence.' And as, in mid-June, France surrendered, he predicted: 'Britain will die hard and heroically, even if she has to.'

By now, however, Congress was worried by Gandhi's non-violence in relation to the war, and India's defence in particular. On 21 June, on the eve of the Franco-German peace signature, it departed from its non-violent principles and decided that it could 'not go to the full length with Gandhi'. It was a painful wrench, wrote Nehru, to break with their cherished and well-beloved leader.

At the end of June, as the German general staff began planning the invasion of Britain and Churchill rallied the British for a last stand, the Viceroy was parleying with Gandhi and Jinnah in Simla, hoping to instil in them some enthusiasm for Britain's war effort. In return he offered Indians a greater share in the government. He saw the two leaders separately, although attempts were made to get them to meet. Gandhi hesitated. 'Adversity makes strange bed fellows,' he joked. Jinnah, staying at the Cecil Hotel, said: 'I am willing to see him if he wishes, but don't say so.' Gandhi then was asked if he wished to see Jinnah. 'It would be a lie if I were to say yes,' replied the disciple of truth. 'But if Jinnah wishes to meet me I will walk on bare feet to the Cecil Hotel.' He was spared the walk, for the Viceroy himself finally got them together. 'In each other's presence', he wrote, 'they refused to say one word that mattered, contenting themselves with a few sharp digs at t'other.'

Out of the talks came a Congress demand for full and immediate independence in exchange for full cooperation in India's defence. The Muslim League were less exacting. They would not interfere with the war effort; on the other hand, they would not agree to any constitutional changes without Muslim approval, or without Muslim-Hindu equality in the government.

To these conflicting demands the Viceroy replied, on 8 August, with a cautious offer. It was decidedly not the moment, he explained, when the Empire was struggling for its very existence, to make fundamental constitutional changes. For the present he was willing to have more Indians join his executive council. But after the war Britain, he promised, would give India a new constitution – on one condition. She would not hand over power to an Indian authority which was denied by other powerful elements in Indian life. In other words, Britain now agreed to a Muslim League veto on Congress policy. 'All I have to do now', remarked Jinnah sarcastically, 'is to wait for the next Congress move, and to counter it. I have no doubt that Nehru will play into my hands.' Nehru angrily rejected the offer. 'Dominion status is dead,' he said.

Perhaps the most extraordinary thing about the 'August Offer' was that it was ever made at all. Britain herself was at this moment making a last ditch stand for her own freedom. It was a time when the King-Emperor, with almost indecent sang-froid, wrote to his mother: 'Personally I feel happier now that we have no allies to be polite to and pamper.' It was a time when, in Churchill's words, His Majesty's Government 'viewed with stern and tranquil gaze the idea of going down fighting amidst the ruins of Whitehall'. A time, too, when the British prime minister rallied his compatriots 'to brace ourselves to our duties and so bear ourselves that, if the Empire and its Commonwealth last for a thousand years, men will say: "This was their finest hour."' It was not, however, a time when India's or anybody else's problems were uppermost in British minds.

Back in May, on the 24th, Empire Day, the King-Emperor had warned his five hundred million subjects that Hitler was seeking 'the overthrow, complete and final, of this Empire and of everything for which it stands, and after that, the conquest of the world'. Incredibly, the very same day, Hitler, the victorious war-lord, had astonished his generals (General Blumentritt, who was present, has left an account) by speaking 'with admiration of the British Empire, of the necessity for its existence and of the civilization that Britain had brought into the world. All he wanted from Britain was that she should acknowledge Germany's position on the Continent.'

Less than two months later, on 19 July, Hitler, now master of Europe, made his 'final appeal to common sense'. The bargain was still on: Europe for him, the Empire for Britain. Otherwise: 'I prophesy that a great Empire will be destroyed, an Empire which it was never my intention ... even to harm.' Within the hour, the BBC, on its own initiative, had replied in German, rejecting Hitler's offer. The radio and press were quick to follow. Their reply was one that came from the hearts of the British people. In Churchill's words, they 'courted the horrors of invasion and disdained a fair chance of peace'.

During his speech, Hitler had jibed at British leaders who had declared that 'if Britain should perish, they would carry on from Canada ... where the money and the children of those principally interested in the war have already been sent'. As one of those principally interested, the King-Emperor had flatly refused to go to Canada.

Instead, he had a shooting range set up in the garden
of his London home, Buckingham Palace, where he practised with revolver and machine-gun. A crack shot, he
was determined, if the Germans invaded, to lead the
British resistance.

It was only when the bombing attacks crept nearer
London that someone realized that there was no royal
bomb-shelter. A housemaid's room was hastily converted
into a make-shift bunker. As the Luftwaffe reduced London's East End to rubble and the civilian death-toll
mounted, the King and Queen moved about among the
ruins sympathizing, encouraging. 'The destruction is so
awful', said the Queen, 'and the people so wonderful.'
And once, from a group of survivors came a cry, 'Thank
God for a good king!' 'And thank God for a good
people!' the King answered feelingly.

He and the Queen were nearly killed when on 13
September, bombs hit Buckingham Palace. 'We saw two
bombs falling into the Quadrangle,' said the King. 'We
saw the flashes and then heard two resounding crashes
as the bombs fell about 30 yards away ... We looked
at each other and ... wondered why we weren't dead.'*

The King-Emperor, as Lieutenant Prince Albert, had
been in the thick of the action twenty-four years earlier
at Jutland – a great experience he had called it. But the
bombing shook him badly. He thought it 'a ghastly experience' – surely only because total war had struck at his
own home. It was different from being with the guncrew
aboard HMS *Collingwood*. Churchill, however, found
him 'exhilarated by all this, and pleased that he should
be sharing the dangers of his subjects' – an opinion confirmed by the Queen. 'I'm glad we've been bombed,' she
said. 'It makes me feel I can look the East End in the
face.'

This was only the beginning. Before the war was over,

* The King-Emperor's own account given here is compiled from
an entry in his diary and an account he wrote for Mr Winston
Churchill, reproduced in the latter's *Second World War*, vol. II.
They differ only in detail.

Buckingham Palace would be hit nine times, but never did the King and Queen shrink from the danger. Later, as the King's equerry, I stood behind him during an investiture at Buckingham Palace, uncomfortably aware of the flying bombs which roared overhead, while the windows vibrated with their shindy. But the King, unperturbed, continued to pin on medal after medal, chat with each recipient and shake his hand. Only once did he turn and look through the window – in time to see the evil, stunted silhouette of a V.1 flying bomb as it darted past a few hundred feet above. And when, one night during dinner, one of Werner von Braun's supersonic V.2 rocket missiles (you never heard them coming) exploded with a sudden almighty crash, the King asked me quietly: 'Perhaps you would find out where that one fell.' It had hit a pub next to Selfridges in Oxford Street, killing over a hundred people.

On 15 September 1940, the Battle of Britain reached its culminating date, as Churchill called it. That day Gandhi told Congress: 'I do not want England to be defeated ... It hurts me to find St Paul's cathedral damaged.' It was not because he loved the English and hated the Germans, or that he claimed any superiority for the Indians – 'we are all tarred with the same brush,' he said.

Despite this naïve profession of neutrality, Gandhi asked the Viceroy, a few days later, if Congress might launch non-violent propaganda against Britain's war effort – he wanted complete freedom of speech. Patiently, Linlithgow explained that he could not grant Indian pacifists more freedom of speech than was allowed to British conscientious objectors, who were free to practise their faith but not to preach it to others. Linlithgow admired Gandhi. 'There is not a shadow of doubt that he is the one real figure which appeals to the popular imagination.' On the other hand, as he warned Amery, Secretary for India: 'I have now little doubt that he is bent on mischief ... The conflict which I have laboured so long to avoid may now be imminent.'

The Viceroy was not mistaken. On 17 October, Gandhi

launched a new disobedience campaign, but this time of a symbolic kind. He selected individual Congress leaders, charged them to deliver anti-war speeches and thus court arrest and imprisonment. Gandhi's first candidate for this self-immolation process was the gentle, studious Vinobe Bhave, one of his most devoted disciples. Next came Nehru, who was arrested – on a different charge, sedition – before he could shout any anti-war slogans. He received a harsh four years' sentence. Churchill was stunned at this treatment of a fellow old-Harrovian and ordered that Nehru should be considered as an internee, not as a criminal. But Nehru felt bitter. 'Instead of the intoxication of the thought of freedom', he wrote later, 'we experienced the aching frustration of its denial ... All this talk and ritual of parliamentary debate in England, of rounded and pompous utterance, was just political trickery ... The claws of imperialism would continue deep in the living body of India. And that was the measure of that ... freedom ... for which Britain claimed to be fighting.'

Vallabhabhai Patel followed Nehru, and so the process went on. Gandhi obligingly suspended it over Christmas and New Year. But turkey and plum pudding failed to deflect the zeal of the British. They arrested Congress president Azad during the truce. Gandhi extended the campaign to the provinces, to the 'four-anna members'.* There was little enthusiasm, but occasionally comedy. Sampuran Singh, from the Punjab, volunteered for *satyagraha*. Brought to trial, he put up a spirited defence (against all the principles of non-violence). He was fined one anna and freed. The press began to protest that *satyagraha* was becoming a farce and called a halt to it. By the summer of 1941, Gandhi's peace campaign was dead – killed by the human instinct of self-preservation.

A fierce display of this basic instinct by an officer of His Majesty's navy occurred about this time. It was to have an important bearing on India's future. The occasion was the sinking of the destroyer *Kelly* on 23 May

* 1 anna = 2 cents.

1941 during the Battle of Crete. Hit by a Junkers dive bomber, she capsized at 34 knots. As she turned over, her captain's one thought was: 'I must be the last to leave her alive.' He clung to the gyro compass pedestal. Then: 'I took an enormously deep breath as the water closed over my head ... I suddenly felt my lungs were going to burst ... I had to kick hard to fight my way to the surface.' He broke surface, gasping for breath. 'At this moment, up bobbed one of our Stoker Petty Officers', who saluted his captain and cracked: 'Extraordinary how the scum always comes to the top, isn't it, sir?' The 'scum' was Captain Lord Louis Mountbatten, India's future Viceroy, and her last.

While Gandhi persisted that wars could be won by non-violence, his view was not shared by the Zionists. Weizmann and Ben Gurion wanted a Jewish army to fight alongside the British. Ironically enough, some of the Jewish fighters' most spectacular successes were to be made against the British.

As thousands of Palestine Jews queued up to register for national service, the High Commissioner, Sir Harold MacMichael, informed Ben Gurion that the White Paper land purchase restrictions were now to be applied. Ben Gurion was flabbergasted. The consequences, he warned, would be disastrous. 'The policy strikes at the very heart of the Jewish National Home by depriving Jews of the right to settle on the land and compels them as in the Diaspora* to be town dwellers.' The Jews' age-long aspirations to become rooted in the soil of their ancient homeland was frustrated at a time when millions of Jews were being mercilessly persecuted. It was racial discrimination to confine Jews to a small pale of settlement such as only existed in Nazi Germany. The Mandate, concluded Ben Gurion, had ceased to exist.

A wave of anger swept the Yishuv, rousing in the breast of one, Abraham Stern, a violent insane fanaticism against all opponents of Zionism – Nazis, British and, worst of

* Jewish community, apart from the Yishuv, dispersed throughout the world.

all, Jews who opposed him. A brilliant scholar and poet, Stern dreamed of a Jewish kingdom stretching from the Nile to the Euphrates. His followers called him Yair, 'the illuminator', after a Jewish hero of Roman times. Stern decided that the present time was one for more heroics. He broke away from the Irgun (which he and another student, David Raziel, had created) and formed his own group, the fanatical terrorist Lehi – known more commonly as the Stern Gang.

The Irgun themselves were eager for rebellion. They too believed in terror, in martyrdom for the cause. The Irgun called Ben Gurion a coward, and they felt contempt for Haganah because of its strict observance of *havlagah*, self-restraint or non-retaliation. But Haganah was not sleeping. By 1939, it had created secret arms stores throughout the country. Its grenades and bombs were being manufactured clandestinely. No one was quite sure whether Haganah was illegal or not. Officially it was. Ben Gurion denied all knowledge of its existence. The British closed their eyes to its activities, but, to keep the record straight, they recruited from its ranks, trained and armed twenty thousand Jewish Special Police, calling them, ingenuously, the Legal Haganah.

But it was a Haganah scout force that headed the British invasion of Syria in July 1941. In a bloody battle with French Somali units at Fort Gouraud, one of the Haganah men lost his left eye. His name was Moshe Dayan, future chief of staff of the Israeli army.

Haganah and Irgun were at this time on the point of reconciliation, but Ben Gurion scotched the idea. He saved Haganah's reputation, but by sparing Irgun the restraining influence of *havlagah* he left them with a free hand – and a free conscience – to indulge in terrorism.

The Zionists longed to fight Nazism under their own blue and white banner, emblazoned with the Star of David. In June 1940, as Britain made feverish last-minute preparations to face the German onslaught, Weizmann took up the argument with Lord Lloyd. The Jews, too, he asked, should be allowed to organize the defence of the Holy Land. 'Time presses,' he said. 'Delay may mean the annihilation of half a million Jews in Palestine ... If we have to go down, we are entitled to go down fighting, and the Mandatory Power is in duty bound to grant us this elementary human right.' To Churchill, Weizmann wrote in August, saying that, if the British had to withdraw from Palestine: 'The Jews would be exposed to wholesale massacre at the hands of the Arabs, encouraged ... by the Nazis.' Once again, he begged for 'the elementary right' to bear arms. His eloquent and moving argument would doubtless have made a greater impression had not Churchill, in exhorting the British to fight on the beaches, in the hills and in the streets, envisaged their doing so with clubs and home-made spears because there were not enough rifles to go round.

Early in September, Weizmann had lunch with Churchill at Chequers. By the time it was over, he had obtained the Prime Minister's approval for a Jewish army. It was to be organized like the Czech and Polish armies and to consist of ten thousand men, including four thousand from Palestine, and its commander was to be Orde Wingate. But by March 1941, the Jewish army had to be postponed through lack of equipment – a pretext that the Zionists naturally disbelieved, though it happened to be true. Wingate himself, now leading Haile Selassie's guerillas in Ethiopia, was also starved of equipment.

When in June 1941, Hitler invaded, Russia, Weizmann once again had to be told 'since the Government have to give every aid to Russia, it will not be possible to form a Jewish division'.

If the Zionist felt despair over their army, they were moved to hatred by the British immigration policy. Since Hitler came to power in 1933, a new type of immigration had developed, via the Black Sea and eastern Mediterranean ports. Haganah's Moddad le Aliyeh Beth ('Illegal' Immigration Committee),* created in 1937, operated

---

* There were two immigration organizations, Aliyeh Aleph (*A*) which the British called 'legal' and and Aliyeh Beth (*B*) which the British called 'illegal', the Jews 'unpermitted'.

through its agents in anti-Semitic countries, who selected the most likely-looking immigrants. By 1940, the monster Eichmann himself was taking a hand at the despatching end of 'this interesting business' as he called the shameful human traffic which rivalled the slave trade in horror and human degradation. He entrusted the shipping side to a rich Viennese Jew, Storfer. Eichmann did not select – all Jews were undesirables. They were simply rounded up by the Gestapo and, having paid an exorbitant price for passports and exit permits, were herded like cattle into small boats, and transported down the Danube. Transferred to leaking, rickety, vermin-infested freighters and cattle boats, they then set out on the dangerous and terrible odyssey across the Black Sea, via Istanbul, to Palestine. Some of the 'coffin-ships' never reached Palestine, like the *Salvador* which sank with 204 refugees, 66 of them children. Others were able to land their passengers clandestinely, but most were intercepted. 'The British Navy was always on the watch,' wrote Albert Hyamson. 'This was the great safeguard, for it was known that no immigrant ship once seen would be left to sink with its human cargo.'*

On arrival at Haifa, the 'illegal' immigrants (Zionists always used inverted commas) would be transferred to a sea-worthy vessel for shipment to far-away Mauritius, extravagantly depicted by Zionist propaganda as another Devil's Island. A lucky few, as Hyamson says – the sick, pregnant women, perhaps orphan children – would be treated as exceptions and allowed to land.

Throughout 1941, the lamentable traffic in human lives to Palestine continued, with its immeasurable toll of death on the high seas and deportation of the survivors, exacerbating the conflict between the Palestine government and the Jewish people.

* *Palestine under the Mandate* (London, 1950).

7

Distrust 1941-2

On 7 December 1941, the Japanese attacked Pearl Harbour. At the same time they also landed in Malaya. Their possession of air bases in French Indo-China gave them complete mastery of the air. On 10 December their torpedo-bombers sank the great warships *Prince of Wales* (the Navy's newest and finest, in which Churchill and Roosevelt had recently met), and *Repulse*. 'It is a national disaster,' wrote the King-Emperor to Churchill, who himself, on hearing the news, said: 'I never received a more direct shock.' By Christmas Day, Hong Kong was in Japanese hands. That evening the King-Emperor broadcast to the Empire. 'Truly, it is a stern and solemn time,' he said. 'But as the war widens, so surely our conviction deepens the greatness of our cause.'

Conviction, of the deepest kind, was indeed needed as more disasters followed. On 15 February 1942, Singapore, the island-fortress deemed impregnable, surrendered. Churchill, who had attempted to rally the defenders with the message: 'The honour of the British Empire and of the British army is at stake', had instead to witness what he called the greatest defeat in British history – and this at the hands of an Asiatic people. The King-Emperor was despondent, but phlegmatic. 'I am depressed by the loss of Singapore,' he wrote. 'We are going through a bad phase.'

On top of the Far East disasters, there now occurred, under the noses of the British public, yet another blow at the Navy's prestige as the German warships *Scharnhorst* and *Gneisenau* steamed unscathed up the Channel from Brest. One of the searching aircraft was piloted by Michael Weizmann, son of Chaim. On the eve of his departure to the US, the Zionist leader was called to the telephone to be told: 'Your son is missing.' Stunned with grief, Chaim Weizmann reflected bitterly that his son had fallen in a cause for which the Zionist flag had not yet been unfurled.

'These reverses will continue for longer still,' the King-Emperor forecast two days after the fall of Singapore. But when, a week later, Churchill warned him gloomily: 'Burma, Ceylon, Calcutta, and Madras in India and part of Australia may fall into enemy hands', the King-Emperor's sang-froid momentarily failed him. 'Can we stick together in the face of all this adversity?' he asked his prime minister, but without waiting for a reply he added: 'We must somehow.' But he was finding it hard to stick to his convictions. 'I cannot help feeling depressed at the future outlook,' he recorded. 'Anything can happen.' It did. A week later Rangoon fell to the Japanese. But by now the King-Emperor, apparently immune to disaster, had taken a firm hold on himself. Writing to Roosevelt early in March, he said: 'Japan ... has not counted the cost we shall mete out to her with our combined strength ... Victory is without any doubt to be with us.' This was pure, naked faith, and it was needed. By the end of May the British had been driven out of Burma and the King-Emperor no longer ruled over the Golden Land – a mere fifty-seven years after Queen Victoria had informed King Thibaw that Burma, during Her Majesty's pleasure, was part of Her Majesty's dominions. The British Emperor had lost Hong Kong, Singapore, Malaya and Burma to the Emperor of Japan. The Mikado's troops now stood on the frontiers of the Indian Empire.

With the invading Japanese, back came Aung San to his native land, in the guise of a Japanese colonel, as chief of staff to Colonel Suzuki, commander of the Burmese Independence Army, whom the Burmans called Bo Mogyoe, 'General Lightning'. During his stay in Japan, Aung San had been joined by other young Burmese rebels. In all they were thirty – the 'Thirty Heroes'. The Japanese put them through a stiff training course – day and night exercises and basic rations. As Bo Let Ya, one of the thirty, said, 'We were all looking like scarecrows.' But Aung San, according to Brigadier Maung Maung, his aide, admired the tough Japanese methods. They made men who were efficient tools to serve the national cause. They had raised Japan, in an incredibly short time, from feudalism to modern nationhood. Aung San realized that a national struggle like Burma's needed iron-willed leaders.

The Japanese came to respect Aung San, though he felt no particular respect for them. In deference to Japanese custom, he bowed before the Imperial Palace, but 'I did not believe in the divinity of the Emperor', he confessed, 'and do not like monarchy in any form. I bowed out of courtesy and had no intention of becoming his subject.'

Any more than he intended to become once again the British Emperor's subject. On the contrary, Aung San, at the head of the Burmese Independence Army, had committed treason in making war against the King-Emperor.

But as he marched north from Moulmein to Rangoon, Aung San felt unhappy. 'The Japanese, from the start, broke all the promises they gave us.' Clashes between Burmese and Japanese soldiers became more frequent. Bo Let Ya (soon to succeed Aung San as chief of staff) said: 'The Japanese were overbearing; they began to bully our boys.' Only General 'Lightning' Suzuki remained loyal to them. When they reached Rangoon on 10 March, he wanted to declare Burma independent, but that, his superiors told him, was for later.

Aung San was now promoted General Commanding The Burmese Independent Army, with colonels Ne Win and Zeya as field commanders. At the BIA's inception in Bangkok in December 1941, each one of the Thirty had drawn blood from his arm to drink the oath of loyalty. Aung San suggested they should each pick a name which would give pride and purpose to their sacred mission. 'We felt a few inches taller with new names,' said Bo Let Ya. They gave Aung San the title 'Bogyoke', an affectionate term meaning 'Chief'.

Soldiering under the name of General Te Za, Aung San now led the BIA on northwards beyond Rangoon in the wake of the retreating British. As a Japanese general, Aung San was obviously not made for the part. He was

often so wrapped up in thought – about Burma's struggle
– that he would do up his tunic buttons the wrong way
and buckle his sword on so that it trailed almost hori-
zontally on the ground. Once he complained that his boots
were pinching, only to discover that he had them on the
wrong feet. Though he wore breeches – and slept in them
– he preferred a *longyi* for comfort. His few spare clothes
were rolled into a small bundle and wrapped in a *longyi*.
Playing commander-in-chief bored Aung San. 'He never
took his role so seriously as to insist on military honours,'
never called pompous military conferences, said his aide
Maung Maung. He never took a bath either, in all the
weeks of marching between Rangoon and Mandalay.
Aung San told Maung Maung that a revolutionary should
have few wants, and eat and sleep where he could.

Thus, first by river-boat, then in an old Ford Sedan,
General Aung San led his rebel army (Maung Maung
called it a rabble army) in pursuit of the King-Emperor's
forces. The experience so exhausted him that he landed
up in hospital. 'That was the end of our peace,' said Bo
Let Ya, already there. 'Aung San made noises or sang.'
And he never allowed his nurse, Ma Khin Kyi, out of
his sight. Shortly after, he married her.

After the long road to Mandalay, the BIA was re-
organized and called the Burma Defence Army. By then
the Burmese had no illusions about the Japanese. U Nu,
Aung San's closest confidant, described how Japanese
propaganda thrilled the people. 'A Burmese prince is
coming as a leader in the Japanese army.' But the Japanese army itself came as an unpleasant surprise. Under the
scorching midday sun at Mandalay, 'the poor people were
so keen to meet their great ally that they did not even
notice the heat'; but after greeting the Japanese, said
U Nu, 'their faces were no longer joyful and exultant'.
One of them told him: 'We expected the Japanese commander to be very thankful for our bowls of rice, but all
he did was to give us a hard slap in the face.' Word spread
like wildfire that the Japanese were a tough crowd – so
tough in fact that the Burmese began to think that they

might, after all, stand a better chance with the British.

Meanwhile, the British-Indian forces, minus tanks and transport, were racing against the invaders and the approaching monsoon. Accompanied by a weary, straggling mass of refugees and wounded, they laboured up the jungle tracks which led over the mountains to Imphal, just inside India's eastern frontier. Another route wound up from the steamy, malarial Hukawng Valley in the north to the Pangsau Pass.* Many died before they got there. Those who reached the pass called it Hell's Gate. Yet it led to Heaven – India and safety.

Or comparative safety. For, as Prime Minister Churchill had warned his new ally, President Roosevelt, eastern India was threatened with invasion, 'with incalculable internal consequences to our whole war plan'. General Wavell, Commander-in-Chief in India, was begging for reinforcements – 'if not, we run the risk of losing India'. To the Anglo-American allies, India was a vital base.

To neither of them were Gandhi's views on India's defence reassuring. 'I would say to an aggressor', Gandhi had declared, 'you may destroy my churches, my hearths and my homes, everything but my soul. I will not defend my country with your weapons. I will simply refuse to cooperate with you.'

Nehru, who had been released prematurely at the time of Pearl Harbour, disagreed with his master. As the Japanese approached India, he declared: 'It would be preposterous indeed to advise the people to offer passive resistance.' Winston Churchill's opinion was a typically trenchant one. He wrote later: 'No portion of the world's population was so effectively protected from the horrors and perils of the World War as were the peoples of Hindustan. They were carried through the struggle on the shoulders of our small island.' British debts to India were piling up. 'We were being charged nearly a million pounds a day for defending India from the miseries of

* The author took this route by car in 1956. At one stage it took him 7 days to cover 25 miles.

invasion which so many other lands endured'. Nevertheless, he added: 'Two and a half million Indians volunteered to serve in the forces ... The response of the Indian
peoples ... makes a glorious final page in the story of our
Indian Empire.'

In face of the Japanese threat, Churchill formed an
India Committee, whose president was Clement Attlee,
deputy prime minister. Its decisions concerning 'this India
business', as Churchill called it, must, he insisted, obtain
the King-Emperor's consent, 'as the rights of the Imperial
Crown are plainly affected'. So too were the interests, if
not the rights, of the US president – as Commander-in-
Chief of the US forces now beginning to pour into India.

Now that the Americans were concerned with global
strategy, Churchill did not in the least appreciate their
tendency to offer advice on political issues 'on which they
had strong opinions and little experience'. Even the mild-
mannered Clement Attlee resented the way the Americans
threw their weight about. 'Much of their criticism of
British rule was very ill-informed, but its strength could
not be denied.' Americans, he complained, drew a sharp
distinction between overseas expansion and the Americans' conquest of their own continent, and the virtual
liquidation of its native inhabitants.

The first time Roosevelt mentioned the subject of India
in conversation with Churchill, he received in return such
a tirade that he never raised it verbally again. But early
in March 1942 Churchill cabled the President: 'We are
earnestly considering a declaration of Dominion status
after the war ... with the right to secede.' He emphasized:
'We must not ... break with the Muslims ... a hundred
million people, and the main army elements on which we
must rely ...; also ... our duty towards thirty to forty
million Untouchables and our treaties with the Princes'
states ...'

A few days later, the President, in his most disarming
manner, submitted his views on the subject 'which of
course all you good people know far more about than I
do'. As tactfully as possible, he reminded Churchill that

after the American Revolution (1775–83), the thirteen rebel British colonies joined in the Articles of Confederation, 'an obvious stop-gap government'. It was 'merely a thought of mine', said the President, that the British might set up a similar kind of temporary government in India. 'Perhaps', he concluded, 'the analogy ... to the travails and problems of the United States from 1783–9 might give a new slant in India and ... cause the people there to ... become more loyal to the British Empire.'

No such happy result was achieved with the thirteen colonies, but the President was reluctant to go further: 'For the love of heaven don't bring me into this ... It is strictly none of my business, except insofar as it is part and parcel of the successful fight that you and I are making.' Churchill commented with a touch of sarcasm: 'This document illustrates the difficulties of comparing situations in various centuries ... where almost every material fact is totally different.'

The Emperor of India summed up the situation of which, after all, he was the central figure: 'FDR had urged Winston to give India a promise of Dominion status now ... The draft declaration states to create a new Indian Union associated with the UK and other [Dominions] by a common allegiance to the Crown, but equal to them ... and free to ... separate itself from ... the British Commonwealth.' But the Emperor was indignant at the prospect of losing India. 'Why mention secession?' he asked. 'Many Indians still want to owe me allegiance as King-Emperor.'

The draft declaration's offer of a post-war Indian Union carried two main reservations: guarantees for minorities, and British responsibility for India's war-time defence. Sir Stafford Cripps, its principal sponsor, flew to India to negotiate it with the Indian leaders. Cripps, austere, vegetarian and a specialist on Indian affairs, was held in high esteem, at least in Congress circles. He shared with Gandhi a taste for nuts and raw vegetables, and was a friend of Nehru's. Jinnah regarded him less fondly – Cripps had recently written some terse comments on the

Muslims, for which he hastened to apologize to the Muslim leader.

Cripps landed in Delhi on 22 March. Colonel Louis Johnson, President Roosevelt's personal envoy, arrived hot-foot, but uninvited, a few days later, to intervene in the complicated parleys. The colonel lost no time in putting over the American case. He told B. Shiva Rao, a leading Hindu journalist: 'We are fighting this war more than the British' – a highly deceptive statement when considered in terms of human, let alone material, losses. Pursuing his theme, the colonel told Rao that as long as India would continue to fight the Japanese to the end and promise also to treat the Muslims and Untouchables fairly, the President would use his influence with Churchill to give India her freedom.

Colonel Johnson then had an off-the-record meeting with Nehru, who spoke of India hitching her waggon to America's star – at which the colonel stoutly declared that the President was determined to support Britain until the end of the war. If the Indian Congress would do the same, they could count on the President's sympathy.

Soon after his arrival, Cripps showed the draft declaration to Gandhi, who did not react kindly. 'If this is all you have to offer,' he said, 'I would advise you to take the next plane home.' But Cripps, undaunted, continued his talks, and, when Colonel Johnson arrived, the British envoy, far from resenting the American, got together with him and produced a formula on the thorny question of defence. Without so much as consulting the Viceroy or the Commander-in-Chief, they submitted it to Congress, who were delighted – the two envoys had calmly divested the Commander-in-Chief of his absolute authority in India's defence.

In his zeal to please the Indians and stung, perhaps, by Gandhi's comment, Cripps not only ignored the Viceroy, but went well beyond his brief. This brought a protest from His Excellency to London, who in turn cautioned Cripps to stick to his terms of reference. Nor was the King-Emperor too pleased with the way his Viceroy was being treated. 'There is no excuse for this,' he noted angrily, 'or for bringing Colonel Johnson, an American, into the negotiations. The latter knows nothing about India ... In fact, the whole matter is in a most unsatisfactory state.'

Indeed, in the cross-currents between London, Washington and Delhi, and in the whirlpool of Delhi itself, the Cripps Mission was foundering. Roosevelt, in a determined effort to save it, cabled Churchill, insisting once more on the idea of a provisional Indian government along the lines of the post-revolution American one. Its final form could be determined 'after a period of trial and error'.

Churchill, touched as he was by the President's solicitude, refused to budge. 'You know the weight which I attach to everything you say to me,' he replied; 'a serious difference between you and me would break my heart.' But the President's mind, he wrote later, was back in the eighteenth century, when the thirteen American colonies were fighting George III for independence.

Churchill's was the bulldog attitude of not relaxing for one instant his grip on the all-essential purpose of winning the war. Everything, Indian, American, British, world freedom depended on that one thing. This was not the moment for the trial and error experiments advocated by Roosevelt. 'I was responsible', said the British prime minister, 'for preserving the peace and safety of the Indian continent ... nearly a fifth of the population of the globe.' Now that the Japanese had routed the British on land and in the air, and driven the British navy from the Indian Ocean, 'our forces', said Churchill, 'were slender and strained to the full'. But he still believed that there was 'the hope, and the chance to preserve from hideous and violent destruction the vast, ancient Indian society over which we had presided for nearly two hundred years'. For Churchill, there was no question, simply in order to please American public opinion, of abandoning the Indian peoples 'to anarchy and subjugation ... by allowing their base of operations and the gallant

back on the Cripps offer. The days of the British Raj were numbered. Churchill said as much, at the end of July 1942, to the King-Emperor, who reacted fiercely. 'He amazed me', wrote George VI, 'by saying that his colleagues and ... Parliament were quite prepared to give up India to the Indians after the war. Cripps, the Press and US public opinion have all contributed to make their minds up that our rule in India is wrong and has always been wrong ... I disagree and have always said India has got to be governed.'

Governed it would be, but not – at least in the immediate future – without difficulty. For as the British in India prepared to meet invasion, they heard first a murmur, then a rending shout on the lips of millions of Indians: 'Quit India!'

Defeat, ignominy, the threat of insurrection and invasion – such was the Empire's sorry fate, for the moment, in the Far East. In the Middle East, its fortunes were scarcely better. Rommel's Afrika Korps were within striking distance of Cairo, lynch-pin of middle-eastern imperial strategy. Since the beginning of 1942, the Desert Fox had driven the 8th Army back over five hundred miles to El Alamein, where it stood at bay. The final battle would be vital for the British, probably for the outcome of the war. Besides, a British defeat would mean the annihilation of half a million Palestinian Jews.

The 8th Army was an imperial army in the truest sense, with its British, Australian, New Zealand, South African and Indian contingents. Many were the sons of Yishuv who won glory in action with British units. Attached to the King's West African Rifles was a company of four hundred Palestine Jews, under Major Liebmann. Near Bir Hacheim, stoutly defended by the 1st Free French Brigade, Leibmann and his men fought a heroic and very costly action. When the Germans called upon them to show the white flag of surrender, Leibmann replied: 'We know only one flag, the blue and white one of Zion.' Yet the flag of Zion had still not been officially unfurled at the head of an all-Jewish army. In fact the Jews were in a dilemma over Ben Gurion's policy of fighting both the war and the White Paper. For the more they fought the White Paper, with their 'illegal' immigration and their hate-ridden anti-British propaganda, the less were the British inclined to trust them with an army of their own. Already, the British had raised the Palestinian Buffs, a Palestinian battalion, preponderantly Jewish, the remainder Arab, attached to the East Kent Regiment (the Buffs). There was also the Jewish Settlement Police, the legal Haganah. And now that Rommel's Afrika Korps threatened annihilation to the Yishuv, the Jewish authorities sent out a call to arms. 'The best of our sons are taking part in the struggle,' it ran. 'Should the fight approach the borders of Palestine, we shall all form a wall for its defence.' Palestine Jews rushed to join up in the British armed forces.

In June 1942, Weizmann, in a letter to Churchill, renewed his plea for a Jewish army fighting under their own flag alongside the armies of the United Nations. Churchill, despite his Middle East advisers, brought all possible pressure to bear. In August 1942 the Palestine Buffs were re-formed as the Palestine Regiment. But further than that the Palestine government refused to go. They had their reasons. Their intelligence had just discovered that former members of Haganah serving in the British forces were still under Haganah orders. It was known too, that Haganah – as well as the Irgun and the Sternists – were secretly discussing the use of force against the British. The theft of British arms and munitions by Jewish soldiers was common. The British army, already fully extended, had to deploy men to guard ports, depots and munitions-transport – all this at a time when Weizmann found it necessary to give a solemn warning to General Marshall, US Chief of Staff, of 'what faced us [Jews in Palestine] if the needed munitions did not reach the British in time'.

Revolt threatened in Palestine, rebellion in India. Jewish and Indian patriots, distrustful of British intentions, believed their best course was to turn against Britain and usurp power to themselves. Burmese patriots had already done so. Ireland too – she stood aside from the struggle. Yet it was an Irish poet who at this moment of England's darkest fortune, spoke for those who still believed in her:

> Through the dense fog of war
> I see nothing clearly
> Nothing at all, nothing at all
> But one fixed star:
> England's star merely
> By it I stand or fall,
> Loving her dearly.*

* Conal O'Riordan, quoted, from *Punch*, 1 July 1942, by Sir John Wheeler-Bennett in *King George VI* (London, 1965).

8

Rebellion 1942–5

At no moment in its history had the British empire been in such peril. The Japanese stood on India's eastern frontier. In the west, the German armies in Russia had advanced as far as the Don, and in North Africa, Cairo was within their grasp. The Axis strategy was clear: an east–west link-up, a victorious handshake over the prostrate bodies of India and Palestine after the elimination of Britain, protector (much as they resented it) of their liberties.

It was the moment that the Indians and the Palestinian Jews decided to make an independent bid for liberty by striking at Britain, who regarded their action, legitimate and urgent as its motives may have been, as a treasonable attempt to sabotage her own unflagging and costly efforts in the defence of liberty. In the heartless reckoning imposed by war, Britain too had a legitimate view-point. She clung doggedly – blindly too, but that was part of her strength – to the one essential, victory. Without the defeat of Germany and Japan, and all their abominable paraphernalia of crime, it was idle to dream of freedom or even survival.

The 'Quit India' resolution was approved by the Congress Working Committee on 14 July 1942. Gandhi was its inspiration and its acknowledged leader. For the last three months he had been pressing the British. 'Leave India to God or to anarchy' was his theme. Now, as Congress demanded that 'British rule in India must cease immediately' – if not, it would use all its 'non-violent strength' – Gandhi declared, on a not so non-violent theme: 'After all, it is open rebellion.'

On 8 August, the All-India Congress Committee ratified the resolution. 'The peril of to-day necessitates the ending of British domination,' it declared. 'Only the glow of freedom' could release India's energies and enthusiasm for winning the war. Gandhi now rallied his followers with a new battle-cry, 'do or die!'

Before he himself could do either, the British – the very next day – arrested him along with other Congress leaders. Sedition was the charge, but the Viceroy ordered that Gandhi was not to be treated as a common criminal, but as a state prisoner, and lodged in the Aga Khan's palace near Poona. Nehru and others were interned in Ahmednagar Fort, in Bombay presidency.

Violence, not non-violence, immediately swept India – violence which had clearly been planned beforehand by the Congress high command. Government property was the main target: 550 post offices were attacked and telephone lines cut in over 2,500 places; miles of wire were rolled up and removed, to be transformed, no doubt, into copper bangles for Indian ladies; seventy police stations were assaulted and policemen murdered and burnt alive. At Singhia, the assistant-inspector's body was transfixed by a dozen spears. At Ballia only two police stations remained standing. Ballia resembled a country which had been fought over and conquered, wrote Hugh Lane, joint-magistrate in nearby Benares. The rebellion was 'very reminiscent of what one reads of the Mutiny'. The Congressites ransacked over 250 railway stations, blew up signal boxes and lifted rails – with specially provided tools. At a station in Bihar, two Canadian officers were dragged from a train by the mob and torn to pieces.

That Congress, despite its profession of non-violence, had carefully planned the rebellion, was further evidenced by the fact that it launched its main offensive in Bihar and the eastern part of the United Provinces – that is, athwart the communications to the eastern frontier where British-Indian forces were preparing to meet a Japanese invasion.

A swift decision by the Indian government to act nipped the rebellion in the bud. It was a courageous decision, too. All except one of the Executive members who made it were Indians, who risked the direct personal consequences. Later, a Congress bulletin admitted that 'the Revolution had been disappointing. The gigantic and sweeping mass uprisings and ... mass attacks that we witnessed in the beginning of our struggle have slowed down and subsided ... while numerous centres of usurper [i.e. British] administration have been attacked ... we have not been able to paralyse the administration comepletely.'

Gandhi meanwhile put the blame for the rebellion that failed squarely on the shoulders of the Viceroy. 'Dear Lord Linlithgow,' he wrote, 'the Government of India were wrong in precipitating the crisis ... Violence was never contemplated.' The British government's offer of post-war independence was frustrating. 'Hence the logical cry of withdrawal first.' To the British claim that it was their job to defend India, Gandhi retorted: 'It is a mockery of the truth after the experiences of Malaya, Singapore and Burma.' Piously he enjoined the Viceroy: 'Do not disregard this pleading of one who claims to be a sincere friend of the British people. Heaven guide you.'

The Viceroy parried Gandhi's thrusts and the wordy duel continued into 1943. 'I seem to be the *fons et origo* of the evil imputed to Congress,' complained Gandhi. He was prepared to wait six months 'in the hope that the Government will admit that they have wronged innocent men'. The period was ending. 'So is my patience,' said Gandhi with an unconscious Hitlerian touch. 'The law of *satyagraha* prescribes a remedy, "Crucify the flesh by fasting".' He fixed the fast for February.

Replying, Linlithgow told Gandhi that he was frankly and profoundly depressed by Congress policy, particularly as 'while it gave rise to violence and crime ... no condemnation ... should have come from you'. But Gandhi was in no mood for contrition. 'I have not any conviction of error,' he replied. He had no control over the violence which had occurred and, anyway, disbelieved the press reports. 'I am as confirmed a believer in non-violence as I ever have been. I have condemned openly any violence on the part of Congress.' He refused to plead guilty. 'Convince me that I was wrong,' he challenged the Viceroy, who thundered back: 'We are dealing with facts in this matter.' And the facts were that the Congress 'Quit India' resolution had declared a mass struggle and appointed Gandhi as its leader. 'A body which passes a resolution in these terms is hardly entitled to disclaim responsibility for any events which follow it.' Then, for the high-priest of non-violence, the most unpleasant fact of all. 'There is evidence,' pursued the Viceroy, 'that you and your friends expected this policy to lead to violence; and that you were prepared to condone it; and that the violence which ensued formed part of a concerted plan.' There was ample evidence too, the Viceroy added, to prove that the campaign of sabotage was conducted on secret instructions from Congress, and that well-known Congressmen had committed acts of violence and murder. Congress, he was well aware, had an underground organization (one of its most active members was the wife of a member of the All-India Committee) 'which actively engaged in planning the bomb outrages and other acts of terrorism that have disgusted the country'.

The Viceroy argued like any law-abiding British citizen. To accept Gandhi's point of view would be to ask that the Indian government, whose job was to maintain law and order, 'should allow subversive and revolutionary movements, described by yourself as open rebellion, to take place unchallenged; that they should allow preparations for violence ... for attacks on innocent persons, for the murder of police officers and others to proceed unchecked ... Your statements ... that there was no room left for negotiation, and that after all it was open rebellion, are all of them grave and significant, even without your final exhortation to do and die.' The Viceroy deeply regretted Gandhi's intention to fast – because of his health and age, and the fact that such a fast was a form of political blackmail.

Despite this viceregal indictment, Gandhi remained impenitent. 'If then I cannot get soothing balm for my pain, I must resort to the law prescribed for *satiagrahis*, namely, a fast' – which he postponed to 10 February. 'My wish is not to fast unto death, but to survive ... This

fast can be ended sooner by the Government.' The Government offered to release Gandhi, but he refused. If
released, he would not fast at all. At that the Government
told him: 'You may invite your own doctors and your
friends. We disclaim responsibility for your fate.' Gandhi
began his fast cheerfully, but quickly weakened. On the
sixth day his doctors announced that his condition had
further deteriorated. On the eleventh day his wife Kasturbai prayed for him before a sacred plant. Gandhi's end
was very near. He was persuaded to drink water mixed
with juice of the *moosambi* fruit. Suddenly, he began to
pick up and by 25 February was out of danger. His amazing recovery was believed by many to be an act of God.
Others put it down to glucose – mixed with *moosambi*
juice. God or glucose, the Mahatma's weight increased by
one pound during the last week of the fast. The explana-
tion, according to an Indian source, was that as soon as
it was clear that the Government refused to budge, Congress ordered stimulants to be given to the dying Mahatma. By 2 March, when the fast ended, he was on the
mend.

Linlithgow's problems – emotional as they were, as well
as political – were made no easier by outside intervention.
He asked the India Office to stop 'this flow of well-mean-
ing sentimentalists from the USA to India, so that we
may mind here what is still, I suppose, our own business'.
The Chinese Generalissimo, Chiang Kai Chek (and
Madame) had been badgering President Roosevelt about
India. Their interference elicited a tart note from
Churchill to the President: 'I take it amiss that Chiang
Kai Chek should ... make difficulties between us ... in
matters about which he has proved himself most ill-
informed.'

The President's envoy in Delhi was a suave, distin-
guished diplomat, William Phillips. Linlithgow liked
Phillips, but had to dissuade him from his belief that he
shared equal responsibility with the Viceroy for solving
India's problems. As Gandhi's fast neared its climax,
Phillips told Linlithgow of the President's concern. 'What

would happen if Gandhi died?' asked Phillips. 'There would be six months of unpleasantness,' was the Viceroy's lofty answer. 'After which the prospect of a settlement would be greatly enhanced by the disappearance of Gandhi, who has for years torpedoed every attempt to reach one.'

Phillips wrote a penetrating report to the President: 'From the British point of view, their position is not unreasonable. They have been in India for 150 years and ... generally speaking internal peace has been maintained. They have acquired vast vested interests in the country and fear that their withdrawal would jeopardize these interests. They realize that new forces are gathering ... and they have therefore gone out of their way to offer freedom to India as soon as ... Indians themselves can form a government. This the Indian leaders have been unable to do ...'

It occurred to Linlithgow that the size of the American mission in India was out of all proportion to its work. No doubt, he concluded, they were there with an eye on the future of those British vested interests.

As Linlithgow left India in October 1943, Gandhi took a parting shot at him. 'It has cut me to the quick', he wrote, 'to think of you as having countenanced untruth ... I hope and pray that God will some day put it into your heart to realize that you ... have been led into grievous error.' But the departing Viceroy still had the measure of the Mahatma. 'I must be allowed', he replied, 'as gently as I may, to make it plain to you that I am quite unable to accept your interpretation of the events in question. As for the corrective virtues of time and reflection, evidently these are ubiquitous in their operation and wisely to be rejected by no man.'

The man who had scored out of the Congress–Government dispute was Jinnah. Always true to his belief in constitutional methods, he had seen Muslim League ministries elected in three provinces. He glowed with pride now that his claim that the League was the Muslims' sole representative was vindicated. There was no need for him to bargain with Congress. 'My men are in power,' he told journalist Durga Das. 'I am in the happy position of being able to extract the best terms.' Before long, Gandhi would discover the truth of this remark.

The Muslim minority of India was heading, though it hardly knew it, for nationhood. No such proud destiny was shaping for Palestine's Muslim majority. Events were sweeping the Palestinian Arabs on towards their tragic fate, as a multitude of stateless refugees in a squalid homeland of hovels and hutted settlements.

The underlying cause of the Palestinian Arab tragedy was *Endlösung*, the final solution, total extermination of European Jewry, now in full-scale operation by the Nazis, with whom – terrible irony – the Palestinian Arabs' temporal and spiritual chief, Haj Amin, Mufti of Jerusalem, was presently hob-nobbing in Berlin. With Hitler's blessing, Haj Amin was raising a Muslim Army of Liberation. Its main unit was a division of SS, the 13th Handschar, recruited in Bosnia and fitted out with fezzes emblazoned with the death's head emblem of the Huns. Hitler agreed to the Mufti's demand that no Jews were to be ransomed. All were to be exterminated – that diabolical clergyman remarked that this would provide 'a comfortable solution to the Palestine problem'. With Eichmann, Mufti Haj Amin visited the gas chambers at Auschwitz, where hundreds of thousands of Jews were to be murdered, two thousand at a time, by prussic acid gas. Monoxide gas was used to kill eighty thousand in six months at Treblinka. The same poisonous fumes exterminated three thousand victims at a time in the four chambers at Belzec. Auschwitz, Treblinka, Belzec – names which will forever shame the human race. Yet they represented but a small measure of Nazi atrocity. The estimate of six million Jews who perished in extermination camps or before the firing squad was considered on the low side by Gestapo chief Heinrich Himmler.

The desperate need to rescue the victims of *Endlösung* and to put an end to Jewish homelessness increased Ben

Gurion's determination. His sole and sacred purpose now was a Jewish state in Palestine, where Jews would be safe at last after 2,000 years of persecution. Ultimately, it meant ousting both the Arabs and the British from Palestine.

But the salvation of the Palestine Jews had yet to be achieved – by British Empire troops. West of Cairo, at El Alamein, Rommel's Afrika Korps was poised to strike the blow which, if it succeeded, would mean the annihilation of Palestine Jewry. As Montgomery's 8th Army, under the supreme command of General Alexander, made ready for battle, no one, as Weizmann later wrote, remembered those agonizing days more vividly than the Jews of Palestine. Only the British 8th Army could save them.

On 30 August, Rommel made an initial thrust. It was repulsed, at a cost of 2,000 8th Army men killed. An Empire battle, Churchill called it, in which the Mother Country bore the brunt. But the main battle had yet to come, and Churchill waited anxiously for the codename 'Zip', inspired by the fastener of his oft-worn 'siren suit'. At last came Alexander's telegram: '23 October 1942. C-in-C to Prime Minister – Zip.'

On the afternoon of 4 November the King-Emperor, at Buckingham Palace, was rehearsing with Mr Lionel Logue the Speech from the Throne for the opening of Parliament on the 11th. In the sixteen years that Logue had been helping the King-Emperor with his stammer, they had worked together on every one of his speeches, getting the breathing right to assure a smooth flow of words, altering words which might present an obstacle. King George had given strict orders not to be disturbed during these sessions, so that when the telephone suddenly rang, he looked hesitatingly at Logue. Then he picked up the receiver and after listening a moment cried out excitedly 'Read it out! Read it out!'

'It' was a telegram from General Alexander: 'After twelve days of heavy and violent fighting 8th Army has inflicted a severe defeat on the enemy's German and

Italian forces under Rommel's command in Egypt . . .' As the message ended, the King-Emperor said quietly: 'Good news. Thanks.' That night, in his diary, he gave fuller play to his feelings: 'A victory at last, how good it is for the nerves.' And he told Churchill: 'I am overjoyed.' But it was a further telegram from Alexander that expressed the full elation of victory: 'Ring out the bells. Prisoners 20,000. Tanks 350, guns 400. MT [Motor Transport] several thousand.'

The Jews of Palestine were saved. Between them and the Nazis lay 14,000 dead – British Tommies for the most part.

As *Endlösung* got under way and the ghastly details of the Nazis' genocide by lethal gas trickled through to Palestine, the hearts of the Yishuv hardened against the British. They in turn seemed incapable of relating the growing defiance of the Yishuv with the unspeakable sufferings of European Jewry. In March, from New York, Weizmann cried out in anguish against 'first, the crime; second, the reaction of the world to that crime', for whose execution Germany, 'a great and civilized nation, put power into a band of assassins who transformed murder . . . into a publicly avowed government policy . . . of the human slaughterhouses, the lethal chambers, the sealed trains'. The other side of this monstrous story was the 'apathy of the civilized world in the face of the immense, systematic carnage of human beings'. Weizmann implored: 'Let the gates of Palestine be opened to all who can reach the shores of the Jewish homeland.' At the same time, from the heart of Palestine, Ben Gurion roared defiantly: 'We shall not cooperate with the White Paper government . . . There is one people in the world without a home . . . There is no salvation but for them to return here, whether they have in their hands an official scrap of paper called an immigration certificate, or not.'

For the Yishuv it was now an all-out fight against the White Paper, war or no war, with the Jews openly or secretly violating the law. Land purchase restrictions were disregarded and 'illegals' continued to filter in. 'During

March 1943', the Palestine government stated, 'there was a notable increase ... of thefts of arms and explosives from military establishments.' The report mentioned 'a large-scale stealing racket connected with Haganah and with ramifications throughout the Middle East.'*

In April 1943, the Jews of the Warsaw ghetto rose – thirty thousand armed with old guns, crowbars and bombs made out of tin cans against the panzers, the stukas, the gas and heavy guns of the German Wehrmacht. Over their single radio transmitter, the Warsaw Jews begged for arms to be parachuted in, but, as Ben Hecht, the Jewish-American writer, wrily observed, 'Not a cap pistol fell from the sky.' With desperate incredible heroism the Jews fought on for four weeks, till all were killed or maimed. 'They were a little souvenir that glinted in Europe's garbage can.'

The glint caught the eye of the Yishuv, especially of its fanatical patriots, the Stern Gang, who called themselves the Lehi, freedom fighters of Israel, and their brothers in arms, the Irgun. The grotesque, macabre merry-go-round began to gather momentum: Jewish terrorists were out to assassinate British, who were busy killing Germans to prevent them from murdering Jews.

The tide of war had at last turned in favour of the British. From North Africa, on 4 February 1943, had come another of General Alexander's famous telegrams: 'His Majesty's enemies, together with their impedimenta, have been completely eliminated from Egypt, Cyrenaica, Libya and Tripolitania.' From Algeria, US–British forces were driving eastwards in the rear of the Afrika Korps. On 13 May it surrendered, together with its Italian allies. 'It is an overwhelming victory,' remarked the King-Emperor triumphantly.

He immediately set off on a tour by air to visit his victorious armies. The journey, he knew, was a risky one, so he saw his solicitor before leaving. 'I think it better to leave nothing to chance,' he remarked. And to his mother, Queen Mary, he wrote: 'I wonder if I should

* *Survey of Palestine 1945-46*, HMSO.

go? But I know I shall be doing good in visiting those men who have done such wonderful deeds for their country.' The visit was rewarding. 'The men looked fit and well,' he noticed, 'and the smiles on their faces showed that they were pleased with what they have done.' There was a side-trip to Malta, after naval C-in-C Cunningham had agreed that the risks would not be prohibitive. Standing on the bridge of the cruiser *Aurora,* the King-Emperor entered Valetta Harbour. 'It was a very moving moment,' he related. Church bells rang out and dense crowds of Maltese cheered from the quayside. They called their island the King's Island, for a message from the King-Emperor had told them: 'I award the George Cross to the Island Fortress of Malta to bear witness to a heroism and devotion that will long be famous ...'

The British, with their Empire and allied comrades, had fought a long and terribly costly campaign in North Africa and the Mediterranean. The victorious allies, among them Jewish units, now swept on to the shores of Italy.

With the Yishuv out of danger the time was ripe, the Yishuv patriots decided, to rise in open revolt against their British rulers. The Irgun had so far kept to their truce with the British. Not so the Sternists, whose toll of selected victims was mounting. The most dangerous of the captured Sternists were interned in the prison camp of Latroun, hard by the French Trappist abbey of Les Sept Douleurs on the Jerusalem–Tel Aviv road. For ten months during 1943, they tunnelled under the camp's barbed wire fence. On the morning of 2 November, a British sergeant entered No. 4 Hut. It was empty. Beside a gaping hole in the floor lay a book, a best seller in England: *The Escaping Club.*

A few weeks later, it was zero hour for the Irgun. One day in January 1944, their call to revolt rang out, a message pasted to walls throughout the Holy Land: 'Four years have passed since the war began and all the hopes that beat in your hearts then have evaporated ...

We have not been accorded international status, no Jewish Army has been set up, the gates of the country have not been opened. The British regime has sealed its shameful betrayal of the Jewish people ... There is no longer any armistice between the Jewish people and the British Administration in Eretz [Israel] ... Our people is at war with this regime – war to the end ... This then is our demand: immediate transfer of power ... to a Provisional Hebrew Government.'

The Irgun's uneasy truce with the British was over, although they resolved not to attack military installations while the war lasted. Irgun's chief, Manachem Begin, immediately sought the blessing of Ben Gurion. 'If Ben Gurion would lead us in the struggle against British rule, we would follow him.' This was the last thing that occurred to Ben Gurion. He refused to see Begin, but instead sent Moshe Sneh, member of the Haganah committee. Sneh told the Irgun leader: 'You hold in your hands an instrument capable of determining the fate of the people. But we [the Jewish Agency and Haganah, its armed force] regard ourselves as responsible for the people's fate.' The Jewish Agency, he said, was in touch with Churchill, who had recently told Weizmann: 'You may be sure that at the end of the war you will get the biggest plum in the pudding – that is, a good partition scheme.' 'The Irgun's activities', said Sneh to Begin, 'are liable to frustrate the good prospect and at the same time interfere with our preparations for revolt. A people can only have one policy.'

'I don't agree,' argued Begin. 'Unless we fight we shall get nothing. There is no longer any possibility of putting any trust in British promises. Our people is under foreign rule and there can only be one policy: a struggle for liberation.'

Begin apparently took no account whatever of the fact that the British, not to mention that they had just saved Palestinian Jewry from the gas chambers, were at this moment massively engaged in the greatest battle for liberation the world had ever known – a battle of which one of the principal objectives was to free the Jews and other enslaved people from the Nazi death camps.

On the afternoon of 5 June 1944, the King and Queen and their two daughters were having tea on the grass beneath the wall of the east terrace at Windsor Castle, whose first grey stones William the Conqueror had shipped nine centuries ago from Caen in his native Normandy. The King, I noticed, seemed absent: he hardly spoke, but gazed fixedly towards the south, where the ground sloped away to the wide green swathes of the Great Park. I did not know, but his thoughts ranged far beyond to the South Coast ports, to the Armada of ships and the men in them who were at that moment about to set forth on the greatest sea-borne invasion in history – the Conqueror's invasion, on a gigantic scale, in reverse. Its objective was the beaches of William's native Normandy.

Next day, 6 June, the world learnt that the Allied Army of Liberation had landed in Nazi-held Europe. Until this moment – that is, during nearly five years – Britain, world-wide, had more men in the field, in the air and on the high seas than any of her allies, though from now on the formidable strength of America's manhood would prove to be the deciding factor. British forces, alongside their American allies, and the free forces, including the Jewish Brigade Group, of the Nazi-enslaved peoples, were furiously fighting their way towards Germany's frontiers – and the extermination camps within them. The liberation of the Jews was at hand.

The King-Emperor had called upon his people to observe 'a vigil of prayer as the great crusade sets forth', as it had done from the ports and airfields of Britain, 'Fortress Britain', which the British had defended at great cost to serve ultimately as a base for this army of liberation. 'Four years ago,' said the King-Emperor, 'our Nation and Empire stood alone against an overwhelming enemy ... Tested as never before ... the spirit of the people, resolute, dedicated, burnt like a bright flame ... Please God both now and in a future not remote the predictions of an ancient psalm will be fulfilled: "The Lord will give strength unto this people. The Lord will give this people the blessing of peace."'

The object of this pious prayer was somewhat blurred in Palestine, where the people who laid first claim to be the Lord's were fighting their own war of liberation against the British liberators of their European kinsmen. Their principal target was His Majesty's High Commissioner, Sir Harold MacMichael.

About this time, Churchill was slowly coming round to the idea of a separate Jewish force under their own flag, for he told the Commons that 'that race which has suffered indescribable torments from the Nazis should be represented as a distinct formation among the forces gathered for the final overthrow'. The Jewish Combat Force – Hayil – marched henceforth under its blue and white flag with the Star of David.

On the flag's design Churchill decided to consult the King-Emperor himself. 'George VI had decided views on such matters; moreover his expertise was very great. He had a keen eye for detail and was punctilious on questions of ceremony. One day he told me: "You know you are wearing one of your medal ribbons upside down." A few days before he opened Parliament, he called at Garrards, the court jewellers, for a final fitting for the crown, which he took back with him. Next day he sent for me. I entered his study and to my amazement there stood the King, dressed in a pinstripe suit, with the glittering crown on his head. He laughed. "I know I look funny," he said. "But I'm only practising. The crown weighs a ton."'

Later that year, Churchill had long friendly discussions with Weizmann about the prospects for a future Jewish state. He was therefore aghast to learn that Lord Moyne, his life-long friend, whom he had appointed Minister of State at Cairo, had been shot dead by Palestine Jews. Members of the Stern gang had been ordered to do this and the repercussions of their deed rebounded throughout Jewry. Churchill, friend of Zionism, told the House of Commons: 'If our dreams of Zionism are to end in the smoke of the assassins' pistols and our labours are to produce a new set of gangsters worthy of Nazi Germany, many like myself will have to consider the position we have maintained so consistently ... in the past.' So deeply did he feel that, during his remaining eighteen months as prime minister, he never again discussed the question of a Jewish state. Nor did he see Weizmann again.

Weizmann, too, was deeply affected. 'Political crimes of this kind,' he deplored, 'are an especial abomination as they make it possible to implicate the whole community ... Palestine Jewry will ... go to the utmost limit to cut out, root and branch, this evil from their midst.'

A forlorn hope, as it turned out. But the Jewish Agency, furiously energized by its chairman, Ben Gurion, did make an effort to stamp out the terrorists. Ben Gurion proclaimed a four-point plan 'for the liquidation of the terror'. Anybody caught aiding the terrorists, or in possession of terrorist literature, was to be driven out of his job – or school, in the case of children. The next step: 'It is forbidden to give shelter or refuge to these criminals who endanger our future.' Thirdly, the Yishuv was not to submit to their threats. Finally – and this hurt – the Yishuv were asked to cooperate with the British. 'Without helping the authorities ... we shall not succeed in destroying this plague.'

So 'the season', as it was called in the Yishuv, a desperate manhunt, opened. Haganah deployed thousands of their men to track down the terrorists. Suspects were dismissed from factories and schools. Known Irgun men were seized and handed over to the British, who themselves located hundreds more on information from Haganah. The spectre of civil war haunted the Yishuv. Menachem Begin and his Irgun lieutenants asked themselves: 'Have we the right to continue?' After long searchings of conscience they decided they had; with the extermination of Jews in Europe in full swing, violence, terrorism – anything but words – must be used to force open the gates of Palestine.

As time went on the inner councils of the Jewish

Left King-Emperor
George V and Queen
Mary pictured in
1917

Below The first
Empress, Victoria,
with the Prince and
Princess of Wales

Left Edward VIII
in naval uniform
during his brief
reign before his
abdication

Below George VI,
the last King-
Emperor, and Queen
Elizabeth after the
coronation ceremony
in May 1937

Left Winston Churchill as Prime Minister during the Second World War

Below Lord Pethwick Lawrence, then Secretary of State for India, with Mahatma Gandhi, 18 April 1946

Left Indian leaders Nehru and Jinnah in May 1946: their ways were soon to part

Below At a conference with the leaders of the Congress and the League on 2 June 1947, Lord Mountbatten, Viceroy of India, announces the British plan to transfer power to two new dominions, India and Pakistan

Right Clement Attlee, Prime Minister when India first became a republican member of the Commonwealth

Below Moslem refugees preparing to flee from the New Delhi area after the partition of India and Pakistan

Above Eamon de Valera as commandant of the Irish Volunteers at Boland's mills

Left The General Post Office in Dublin after the Rebellion had ended in April 1916. It was from here that the Republic was proclaimed on Easter Day

Left Aung San, Vice President of the Burmese government, with Pandit Nehru

Below A boat carrying 'illegal immigrants' into Israel, captured by the British in 1946

Left The Grand Mufti of Jerusalem

Below Ben Gurion (right) with President Weizmann (centre) and Dr James MacDonald, US Ambassador, in 1951

Agency became less decided and the Agency vacillated lamentably between condemning the terrorists and covering up for them. Very naturally, its first thought was to keep the Yishuv united in the struggle for a Jewish state. Eventually Haganah joined forces with the Irgun and the Stern gang in a united resistance movement against the British.

The Jewish freedom-fighters, for all their fanaticism, lagged behind the Burmese in the treasonable pursuits of waging war against the King-Emperor. But the Burmese, very sensibly, were having second thoughts. They had two good reasons: first, the Japanese, despite their genteel talk of Asian co-prosperity and Burmese independence, had not proved to be the generous sponsors of freedom that the Burmese nationalists had imagined. Secondly, the Empire of the Rising Sun had passed its zenith. By 1944, the Japanese armies were being routed.

A year earlier, in August 1943, the Japanese had declared Burma an independent state. A treaty of alliance was signed at a solemn ceremony in Rangoon – at Government House, which the British governor, Sir Dorman Smith, had so recently and hastily vacated. He was now 'governing' from the cool and distant heights of Simla, sustained by certain Burmese who had the loyalty, and the physical stamina, to follow – on foot.

Appointed Premier of 'independent' Burma, Dr Ba Maw had the *toupet* to declare war forthwith against Britain. Aung San, as War Minister, was charged with 'direction of the troops'. He was already wondering how to direct them in the opposite way to that envisaged by Dr Ba Maw. Aung San and his inner circle of revolutionaries held secret meetings at Thakin Mya's house in Rangoon's Golden Valley, where they argued endlessly about how to handle the Doctor and place their own men in the key positions, with the object of rising against the Japanese.

While the Burmese nationalists planned their rising, the British, too, were preparing to strike back at the

Japanese. Captain Lord Louis Mountbatten, who, in early 1941, had nearly gone down with his ship, the *Kelly*, was now, as an acting admiral, Supreme Allied Commander of Land, Sea and Air Forces in south-east Asia. Under him were over a million men, the great majority of them British and Indian, with a sizeable force of Americans and lesser ones of Chinese, French and Dutch.

Churchill gave him instructions to engage the enemy as closely as possible and wear him down by attrition. This eventually boiled down to the reconquest of Burma.

Mountbatten set up his headquarters in Delhi* in October 1943. In that same month, from far away in the Karen Hills, beyond the Irawaddy, in Burma, a radio message reached the Delhi headquarters. Major Seagrim – 'Grandfather Longlegs' – of Force 136, the British clandestine organization working with the Burmese, had at last re-established contact with the outside world. In November, Seagrim's Karen assistant, Po Hla (a graduate of Rangoon University), reported that the Karens in the Burma Defence Army were plotting against the Japanese.

Commanding the BDA's Karen battalion was Kya Doe, one-time gentleman cadet of the Royal Military College, Sandhurst. One day in November, Kya Doe was taken to see Aung San at the BDA's headquarters in St Philomena School, Rangoon. Kya Doe, a little apprehensive, was soon reassured by Aung San's boyish grin. He commented later, in the jargon of Sandhurst: 'You couldn't help liking a bloke like this.' Kya Doe soon realized that the BDA was part of a bigger scheme of things.

The Japanese were staking everything on an invasion of India. In February 1944 they launched their long-awaited attack, striking first towards Chittagong, on the Arakan front in the south, then at Imphal, on the central front. General Mutaguchi, commanding the Japanese 15th Army, told his troops: 'You are invincible. Chittagong will be reached in ten days. India is longing to be liberated by Japanese arms and will welcome you!' The

* They were transferred in April 1944 to Kandy, Ceylon.

March on Delhi had begun.

It was now that the much-vaunted Indian National Army was given a chance to show it mettle. The INA, numbering some twenty thousand, was under the leadership of Subhat Chandra Bhose, plumpish one-time Congress president, rival of Nehru, open advocate of terrorism, but hailed as a 'true patriot' by Gandhi. The rebel army, enlisted by the Japanese from captured Indian army soldiers, was to spearhead the March on Delhi and rally the populace against the British. For this role the INA soldiers had been adequately brainwashed to induce them to forsake their comrades (who, true to their soldier's oath, preferred the ordeal of a Japanese prison camp), and risk being charged, if captured, with waging war against the King-Emperor – an occupation which they quickly discovered was highly dangerous. The 'Jiffs', as the British-Indian troops called the INA, were shown no mercy, least of all from the sepoys and Gurkhas of the Indian Army. One of the INA's proudest units was the Gandhi Brigade. Wisely, it decided to adopt the Mahatma's principles of non-violence, and surrendered in large numbers. The Japanese, disgusted, relegated the remainder to porters.

In the jungle-covered Arakan Yomas (hills) and on the Imphal Plain, Mutaguchi's 15th Army became locked with General Slim's 14th Army in a critical battle for India. Further north, the enemy was harassed by jungle-fighting units – Wingate's 'Chindits' and by US General Merril's 'Marauders' – and by the Chinese divisions led by US General (Vinegar Joe) Stilwell, Chief of Staff to Generalissimo Chiang Kai Chek (the Peanut, as Stilwell called him).

By now, on the Arakan front, the 'Invincible Jap' had been beaten. When the south-west monsoon broke in May, the Japanese surrounding Imphal expected the British to do the normal thing and stop fighting. Instead they broke out and, by June, Slim's 14th Army was pursuing the Japanese 15th Army eastwards. On the third of August, Myitkyina in the north fell to Stilwell's

Chinese, after the Japanese commander, Mizarami, had committed *hara-kiri*.

Two days before the capture of Myitkyina, Aung San, braving the dreaded Kempetai (Japanese Secret Police) publicly declared that the Japanese idea of independence was worthless. During the months that the 14th Army were driving the Japanese back from the Indian frontier, Aung San and his inner circle had been shaping their plans for a rising against the Japanese. But a dispute had flared up with the communist underground, led by Thakin Soe, who accused Aung San and his 'fascist associates' of betraying Burma to the Japanese. Cleverly, Aung San threw back the charge by creating the Anti-Fascist Freedom League – AFPFL. Its manifesto of August 1944 called on Burmans to rally to the Victory Flag (red with a white star in the top left-hand corner) in the cause of 'independent Burma'. Aung San had delivered the revolution.

The 14th Army had pushed the Japanese back to the Chindwin, the great river running through western Burma, by October. The monsoon was now over and the 14th Army, well in its stride, was raring to get across the Chindwin and on towards the open plains around Mandalay, where General Slim intended to fight it out with the Japanese before turning south to take Rangoon. The Cabinet in London, however, decided otherwise. They had just concluded that the German war would last till the spring of 1945. Reinforcements intended for the 14th Army could not be spared. The capture of Rangoon – 'Operation Dracula' – must be postponed until after the 1945 monsoon. From the Supreme Commander downward there was disappointment, but to the King-Emperor there came a thought for his 'Forgotten Army'.

He was always thinking of his soldiers and sailors and airmen, and no one understood better than his own wife. 'He feels so much not being in the fighting line,' wrote Queen Elizabeth, who a few months earlier had waved him farewell at Northolt Airfield, near London, when he had flown off to see General Alexander's army in Italy.

As I watched him kiss the Queen good-bye, I thought of that poignant French saying, so agonizingly true, 'Partir, c'est mourir un peu.' Neither wanted to part, but it had to be done. The journey did not hold the same dangers as the one he had made the previous year to North Africa and Malta. But it was not without its risks. Irreverently, he reminded me of a schoolboy going back to start a new term. The separation was all the harder because it only happened once in a while and one was not hardened. Mechanically, he climbed up the ladder into the four-engined York aircraft, then turned and waved, forcing a smile. Then he was gone.

His tour was a great success. Now he wanted to fly off again to see an even more forgotten army – the one in Burma. 'A visit from me would buck them up,' he told Churchill. Besides, he could meet his Viceroy and Indian leaders in Delhi. But Churchill would not hear of it. The political situation, he objected, was too obscure. The Emperor of India would be expected to make a declaration, and there was nothing for the moment to say. Yet again the Emperor's desire to visit his Indian empire was frustrated – and time was running out.

I had by now been on the King-Emperor's staff for some months. It was on a wet, foggy day in February 1944, as the Japanese launched their invasion of India, that I had been summoned to Buckingham Palace. The idea of finding myself, a young nobody, closeted alone with the King-Emperor, unnerved me somewhat. But a kind old courtier reassured me: 'Be yourself', he said, 'and if the King raises his voice or shouts, don't be rattled. This sometimes happens.' Fortunately it did not. As I stood before him in his green-carpeted study, the awesome image of His Most Excellent Majesty, Defender of the Faith, Emperor of India, vanished. I saw a slight, clean-cut figure in naval uniform, a rather shy man, quiet and composed, for whom I felt an immediate and natural sympathy. All the more so because sometimes during his audience his conversation came to an abrupt and silent standstill. Being an occasional stammerer myself made me feel more warmly towards him. I heard myself saying something, a few words for him to hang on to and get started again. It worked well and he smiled a wide warm smile which revealed a row of big well-set teeth.

The King-Emperor was undeniably *sympathique*, that French word for which the Anglo-Saxons have no equivalent. His looks and his whole allure were reassuring, likeable. The conversation turned around fairly banal things. As a one-time pilot himself, the King-Emperor's interest in my flying experiences was obviously genuine. When did I learn to fly? At the age of eighteen, I replied. 'I was in my twenties when I gained my wings' he told me, almost bashfully. But he was the first prince of the blood ever to have done so. 'How many victories have you?' he asked. Then 'You were shot down?' 'Yes, sir. I made a brolly-hop each time'. He laughed at the expression 'brolly-hop'. And when I added 'Your Majesty's brother the Duke of Kent once visited us – we liked him very much', the King-Emperor was visibly moved. Prince George of Kent, his favourite brother, a Group Captain in the RAF, had been killed in a flying accident in 1942.

The King-Emperor went on. 'We have met before?' he asked with disarming simplicity. 'Yes, sir. You once gave me a medal here at Buckingham Palace and another at Duxford (a fighter base near Cambridge). Later you visited my squadron at Debden ...' 'And you all had the top buttons of your tunics undone?' he cut in; the King-Emperor had a prodigious memory. 'Yes, sir' and this time it was I who replied somewhat bashfully, 'that has always been the tradition in fighter squadrons'.

The conversation lingered on pleasantly for a while. Then – the royal technique that I was to discover later – he smiled a warm smile and said shyly, but quite abruptly 'Well, goodbye' and shook my hand.

Two weeks later I reported for duty at Buckingham Palace. There was a sharp air raid that night from 'lightning bombers' which swooped from a great height above their bases in the Pas de Calais. No one had mentioned the existence of an air raid shelter so I sat there alone in the dark in that enormous house while the blast of bombs and anti-aircraft guns mingled in a deafening shindy. The King and Queen, long since hardened to the London raids, were no doubt sleeping peacefully in their quarters on the opposite side of the palace.

But there were occasions when they were advised to go down to the basement shelter. We of their household would also settle down to an uncomfortable night in its cramped and draughty confines.

The two princesses, Elizabeth and Margaret, meanwhile lived, as did thousands of other 'evacuee' children, in the country, though their house was bigger than most: Windsor Castle. There the family, dogs, horses and all, were reunited each weekend. They were a loving and lovable family, very close-knit, and these forty-eight-odd hours gave them the chance they all longed for of enjoying each other's company. The weekend routine was simple, with walks or rides in the Great Park; meals, within the limits of the rationing scheme, with the members of their household and, on Saturday evenings, in the spacious Waterloo Chamber, a film. On Sunday they invariably attended Matins in the private chapel of the castle.

During the months that followed, the King-Emperor never showed any outward signs of the crushing strains of kingship, of his dark anxieties as ruler of a vast empire in peril. But once I stood by his side in Windsor Great Park before a plantation of trees. Each one, he explained, represented a colony of his empire. Then, pointing to one, he said rather sadly: 'That is Singapore'; and again: 'There is Malaya and Hong Kong is over there. They have all been lost to the Empire Plantation. Burma too, over there. The time may soon come when we shall have to cut out the Indian tree – and I wonder how many more?'

In India time was indeed running out, as it was in Burma, too. The AFPFL, Burma's independence movement, was getting off the ground. In November 1944, a

Burma Defence Army man, captured by the 14th Army, was dropped at Pegu, near Rangoon. Through him and other agents, Aung San and his 'quisling army' (as Churchill called the BDA) were feeling their way back into the British camp. Backed by Force 136, they were soon demanding money, arms, and supplies. The Civil Affairs Service (responsible for putting Burma back on a peace-time footing) disagreed. Its chief, General Pearce, regarded the AFPFL, and Aung San in particular, with suspicion. They had collaborated with the Japanese and killed British soldiers. They were guilty of treason. To accept their aid now would only put them at an advantage later. And Pearce was not convinced, despite appearances, that the AFPFL represented public opinion. Its sponsors, the Thakins, had won only 3 out of 132 seats at the last pre-war election.

The men who were fighting the Battle of Burma saw things differently. Slim was certain that the BDA could be useful in harrying the enemy and giving him 'an uncomfortable feeling on dark nights'. Mountbatten reasoned that, if the BDA found that they could not fight for the British, they might well decide to fight against them. So on 24 February 1945 he ordered Force 136 to arm Aung San's men. A few days later, word came that the Japanese were despatching the BDA to the front on 16 March.

When the great day came, there was a parade in Rangoon, at which General Kimura, the Japanese C-in-C, took the salute. Bogyoke Aung San made a stirring speech. 'Now is the time,' he said, 'for all to go out and fight the enemy until victory is won.' He carefully avoided saying exactly who the enemy was. Kya Doe, the BDA's Karen Brigade commander, thought that the Japanese suspected what was in Aung San's mind, but that either they felt too embarrassed to do anything about it or simply hoped it could not be true. Which was fortunate for, as Kya Doe said, 'It saved a number of Burmese necks, including mine.'

A few days earlier, the 14th Army had captured Mandalay – a disaster for the Japanese army which caused its supreme commander, Field Marshal Terauchi, to have a stroke (from which he died a year later). On 13 March, General Slim, notwithstanding the Cabinet's pessimism and the fact that his plan was a hasty, hazardous and therefore 'rather un-British' one, issued an operation order. Its main intention was the capture of Rangoon at all costs as soon as possible before the monsoon. There were seven weeks to go. The race was on.

Aung San joined his troops at the front. The British waited anxiously. On the 25th came word that the rising was imminent. Mountbatten ordered Force 136 to back it to the utmost and to tell the BDA men that their service in the allied cause would mitigate their past record of treason – which was not meanwhile forgotten. Forty-eight hours later, on 27 March, the BDA struck, killing several Japanese. That day, Resistance Day, the BDA was re-named the Burma National Army. Aung San, whom Churchill had denounced as 'the traitor rebel leader', was now welcomed as the ally and once again, despite himself, the subject of the King-Emperor.

No such volte-face was thinkable for the leaders of the Indian revolution. They were all in prison. True, one of the first thoughts of the new Viceroy, Lord Wavell, before his departure from London in October 1943 to take over from Linlithgow, was to release Gandhi and Nehru and invite them to join his executive council. Such clemency towards the Indian rebels found no favour in Whitehall and shocked the Emperor. 'I was very annoyed when I heard of it,' he remarked. 'Gandhi is now discredited in the USA and in India, and to let him out of confinement is a suicidal policy.'

Wavell, a blunt-spoken and brilliant soldier, with a strong poetic streak in him, had little knowledge of politics. But in his previous post of Commander-in-Chief, India, he became acutely aware of India's problems. He had never forgiven Gandhi for launching his Quit India campaign at the very moment when, as C-in-C, he was organizing India's scant defences against a Japanese invasion. A stab in the back, he had called it. But now he was Viceroy he was convinced that his mission was to break the political deadlock. He put his ideas to the Cabinet. He would gather together ten Indian leaders, men of wisdom and goodwill – they included, of course, Gandhi, Nehru, Jinnah, and Ambedkar, leader of the Untouchables. He would give them a definite pledge of self-government at the earliest possible date, but on two conditions: first, the successful ending of the war, 'in which the British have made such sacrifices and over-come such odds, with much aid from India'; secondly, that Britain would only hand over power to an Indian government capable of governing. The present deadlock, it was obvious, was due to the Indian leaders' refusal to agree among themselves and their rejection of every offer made by the British. Wavell wanted the Indians themselves to work out a programme which would allow Britain to transfer power as soon as practicable. Failing this, he would carry on with the present government, which was mainly Indian, anyhow.

Wavell's plan got a cool reception by the Cabinet. Churchill, 'menacing and unpleasant', countered with a directive of his own, 'mostly meaningless', as Wavell described it, ruefully reflecting that 'he has always really disliked me and mistrusted me, and probably now regrets having appointed me'. As for the Cabinet, Wavell felt that 'it is not honest in its expressed desire to make pro-gress in India'. But the Viceroy-designate had one staunch supporter, the Secretary of State for India, Leo Amery. When Wavell showed him Churchill's directive, Amery remarked: 'You are wafted to India on a wave of hot air.'

On his arrival in Delhi in October 1943, Wavell found his predecessor, Linlithgow, more sympathetic than en-couraging. The ex-Viceroy did not believe any progress was possible as long as Gandhi remained alive (he was then seventy-four). Wavell had come at a time when, un-known to him, Nehru was writing, in Ahmadnagar prison: 'India is very sick in mind and body.' Her bodily sickness was famine, hideous, creeping and horrible, which hit

especially the rich, fertile province of Bengal. Peasants
and their children, too weak to move, stayed to die in
their mud-hutted villages. The less feeble, hoping for
succour, flocked towards Calcutta, falling in thousands
as they went, until the roads leading to the city were
strewn with corpses. Thousands more who reached Calcutta did so only to drop dead before the palaces of those
whom Nehru called Calcutta's upper ten thousand. For
them life went on regardless. 'There was dancing and
feasting ... and life was gay.' Bitterly, Nehru thought how
this famine revealed the 'ugliness of British rule' – the
abject poverty of millions beneath a veneer of prosperity
for the few. All over the world men were killing each
other in battle, dying for a cause, yet here, in famine-
stricken India, death had no purpose. To Nehru's mind,
the famine marked the culmination and fulfilment of
British rule.

Behind this morbid picture of the British Raj there
were disconcerting facts which reflected little credit on
Indians themselves. Britain had never supplied more than
a tiny fraction of the Indian administration. The majority
were Indians who, since the First World War, had been
admitted to the highest ranks. Viceroy Wavell, as ruler
of four hundred million Indians, presided over an executive council of fourteen, ten of whom were Indians, four
British. The two-chamber legislature was Indian. Of the
eleven provinces of British India (that part of India which
excluded the Princely States), six had Indian administrations. The remainder, where Congress administrations
had resigned in 1939, had temporarily reverted to
'Governor's rule'. In his government services Wavell could
number barely one thousand British – five hundred in
the Indian Civil Service, two hundred in the police and
a few in the medical, engineering, forest, and other services. Otherwise the Viceroy was entirely dependent on
Indians for the administration of his government – and
on Whitehall's approval of his policy.

Gandhi gave his view: 'From top to bottom, the whole
system is corrupt ... A National Government, having the

confidence of the people, alone can tackle the problem.'
The problem was far greater than one of corruption.
Cyclones – Bengal's most disastrous killed eleven thousand people and seventy-five thousand head of cattle –
floods and bad harvests had reduced India's own production. Her chief source of supply, Burma, was in Japanese
hands. 'Surplus' provinces, like the Punjab, were reluctant to part with their unwanted grain. The governments
of Bengal and other afflicted provinces failed to devise an
effective rationing scheme. And as prices rose, the
numberless peasant farmers (who marketed their grain
by the basket) and grain merchants began hoarding.
Months before the famine started, Viceroy Linlithgow
had asked London for relief supplies. But London, partly
because she was beset on all sides by disaster, partly because she argued that famine in India was the Indian,
not the British, government's problem, was not helpful.
Finally the new Viceroy succeeded, after a million and a
half Bengalis had perished, in squeezing a million tons
of grain from reluctant, harassed Britain – who would
herself, within three years, be on the bread-line.

Since Wavell's arrival, no sign had come from Gandhi,
still interned in the Aga Khan's palace at Yeravda, near
Poona. The Viceroy's feelings for Gandhi were far from
tender. The stab in the back of the Quit India rebellion
still rankled with him and Gandhi adamantly refused to
withdraw his resolution – and thus earn his release. He
was unwilling, too, to forgive Wavell for the 'leonine
violence' with which Wavell, as C-in-C, had crushed the
rebellion. Gandhi's view was: 'The whole of India is a
vast prison. The Viceroy is the irresponsible superintendent of the prison ...'

Wavell was as impervious to the Mahatma's charisma
as he was sceptical of his saintliness. To Wavell's mind,
Gandhi was a very tough politician rather than a saint,
and his non-violence far more a political weapon than a
gospel. Gandhi, thought Wavell, despite his professions of
friendship, was a more formidable enemy of the British
Empire than ever de Valera had been. Harshly, the Vice-

roy sized up the Mahatma as a 'shrewd, obstinate, domineering, double-tongued, single-minded politician' – in a word, 'an unscrupulous old hypocrite'. Yet, wondered the bluff, straightforward Viceroy: 'Who am I to judge, and how can an Englishman estimate a Hindu?' By Hindu standards, he admitted, Gandhi may have been a saint.

On the night of 17 July, Gandhi wrote a letter to Jinnah. 'Dear Brother Jinnah,' it began, 'let us meet. Do not regard me as an enemy of ... Indian Muslims. I have always been a servant to you and mankind. Do not disappoint me.' Brother Jinnah, staying at beautiful Srinagar in his houseboat *Queen Elizabeth*, replied that he would be glad to receive 'Mr Gandhi'.

On 9 September 1944, at Jinnah's house, No. 10 Mount Pleasant Road, Bombay, the Hindu leader, in *dhoti* and sandals, and the Moslem, wearing an immaculately cut suit, shook hands warmly and embraced. Jinnah, optimistic, declared to the press: 'We are coming to grips. Bury the past.' But Gandhi's and Jinnah's warm mutual feelings made no impact on the barrier between them: Jinnah's two-nation theory. Against Jinnah's claim for an independent state of Pakistan, Gandhi argued in vain. 'Can we not agree to differ on the question of two nations and solve the problem on the basis of self-determination?' pleaded Gandhi. India, he said, was not the home of two nations, but of one family. If there was to be a division between Muslims and Hindus, let it be 'as between two brothers'. Leading Congressman C. P. Rajagopalachari had devised a formula to meet the case and had recently shown it to Jinnah. Areas in north-west and north-east India where Muslims predominated were to be demarcated and their inhabitants allowed to determine by plebiscite whether they wanted to become a separate nation. This was not at all how Jinnah conceived his dream-state. Contemptuously, he dismissed Rajaji's scheme as 'a shadow and a husk, a maimed, mutilated and moth-eaten Pakistan'. Jinnah wanted Pakistan to be 'a perfect democracy', apparently forgetting that long ago he had said that democracy was unsuited to India.

As the first week of the talks ended, Gandhi complained of Jinnah's Pakistan project: 'I see nothing but ruin for the whole of India.' Jinnah in turn challenged Gandhi's claim to represent all Indians. 'It is quite clear that you represent nobody but the Hindus.' By the end of the second week, Gandhi was writing to Jinnah: 'We seem to be moving in a circle. Last night's talk has left a bad taste ...' As the third week neared its end, it was clear that the talks had failed. Gandhi declared to the London *News Chronicle*: 'I believe Mr Jinnah is sincere, but he is suffering from hallucinations when he imagines that an unnatural division of India could bring happiness and prosperity ...' Jinnah, incorrigible, told the same paper: 'The offer made to us is an insult to intelligence. There is only one practical way of resolving Hindu-Muslim differences. That is to divide India into two sovereign parts, Pakistan and Hindustan.'

Viceroy Wavell expected something better of the talks. 'The two great mountains have met and not even a ridiculous mouse has emerged,' he wrote. 'This surely must blast Gandhi's reputation as a leader.' Jinnah's task had been easy, not that his reputation was enhanced either. 'He merely had to keep on telling Gandhi that he was talking nonsense, which was true.'

Wavell himself was convinced that it was high time that Britain took the initiative. While Gandhi and Jinnah were still talking, he suggested to the Cabinet in London that a small conference of Indian political leaders should be called to discuss the forming of an all-party provisional government. But India Secretary Amery raised every objection, confirming Wavell's opinion that Whitehall's attitude towards India was negligent, hostile and contemptuous. Gloomily he thought: 'There are very dark days ahead for India.'

He put his views direct to Churchill. 'Our name in the world for statesmanship and fair-dealing will depend on the settlement we make with India ... With a hostile India we are likely to be reduced to the position of commercial bagmen.' Wavell did not think the British could, or should, hold India by force. 'The British people will not consent to be associated with a policy of repression.' The present government, Indian-controlled as it was, could not last much longer. It was bound to run into trouble, for which the British would be blamed. The British Civil Services, the framework upon which the administration rested, were, said Wavell, moribund. Senior members were tired and disheartened; in their view the country was going, if it had not already gone, to the dogs. It would be hard to find recruits. The situation was so serious that, if the British did not immediately make an imaginative and constructive move, India would drift inevitably into chaos.

The basis of his plan, Wavell told Churchill, was an Indian provisional government which would attempt, with British help, to find a settlement to India's problems. 'But the real essential,' he insisted, 'is a change of spirit which would convince Indians that British intentions were sincere and friendly.'

Wavell waited two months. Then, on Christmas Day 1944, Amery informed him that he must personally plead India's case before the Cabinet. Three more months passed before the Cabinet agreed to hear him. He flew to Britain on 21 March 1945. Immediately he plunged into discussions, seemingly endless and futile, with the Cabinet. 'None of them like my proposals,' he thought. They told him of their apprehensions, objected to the risks involved, of the dangers and difficulties. But, as the Viceroy noted, 'I stuck very bluntly to my point'; 'I am not going to budge'; 'I stuck to my guns'. When summoned to Buckingham Palace, Wavell got the feeling that the King-Emperor had been forewarned by Churchill that His Majesty's Viceroy was 'casting a spanner in the works'.

At last Churchill received him, apologizing for the delay. 'You must have mercy on us,' he said, and explained that, with so many other problems on hand, he thought India 'could be kept on ice'. Wavell was disturbed to find that Churchill held such old-fashioned ideas about India, and how ready he was to misunderstand the Viceroy's intentions. The Prime Minister seemed depressed and lacking in fire (the fact was, he was then so exhausted after five years of war leadership that he had to be carried upstairs in a chair).

At the end of April, Wavell complained: 'I am tired of being treated as an Untouchable.' He had been talking to the Cabinet for five weeks. With Germany's collapse imminent and the reconquest of Burma nearly complete, he thought: 'We have missed the bus.' The Indian politicians would now be more intransigent.

On 2 May, the Viceroy was again received by the King-Emperor. 'He seemed to consider that my scheme would go through,' noted Wavell. But weeks more of delay and frustration lay ahead.

That very day, an RAF Mosquito pilot flying low over Rangoon saw written on the roof of the gaol: 'The Japs have gone.' Having landed – not very gracefully – on Rangoon's bomb-damaged airfield, Mingladon, he walked into the city – the first of the allied forces to do so. Rangoon was occupied next day. The day after, the monsoon broke. Slim's 14th Army had just won the race.

As the 14th Army had been speeding south to the capital, Supreme Commander Mountbatten wrote to his cousin, the King-Emperor: 'Once we have got Rangoon, do *please* come out. You can easily do a flying visit via Delhi ... It's the one chance you will have of visiting your Indian capital without endless political complications, and you have NEVER before been there, whereas David, your father and grandfather all visited Delhi.' As things turned out, it was the last chance. The last Emperor would never again have another before his empire passed away. The longed-for visit had once more eluded him, on account of a momentous event at home. At 3 pm on 8 May, Premier Winston Churchill announced the surrender of Germany. The European war was over.

9

Victory 1945

Victory in Europe was, in Churchill's words, the signal for the greatest outburst of joy in the history of mankind – joy, however, which was mingled with anxiety. For, on the allied side, none save a handful of the highest (including the King-Emperor) doubted that the Japanese war would last another eighteen months. Despite this, the British heaved a huge sigh of relief. The main ordeal, long, grim and exhausting, was over. Miraculously, almost, the British Empire had survived what looked like certain defeat.

On VE Day the King-Emperor summoned to Buckingham Palace his prime minister, war cabinet, and chiefs of Staff. Turning to Churchill, he said: 'On a famous occasion five years ago – which to most of us seems like fifty – you told us we would get nothing but blood, sweat and tears ... I should say that is a fair estimate of what we did get ... But now you gentlemen get a reward ... You have brought this country – I may say you have brought the whole world – out of a deadly peril into complete victory. You have won the gratitude of millions ... and of your sovereign.'

That evening, the King-Emperor spoke to his five hundred million subjects 'from our Empire's oldest capital city, war-battered but never for one moment daunted or dismayed ... Armed or unarmed, men and women, you have fought, striven and endured to the utmost ...' What was it that upheld Britain through nearly six years of hardship and peril? 'The knowledge that everything was at stake: our freedom ... our very existence as a people; but the knowledge also that our cause was the cause ... of every land where freedom is cherished ... We knew that, if we failed, the last remaining barrier against a world-wide tyranny would have fallen in ruins ... For five long years and more, heart and brain, nerve and muscle, have been directed towards the overthrow of the

Nazi tyranny.'

Churchill's theme was similar. Britain and the Empire, he said, had been in the war from the first day to the last. 'Weary and worn, impoverished but undaunted, we had a moment that was sublime.'

The ecstasy was short-lived. A few days after his sovereign, Churchill, in his victory address, spoke more soberly. 'I wish I could tell you that our toils and troubles were over ... But there is still a lot to do and you must be prepared for further efforts of mind and body and further sacrifices ...' And he uttered a new battle-cry: 'Forward, unflinching, unswerving, indomitable, till the whole task is done and the world safe and clean.' Brave, heroic words which brought little comfort to a war-weary nation.

Churchill lashed viciously at his neutral neighbour Eire and its president, de Valera. His grievance had never ceased to rankle since, in 1940, he had warned Roosevelt that Britain was so hard-pressed at sea that the Merchant Navy could no longer carry enormous masses of feeding-stuffs to Eire through the 'de Valera-aided' German U-boat blockade, 'when de Valera is quite content to sit happy and see us strangled'. Churchill taunted de Valera, whose denial of Eire's ports and airfields to the allies was 'so much at variance with the temper and instinct of Southern Irishmen who hastened to the battle front (despite Eire's neutrality) to prove their ancient valour'.

Once more the old, bitter quarrel came to the fore: 'If it had not been for the loyalty and friendship of Northern Ireland,' railed Churchill, 'we should have been forced to come to close quarters with Mr de Valera, or perish forever from the earth. However, we left the de Valera government to frolic with the German and later the Japanese representatives to its heart's content.'

With cool, heavy irony, de Valera replied a few days later: 'Mr Churchill is justly proud of his nation's perseverance against heavy odds. But we in this island are still prouder of our people's perseverance for freedom throughout the ages.' Eire, he added, had stood alone, not for one year or two, but for several hundred years against aggression – British aggression. 'That Mr Churchill should be irritated when our neutrality stood in the way of what he thought he vitally needed, I understand.'

De Valera thought like the Indian Nationalists and the Palestinian Jews. They all preferred to seek their own destiny rather than go along with Britain on the basis that her cause, as the King-Emperor had said, 'was the cause of every land where freedom is cherished'. Their go-it-alone policy did not, of course, exclude accepting British protection when it was needed – as it had been in India and Palestine.

Burma, on the contrary, which Britain had failed so lamentably to protect, now rallied wholeheartedly to the King-Emperor's cause – if only because it coincided perfectly with her own.

During the second half of April 1945, the agents of Force 136, the British-Burmese underground, had offered Aung San a safe conduct to General Slim's headquarters at Meikhtila, with the General's promise to return him unharmed. Aung San hesitated for three weeks. Then, with his aide Bo Min Gaung, he crossed over to the British lines. His arrival in the dress of a Japanese general at Slim's headquarters caused some surprise. He behaved, however, with the utmost courtesy, although Slim was somewhat taken aback by his demand to be treated, as the representative of the Provisional Government of Burma, as an ally.

Slim told him: 'As far as I am concerned, there is only one government of Burma, and that is His Majesty's. Apart from the fact that you, a British subject, have fought against the British government, I have a well-substantiated case of murder against you. I have been urged to arrest you. You have only my verbal promise to return you to your friends. Don't you think you are taking a considerable risk?'

'No,' replied Aung San, and General Slim, surprised, asked:

'Why not?'

'Because you are a British officer,' came the simple answer.

'Then why', asked Slim, 'were you so keen to get rid of us?'

'I don't dislike the British', explained Aung San, 'I just don't want British or Japanese or any other foreigner to rule my country.'

'You only came to us because we were winning,' Slim chided him.

'It wouldn't be much good coming to you if you weren't,' grinned Aung San.

Slim liked the young Burman, above all his honesty. 'I can do business with Aung San,' he thought and agreed to pay and ration Aung San's Burma National Army fighting units.

To his long list of allies, Supreme Allied Commander Mountbatten now added the BNA, which he renamed (once more) the Patriot Burmese Forces – PBF. Mountbatten realized that, although it was out of the question to recognize the 'Provisional Burmese Government', it would be unrealistic to ignore Aung San's AFPFL party, clearly a genuine political party with wide popular support. But Governor Dorman-Smith (still in far-away Simla) would not hear of including any AFPFL members in his executive council. The AFPFL would first have to obtain the electorate's mandate.

The AFPFL were not all that patient. Their ardour, moreover, was considerably whetted when, two days after Slim and Aung San had hit it off so well, the British government declared their policy for Burma in a White Paper. It turned Burma's political clock back to the thirties. Dorman-Smith called it infuriatingly vague. The AFPFL council, a week later, rejected it. To Aung San it was a challenge to intensify Burma's struggle for freedom.

The Middle East, with its shimmering mirages of Arab unity and a Jewish state, had until 1939 left isolationist America indifferent. But in that year the concessions of the great new oilfield at Dhahran, in Saudi Arabia, were awarded to the Arabian-American Oil Company. Henceforth, Arab oil became a pawn in the policy of the US government which, in the best imperialist tradition, persuaded, if it did not actually force, Saudi Arabia's king, Ibn Saud (no friend of Zionism), to accept its protection. American oil men, toiling in the hot, inhospitable wastes of the Arabian desert, naturally approved. But at home, the powerful American Jewish community were urging the government in the opposite direction, and demanding support for Zionism. America, like Britain, was now uncomfortably impaled on the horns of the Arab-Jewish dilemma.

President Roosevelt's answer to the problem was cheerfully to encourage both sides. In October 1944, he promised to help create 'a free and democratic Jewish state'. In February 1945, on the way home from the Yalta Conference, he met Ibn Saud and, according to Arab League secretary Azzam Pasha, told the King that he would not support the Jews against the Arabs. History also relates that, in the hope of opening the desert-king's eyes to the benefits of Zionism, he suggested that the Zionists, who had planted millions of trees in Palestine, might do the same in Saudi Arabia. To which Ibn Saud replied disdainfully: 'My people are a desert people. They detest trees.'

True story or not, the arid wisdom of the Arabian monarch was not lost on the American president. In March 1945 he told Congress: 'I learned more about the Muslim problem, the Jewish problem, by talking with Ibn Saud for five minutes than I could have learned in the exchange of two or three dozen letters.'

The President's words depressed the Zionists, but he quickly reassured them with a further promise of support. Then, early in April, he wrote to Ibn Saud: 'Your Majesty will doubtless recall that ... I assured you that I would take no action which might prove hostile to the Arab people.' A few days later, on 12 April, President Roosevelt died.

Vice-President Harry Truman stepped up into the

presidency. It was said that 'Roosevelt was for the people, Truman *is* the people'. A few days after assuming office, the new president was warned by his secretary of state, Edward Stettinius, that he was likely to be pressurized by Zionist leaders to support unlimited Jewish immigration to Palestine, and a Jewish state. While the government and people of the US had every sympathy for the persecuted Jews, said Stettinius drily, 'the question of Palestine is a highly complex one and involves questions which go far beyond the plight of Jews in Europe'. As the United States had vital interests in the Middle East, the whole question, counselled Stettinius, 'should be handled with the greatest care'.

This practical if heartless advice was followed up by a reminder to the President of his predecessor's assurance that there would be no decision altering the basic situation in Palestine without full consultation with both Arabs and Jews. But big-hearted Harry Truman felt sceptical of the views of the striped pants boys (as he called them) in the State Department. He decided to base his Palestine policy on two principles: to help the victims of Nazi persecution all he could, and to avoid US involvement in Palestine.

It was unfortunately a policy which was bound to embarrass Britain – unless she did the same thing. But she did not. Though by temperament as sensitive as any people to the misfortunes of others, the British were too pinned down by the Palestine dilemma to give a free and helping hand to Jewish refugees.

To Weizmann's plea for free immigration and a Jewish state, Churchill replied in early June: 'There can I fear be no possibility of the question being effectively considered until the victorious allies are definitely seated at the Peace Table.' In mid-June the Jewish Agency returned to the charge with a new and more precise demand: the issue of a hundred thousand immigration certificates for European Jews. At the same time President Truman made his first move to rescue them. He called for statistics of 'displaced persons'; Earl Harrison, US representative on the International Committee on Refugees, immediately left for Europe.

The Jewish Agency's chairman, Ben Gurion, whom experience had taught to attach less importance to other people's promises than to the Yishuv's capacity for self-defence, had meanwhile arrived in New York. On 1 July he was closeted in an apartment at 455 East 57 Street with a number of wealthy American Jews. For three hours he tried to convince them that the Palestinian Jews would have to go on fighting for their existence against the Arabs. When, at 5 pm, the meeting broke up, Ben Gurion's American benefactors had agreed to support a secret organization, innocently registered as the Sonneborn Institute, for the purchase of millions of dollars' worth of US army surplus equipment and arms, and their shipment, in secret, to Palestine. Though the secret leaked out the British authorities turned a blind eye. All they were to get in return was a mounting wave of terrorism.

Nothing came of the Jewish Agency's request for the hundred thousand immigration certificates. By mid-June Britain was entering the throes of a general election. The war-time coalition government was ended. In proroguing Parliament on the 15th, the King-Emperor addressed the Lords and Members of the House of Commons. 'The grievous sacrifices which my peoples and my gallant allies have had to bear ... will not have been in vain if they lead to an establishment of a new world order based upon justice and human rights ...' Two of his own territories, Burma and Palestine, rather than await the pleasure of His Majesty's government, were fighting against it for a new order of their own. India was biding her time. In more constitutional fashion, she was informed that day by the King-Emperor: 'My Government have authorized the Governor-General* to invite the participa-

---

* The King-Emperor's representative in the eleven provinces of British India was the Governor-General, in the Princely States the Viceroy. The two offices were held by the same man, normally called 'the Viceroy'.

tion of Indian political leaders in the government of British India. I earnestly hope that the invitation will be accepted ...'

From the King-Emperor himself, on 2 May, Viceroy Wavell had understood that his plan for India would go through. But during the rest of the month he had been driven near to despair by the Cabinet's tergiversation. Towards the end of May, as His Excellency the Viceroy waited in a queue outside a London news theatre, the thought struck him: 'This is quite familiar, after all these weeks of waiting on ministers.' At last, on 31 May, he had his final showdown with the Cabinet. Churchill began with a long polemical statement against the Viceroy's proposals. Then Wavell said his piece. 'The PM gave me a good run and did not interrupt.' The Cabinet then adjourned. When it met again late in the evening, Wavell was astonished – agreeably so – that 'the PM made just as forcible an address in favour of my proposals as he had made in their damnation in the morning'. By 11.30 pm Wavell had his decision and Churchill 'exuded good will towards India and myself from every pore'.

Twelve hours later the Viceroy was on his way back to India. On the evening of 14 June, from Delhi, he announced his plan in a radio talk. Indian leaders were invited to confer with him on the formation of a new executive council, in which caste Hindus and Muslims would be equally represented. Except for the Viceroy and the Commander-in-Chief, all council members would be Indian. Finally, good news for Nehru and his Congress colleagues: they were to be freed immediately.

The conference was fixed for 25 June at Simla. The press approved, but Gandhi and Jinnah began to behave 'like very temperamental prima donnas'. Gandhi fussed over definitions; Jinnah wanted more time. Within forty-eight hours of his broadcast, Wavell was wondering: 'Whether I shall ever get my conference, Lord knows.' His private secretary, Evan Jenkins, thought it would be as hard as 'trying to get mules into a railway truck'.

In the event, the conference got off to a good start. But

Wavell, looking round the table at the delegates, summed them up, with a few exceptions, as 'poor stuff'. 'If we can build a self-governing India on this sort of material, we shall have emulated the legendary rope trick.' Five days later, his fear that the conference would 'crash on Indian intransigence' was confirmed – it was obvious that the two main parties had failed to agree.

The real obstacle was Jinnah. He insisted that he alone, as head of the Muslim League, should nominate all the Muslim members of the new council. Wavell could not agree – the Punjab Muslims wanted to nominate their own. During his long talk with the Viceroy, Jinnah appeared to be on the verge of a nervous breakdown. 'I am at the end of my tether,' he admitted, and finally refused to submit any names at all.

On 11 July, Wavell recorded the failure of the conference, 'and so of this fresh effort to make progress in Indian self-government'. Gandhi told him: 'Either you must accept the Hindu point of view, or the Muslim. The two are irreconcilable.' But Wavell, instead of blaming failure on the Hindu-Muslim conflict, bluntly announced: 'The responsibility is mine.' Gandhi replied: 'The world will think otherwise. India certainly does.' Both the world and India recognized that immediate hopes of Indian independence had been wrecked on Jinnah's intransigence – with which Wavell, characteristically, sympathized. It sprang, he said, from 'a real fear on the part of the Muslims ... of Congress domination, ... a Hindu Raj'.

As the Simla delegates returned to the sticky heat of Delhi, other delegates, those of the victorious allies, were gathering at what Churchill called the Peace Table, amidst the faded imperial splendours of the Hohenzollern palace of Potsdam, near Berlin. President Truman seized the opportunity of a *tête-à-tête* with Churchill over Palestine. He asked that as many Jews as possible be allowed into the country. In that case, enquired Churchill, could the British count on American help? No, answered

Truman, true to Roosevelt's promise to Ibn Saud.

On 26 July, in the middle of the Potsdam conference, the count* of the British general election returned Attlee's Labour Party with a crushing majority. The British had dismissed Churchill, their revered and beloved war-time leader. The King-Emperor told him: 'I am ... very sad ... that you are no longer my prime minister. I shall miss your counsel.' And he added ruefully: 'I thought the people were very ungrateful after the way they had been led in the war.' But perhaps the people, judging Churchill by his rallying cry, 'Forward, unflinching, indomitable ...', just felt too tired for further heroics.

Churchill, despite his brave exhortations to the British people, was himself a very tired man. His Tuesday visits to Buckingham Palace when, over lunch, he discussed affairs of state with the King-Emperor, were not to be perpetuated by the new prime minister, Attlee. George VI paid a special compliment to his veteran prime minister on these Tuesday visits. Normally the King's equerry met the King's visitor at the door and conducted him to the King's study. But when Churchill came to lunch, the King came to the door himself, waiting for him at the top of a short flight of steps, over which presided a portrait of King George III ('The man who lost us the United States,' as I once heard Herbert Morrison, Home Secretary in the new Labour Government, jibe, pointing at George VI's ancestor). I was there when Churchill came for one of his last luncheons. He was bowed with weariness and the King watched anxiously from the top of the stairs as Churchill mounted them, advancing the same foot at each step and unsteadily dragging the other after it. The King-Emperor, proffering his hand, almost hauled Churchill up the last two steps.

The King-Emperor received Clement Attlee on the evening of his election and invited him to form a new government without delay – Truman and Stalin were waiting for His Majesty's prime minister and foreign secretary at Potsdam. Attlee suggested Dr Hugh Dalton

* It had been delayed pending the return of voting cards from the forces overseas.

as Foreign Secretary; Dalton himself expected to get the post. But the King-Emperor had another man in mind. 'I disagreed with him and said that . . . I hoped he would make Bevin take it.'

The King-Emperor had a perfect right to advise his prime minister, both constitutionally and in view of his own experience. As his cousin Dickie Mountbatten said to him: 'You are now the old experienced campaigner on whom a new and partly inexperienced Government will lean for advice.' The ultimate decision, however, was Prime Minister Attlee's, and he made it next day. Dalton, meanwhile, was so sure of becoming Foreign Secretary himself that he celebrated with friends at lunch. The celebrations over, he learned that Premier Attlee had named Ernest Bevin for the post.

It was a fateful choice, at least for the Palestinian Jews. Some months earlier, Dalton had boldly formulated the Labour Party's Palestine policy. 'There is surely no hope nor meaning in a "Jewish National Home" unless we are prepared to let Jews . . . enter this tiny land in such numbers as to become a majority . . . Let the Arabs be encouraged to move out as the Jews move in. Let them be compensated handsomely for their land and let their settlement elsewhere be carefully organized and generously financed.' Dalton, as Foreign Secretary, would have accepted Truman's immigration policy. Yet the result might well have been fatal for the Zionists, for the problem would have lost what Dr Abba Ebban called the 'unendurable tension' which precipitated the birth of the state of Israel.

The meeting that evening of 26 July between the King-Emperor and his prime minister was full of portent both for the future state of Israel, for Britain and, not least, for Bevin, the one-time tram conductor and mineral-water roundsman who, fifteen years earlier, had championed the cause of Jewish immigration to Palestine. Though Ernest Bevin was a proven friend of the poor and the downcast, his Palestine policy was to suggest otherwise.

The King-Emperor, who judged men as he found them,

not by appearances, took to Bevin, a massive man in ill-fitting clothes, with a rolling gait, thick lips, flabby jowl and pudgy hands, one of which was invariably in his pocket as he slouched into the King-Emperor's study. Shocked by his manners, I said to the King-Emperor: 'He might at least take his hand out of his pocket when he shakes hands with Your Majesty.' The King reproved me gently: 'Bevin is a good man. I like him. He is a real Englishman. That is more important than his earthy manners.'

Bevin had a broad sense of humour. Before leaving for the Paris conference, he came to see the King. I asked the Foreign Secretary: 'Are you taking Mrs Bevin to Paris with you?' 'Certainly not,' he replied. 'Taking your wife to Paris is like taking a sandwich to a banquet.'

The Labour victory was hailed as Zion's victory. The Yishuv rejoiced, and people danced for joy in Tel Aviv's streets. The Jewish Agency sent hearty greetings. 'We are confident,' its message went, 'that you will act at once for the salvation of the suffering remnants of our people ...' But the dissidents, the rebel Irgun and Sternists, hiding in their cellars, had no such happy illusions. The Irgun declared that 'only the war of liberation ... will bring salvation to our oppressed people ... To war, war till the end, war till Victory!'

Two days before the general election result, President Truman addressed a letter to Premier Churchill. The new premier, Attlee, found it on his desk. The letter said: 'The drastic restrictions imposed on Jewish immigration by the British White Paper of ... 1939 continue to provoke passionate protest from Americans ... I ... hope that the British Government may find it possible to lift the restrictions ...' Attlee promised to give early and careful consideration to the memorandum. Potsdam over, Truman confirmed his Palestine policy at a press conference in New York. 'We want to let as many of the Jews into Palestine as it is possible.' But, he added firmly: 'I have no desire to send 500,000 American soldiers there to make peace ...' Big-hearted Harry Truman's policy was fine for the Jews and the GIs. It was anything but for the bankrupt British government and its home-sick soldiers who were left holding the dirty end of the Palestine stick.

On his way home, President Truman had met the King-Emperor in Plymouth Sound. The King-Emperor found that the President 'understood European difficulties from a new stand-point', a surprisingly gracious tribute considering how much Truman had done in his four months as president to add to British difficulties with his handling of the Palestine problem and his signature, on VE Day, of the document (which he did not even read) ending Lend-Lease. 'A great shock,' Attlee described it, 'the tap was turned off at a moment's notice.'

Four days after the King-Emperor and the US president had met, the first atomic bomb devastated Hiroshima, leaving seventy-five thousand people dead and dying. Three days later it was the turn of Nagasaki, where thirty-nine thousand more Japanese civilians were liquidated. By 15 August the Japanese war was over.

'The war is over,' said the King-Emperor in an Empire broadcast that evening; '... those four words have for the Queen and myself the same significance, simple and immense, that they have for you.' The struggle had cost Britain dearly. 'We have spent freely of all that we had,' he continued. 'There is not one of us who has experienced this terrible war who does not realize that we shall feel its ... consequences long after we have forgotten our rejoicings today.' He sensed already, perhaps, that he spoke more for himself than for most of his subjects. But whatever the cost, the British Empire could feel proud. 'We stand with our whole Empire in the forefront of the United Nations.'

Worn out, the King-Emperor repaired to Balmoral, his home in the Scottish highlands where, as he said, 'one can get out and away from it all'. On 3 September 1945, he wrote in his diary: 'The final surrender of Japan was signed ... yesterday. Thus ended the World War which started six years ago today.'

The King-Emperor, not yet quite fifty, was still in the prime of life. But he and his empire had been through a terrible ordeal – which neither were to survive for long.

10

Cry Freedom! 1946

On VE Day the King-Emperor had said that 'our cause was the cause of every land where freedom is cherished'. Now that cause was won, his own subjects were the first to jump on the freedom band-waggon.

Aung San of Burma did not lose a moment. Now that his erstwhile Japanese friends had been defeated, he confronted Burma's new liberators with a demand for freedom. At a mass meeting on 19 August in Naythuyain Hall, Rangoon, he said: 'The conscience of the world is deeply ... troubled about the plight of nations which remain under foreign rule ... These are imperialism's last days. Look at Europe, where people are banishing their kings ...' A confirmed anti-monarchist, Aung San did, however, covet a crown, 'not to wear on my head, but the crown of freedom for Burma'.

The British did not feel at all that complacent. Their failure to defend Burma had left it the most devastated of all the King-Emperor's possessions. They thought quite honestly that it was they who should govern Burma and set it on its feet again. The Burmans were manifestly incapable of doing so on their own, of restoring law and order and rebuilding the economy. So Britain must do the job for them. It was all in the latest White Paper, anyhow, which Governor Dorman-Smith had explained already to Burmese leaders, including Aung San. He had tried to reassure them: 'I do not mean to be rigid. I only want to see Burma happy.'

Charitable as British intentions were, they did not in the least please Aung San and the AFPFL. Political freedom did not appear to them an impossible dream, but it could never be realized without economic independence. The AFPFL were determined to prevent British business from laying its hands once more on Burma.

To succeed, the AFPFL needed power, and this lay in its army, the newly named PBF. But here too the British were being tiresome. They wanted (rather naturally) to disband the PBF, but agreed to re-enlist its members, if they volunteered, in the regular Burma Army. Reluctantly, Aung San had to consent, but he invented a clever dodge. He formed a so-called ex-servicemen's association, the People's Volunteer Association, PVO, in which he enrolled 3,500 of his soldiers with the stated object of performing 'social work' -- which, the surprised British noticed, included weapon-drill and tactical exercises in the spacious precincts of the Shwe Dagon Pagoda. Thus did Aung San raise an efficient private army.

Events were leading to a renewal of the struggle for freedom by the private armies of Palestine. Towards the end of August, Earl Harrison reported to Truman that for one hundred thousand European Jewish refugees – the Zionist figure – 'there is no acceptable or even decent solution for their future other than Palestine ... only in Palestine will they be welcomed and given an opportunity to work'. Truman forwarded the report to Attlee with a letter. The issue of another hundred thousand immigration certificates, wrote the President, would solve the tragedy of European Jews whose one passionate desire was to start life afresh in Palestine. Attlee telegraphed back curtly, not to say cynically: 'The immigration certificates available (two thousand) have not in fact been taken up.'

A fuller and carefully reasoned reply followed on 16 September. The British Control Commission, Attlee wrote, had tried to avoid treating refugees on a racial basis. The Nazi death camps contained people from almost every race in Europe – all had suffered the same barbarities. 'If our officers had placed the Jews in a special racial category at the head of the queue ... the effect of this would have been disastrous for the Jews.' Furthermore, in Palestine, continued Attlee, 'we have the Arabs to consider as well as the Jews', and there had been solemn undertakings, by Churchill, Roosevelt and Truman himself, that the Arabs would be consulted. It would be very unwise to break these promises and so set aflame the whole Middle East. This Attlee stated with feeling, for, with Truman's express refusal to involve the US, the entire responsibility for keeping the peace fell on the war-weary, impoverished British.

The President was also asked to remember that the fate of the Arab Muslims of Palestine was tied up with Britain's other major problem, India, where there were some ninety million Muslims 'who are easily inflamed'. Much as the harassed British premier sympathized with the President's request, he would prefer to work out himself a solution easier both on the Arabs and on Britain, and submit it to the 'World Organization' (UNO). Unfortunately, eighteen months were to drag by before he actually did so.

At this moment an Arab – no other than Azzam Pasha, Secretary-General of the Arab League – put forward a plea in favour of the Palestine Jews. Azzam backed Attlee's plan to put the Palestine question to UNO adding: 'Destruction of the Jews by force (as advocated by Ibn Saud) is not a solution.' Talks with the British opened his eyes wider. 'There is a very serious problem ... There are hundreds of thousands of Jews in concentration-camp-like conditions ... We must not take an extreme attitude against the Jews ...' Azzam wanted an understanding with the Zionists 'if they will agree to a compromise based on justice and historical rights'. But Azzam trounced Truman's plan. It was an attempt to get publicity at the expense of the British, he accused.

By now, Zionism's obstinate, warm-hearted sponsor Harry Truman was having trouble in his own back-yard. In his attempt to help destitute European Jewry he had run foul of his State Department, who, in September, sent him another warning. 'No Government', it said, 'should advocate a policy of mass immigration unless it is prepared to assist [with] the necessary security forces, shipping etc. ... The United States should refrain from supporting large-scale immigration to Palestine.'

Regrettably, too, it transpired that there was more to Harry Truman's pro-Zionist policy than pure altruism.

Democratic Party chief Bob Hannegan had reminded him that, during the 1944 presidential elections, New York State's Republican Governor Thomas E. Dewey had attracted the large Jewish vote with the promise of support for a Jewish commonwealth in Palestine. Dewey, it was learned, had further plans in this direction. Hannegan's advice to the President was to forestall Dewey by championing full-scale immigration to Palestine. Let Britain, the Arabs and the State Department go hang!

While Truman and Attlee parleyed, an ominous lull hovered over Palestine. But Ben Gurion had been active. Zionist intelligence had reported that the hundred thousand certificates were never likely to materialize. As he had expected, the Labour Government were going to rat on their flowery promises. Ben Gurion (according to one of his biographers) felt that now Britain had stopped fighting the Nazis, he had no more moral obligations towards her. So the Yishuv must fight the British. Nor, apparently, did Haganah feel any longer morally bound to *havlagah*, its sworn code of non-retaliation, nor towards its leader Golomb's promise to 'step in and finish' those partisans of terrorism, the Irgun and the Stern Gang. Golomb was dead. His successor, Moshe Sneh, had stepped in all right, not to finish the terrorists, but to join forces with them.

Ben Gurion argued that the Jewish people abhorred violence – 'having to bear arms is an affront to our Bible'. But the time, he decided, had come to lay down the Bible and take up the sword instead. On the first of October, Haganah received a top secret order, signed by Ben Gurion. It detailed the action – hopefully bloodless – to be taken in the war against the British: sabotage and attacks on military installations, civil disobedience, the founding of new kibbutzim in the White Paper-forbidden zones and, to people them, an intensification of the activities of Aliyeh Beth, the illegal immigration organization, all of which were bound to make the British get tough – at last – and cause the bloodshed that Haganah wished to avoid.

A second network, Aliyeh Gimmel, was to be organized with headquarters in France, whose burning chestnuts Britain, with her own blood and money, had also pulled out of the Nazi hell-fire, but who also in the rising tide of emotion apparently felt no moral obligation to help, instead of hinder, her harassed saviour.

Attlee had not forgotten the proverb: 'If you have a good dog, don't bark yourself.' After his initial skirmishes with Truman, he left Ernest Bevin to do the barking. On 5 October Bevin summoned Chaim Weizmann to the Foreign Office and blurted out rudely to the aged, half-blind Zionist leader: 'What do you mean by refusing the 2,000 immigration certificates? Are you trying to force my hand? If you want a fight you can have it.'

Weizmann might have felt less reason to feel hurt by Bevin's hectoring tone, as he called it, had he known that the Foreign Secretary was in possession of a telegram, intercepted and decoded by the British Secret Service, from the new Haganah chief, Moshe Sneh, to the Jewish Agency in London. It was dated 23 September and proposed 'that we cause one serious incident. We would then issue a declaration that ... much more serious incidents would threaten British interests ... should the Government decide against us.'

The serious incident occurred five weeks later. On 1 November Sneh telegraphed the Jewish Agency in London: 'We have come to a working arrangement with dissident organizations [i.e. Irgun and Sternists] ... On Wednesday [31 October] ... two British boats were sunk at Haifa and a third at Jaffa. They were engaged in hunting immigrants. The railway lines were cut at 186 points. That night the IZL* attacked Lydda station causing serious damage and ... casualties. The Stern Group seriously damaged the oil refineries at Haifa ...'

Ben Gurion's 'four-point plan for the liquidation of terror', launched a year ago, was dead. Instead of liquidating terror he was now forced to encourage it. The Haganah, whom he had then set at the heels of the terrorists,

* Irgun Zvai Leumi.

now had a working arrangement with them. The 'season' was closed. Kol Israel, the Voice of Israel, Haganah's secret radio station, now acclaimed the heroic deeds of the 'Jewish Resistance Movement', and Menachem Begin's Herut (Freedom) organization rejoiced that the Irgun were at last fighting 'shoulder to shoulder with our erring brothers ... We should humbly thank the God of Israel for the great love, which ... made possible a war of liberation.'

Bevin's reaction was carefully reasoned. If Truman had cut off material aid, in the form of Lend-Lease, to Britain, he was all too ready with advice on Palestine. The advice was not so warmly appreciated, but an American loan, to replace Lend-Lease, was essential to Britain's survival. Obviously, therefore, the US must be let in on Palestine. So on 13 November 1945, Bevin announced in the Commons that an Anglo-American Committee would enquire into the whole question of European Jewish refugees and Palestine immigration.

Bevin was suspected (unjustifiably at this stage) of being an enemy of Zionism. His utterances, which closely followed Attlee's line to Truman, now convinced Zionists, once more unjustifiably, that he was a rabid anti-Semite. Nothing was further from Bevin's intentions. 'The Government', said he, 'does not accept that the Jews should be driven out of Europe, or not permitted to live again in these [European] countries without discrimination, contributing their ability and talent towards re-building ... Europe.' Bevin's error was to ignore the conclusion of Earl Harrison's report that the overwhelming desire of European Jewry was to settle in Palestine. He did not help matters, either, by appealing to European Jews not to 'over-emphasize their racial position'. He said: 'If the Jews, with all their sufferings, want to get too much to the head of the queue, you have the danger of another anti-Semitic reaction.' With the whole of England, from the housewife to the Viceroy of India, waiting patiently in their queues, his allusions were not ill-meant, but the Zionists took them badly. Kol Israel snapped back: 'What

Hitler did in his murderous blitz against the Jewish people is now being repeated ... We are being condemned to live in an intolerable ghetto so as not to deprive Europe of its Jewish talents.'

The Zionists' war of liberation was on. In December 1945, the Anglo-American Committee set to work to the accompanying rattle of the rebels' Bren guns. On the night of 27 December, the Irgun attacked two police headquarters and an arms depot, killing nine Englishmen. The new year, 1946, was hardly in when the Irgun, aided by the Sternists, struck again, this time at Jerusalem prison, whose walls they breached. And yet again, at the police headquarters in Jerusalem and Jaffa, which they reduced to rubble.

Among those who admired these daring attacks, none were more pleased than the Russians. *Isvestia* and *Pravda* reported them fully, if not accurately. The Jewish freedom-fighters felt encouraged. An Irgun communiqué stated: 'Russia *wants* the fight of the Jewish people against the British Mandatory.' Of course she did. Russia was gunning for a place in the Middle East. The Irgun rejoiced that 'the Jewish state will arise only as a result of our struggle against the British and we shall be helped by the Soviet Union'. Disillusionment was to come later, when the Jewish state would have to wage a lone battle for existence against Russia's superbly armed satellites, Egypt and Syria.

The Irgun were impatient of the slow pace set by Haganah. But in February 1946 the Jewish Resistance struck again, and Michael Ashbel, ascetic soldier-poet, wrote a song, 'On the Barricades', which became a hit with the Jewish fighting youth.

Then the Irgun made its most daring raid – on the great army base at Sarafand. The raid miscarried, but the Irgun men escaped with two wounded, who were later transferred to a passing taxi. The taxi was stopped and the men arrested. One of them was Ashbel, the soldier-poet. He was tried and sentenced to death. Addressing the court, he said: 'If your rulers have robbed us of our country, it only means that God has blinded them and decreed their decline and fall.' There was truth in Ashbel's words. The decline of the British Empire was accelerating. Not that, like the empires of the Romanoffs, the Hohenzollerns, of Hirohito and Hitler, it was paying the price of tyranny and conquest. Its ruler, the King-Emperor George VI, was a good and a pious man who had fought fearlessly for freedom all his life. He had led his empire victoriously through a titanic struggle for freedom, which meant that the Zionists were still free to fight on for theirs. But things had gone grotesquely wrong. The freedom-fighters were now fighting among themselves; Ben Gurion was fighting against the King-Emperor, so was Aung San and so were Gandhi and Jinnah.

Yet the King-Emperor still stood without fear or hesitation, as he said, for freedom. Early in January 1946, addressing the delegates of the first Assembly of the United Nations Organization in London, he declared that the UN Charter 'reaffirms our faith in the equal rights of men and women and of nations great and small'. It was the UN's noble duty to put the Charter into effect, 'a duty to which ... I pledge ... my peoples of the British Commonwealth and Empire. They have fought through two great world wars from start to finish ... they did not fail mankind in its hour of deadliest peril ...'

It was for this reason that the British Empire had now spent itself. Freedom and order, as the King-Emperor said, was Britain's watch word and neither could be preserved without the other. He nailed Britain's problem. She no longer had the men, the money, nor the will, to preserve the *Pax Britannica*.

The fight for freedom had told on the King-Emperor, too. He was a very weary, if not yet a very sick man. Outwardly the signs of his crushing fatigue were barely visible. His frame was always lean and spare, his skin and eyes luminous; he wore his fine, fairish hair rather short, his stance was straight, his stride long and measured. He had the stamp of a thoroughbred and his fine, disciplined physique revealed little of the stresses which were tearing it apart from within. Occasionally he would appear absent or doze off, oblivious of the animated company around him. And he kept saying 'I feel burnt out', and to his brother, the Duke of Gloucester, he wrote, just after his UNO speech: 'I have been suffering from an awful reaction from the strain of the war ... and have felt very tired ... I really want a rest, away from people and papers, but that, of course, is impossible.'

For Ashbel, though he did not know it, there was to be a reprieve. For the King-Emperor, though he did not know it either, there was to be none.

If the grim atmosphere of terror was absent from the struggle for freedom in Burma, it was not because the Burmese were less resolved than the Jews to wrest their independence from the British. The Golden Land, until the arrival of General Harry Prendergast in Mandalay sixty years earlier, had been theirs for two thousand years – the time that the Jews had wandered from the Holy Land. Because the Burmans had never left Burma, it could be argued that their claim on the British to hand them back their country was more logical than the Jews' claim to Palestine, which, during the two millennia they had vacated it, had been inhabited by another people. But the solution, if there was to be one, of the Jewish tragedy could not be treated logically. Emotion outpaced logic and emotion meant force; the Jews were finding that it gave quicker results.

The Burmans, on the other hand, had years of experience of the British. Their leaders had a British education – a very different background from that of the Middle-European Jews who were now the power in Palestine. If the British held, as they did, that 'the right to use force as a means of gaining .. political ends is not admitted in the British Commonwealth',* the Palestine Jews, immigrants from Poland and Russia, where violence was a byword, did not give a damn. But the Burmese, under Aung San's persuasion, did.

* *Palestine: Supplementary Memorandum to UNSCOP.*

While not above threatening violence, Aung San was wise enough to consider its use only as a last resort. He was a tough fighter, but a fair one. He made it hard for the British not to like him. When, in October 1945, Governor Dorman-Smith returned to Rangoon from his Simla exile, Aung San did not greet him with the weapons of terrorism, but with a demand, admittedly exacting, that seven of his AFPFL men should be included in the Governor's executive council of eleven. The Governor countered with an offer of two. Like Glenvill Hall's offer to the Zionists of two thousand immigration certificates, it was indignantly rejected. So the Governor surrounded himself with elder Burmans who had remained loyal to the British connection – and one who had not: U Saw, who had collaborated with the Japanese. The choice of U Saw was a fatal one.

Two months later, before an enraptured crowd of twenty thousand gathered at Rangoon's Shwe Dagon Pagoda, Aung San openly challenged the Government: since the Governor had ignored him, he would go all out to get the programme changed. 'Burma's battle for freedom is just beginning,' he cried, but he hoped it would go no further than a battle of words. In January 1946, in his inaugural address as President of the AFPFL, he fired another verbal volley: '... we want to work together to rebuild our country and prepare her for freedom ... the powers that be are flouting public opinion ... we shall not be provoked ... we shall march to freedom.'

Burma was still peaceful, but the people were in a dangerous mood. In March, a Burmese member of the Council, Thakin Tun Oke, once more brought up the charge of murder against Aung San. There was enough evidence to hang him, but the British C-in-C warned that his arrest would mean a national rising. Ignoring the warning, London ordered a warrant to be issued, then, just in time, had second thoughts. It had at last dawned on His Majesty's Government that Aung San commanded more loyalty with the King-Emperor's Burmese subjects than did the King-Emperor himself. Anti-British demonstrations were taking place up and down the country. They were orderly, except at Tantabin, in the Insein District, where the police opened fire, killing three peasants. But Aung San kept his head. He ordered a public funeral, which turned into a picnic, with free transport, tea and lunch packets provided for the twenty thousand mourners.

When, in mid-May, Aung San addressed the AFPFL Supreme Council, he was conciliatory: 'We still offer our hand of friendship, we still desire to come to a peaceful settlement.' But, he warned, 'we are ready for an extra-legal struggle for freedom if necessary. It rests with the British whether they choose to have it or not.' This was the kind of language the British understood – cool and firm. It made an impact in London, where *The Times* had urged early Burmese elections. Dorman-Smith had gone further: 'It is very difficult', he told Whitehall, 'to see how anything short of handing over power ... could ease the tension.' Sixty years after King Thibaw had surrendered his throne to Empress Victoria, her great-grandson faced the prospect of vacating it in favour of Aung San, the left-wing, uncrowned king of Burma.

The anxieties of Governor Dorman-Smith were mild compared with Viceroy Wavell's. As he queued outside a London news theatre earlier in the year, the Viceroy had reflected on the dilatoriness of the Conservative government. Attlee's new Labour ministry, however, were quickly off the mark. They recalled Wavell to London. The Secretary of State, seventy-four-year-old Lord Peth-wick Lawrence, told him of the Cabinet's desire for early action.

Attlee could not wait to liquidate the Indian Empire, whose first Empress, Victoria, had been acclaimed amidst scenes of unimaginable splendour only sixty-eight years earlier. Less than half a century had passed since school-boy Attlee had frenziedly waved his flag as the august and aged Empress passed by on Diamond Jubilee Day. But now the former glories, the glittering splendour, had faded into the dim past. Forgotten were the lavish vice-regal pomp, the imperious ministerial orders which issued from the India Office. Today's Viceroy waited his turn at box-office or bus-stop. Secretary of State Pethwick Lawrence could be seen on Saturday mornings, basket in hand, standing in the fish-queue in the village of Shere, his Surrey home. These were the men who were to be the central figures in yet another attempt to persuade the Indians to agree on how to govern themselves. Queuing had certainly taught both Wavell and Pethwick Lawrence the patience needed for the job.

On 19 September, Viceroy Wavell announced: 'His Majesty's Government are determined to do their utmost to promote ... the early realization of full self-government in India.' Elections, he said, would take place during the 1945–6 cold season. Then, in January 1946, the Government decided to send Pethwick Lawrence as head of a three-man mission to negotiate with the Indian leaders. Much was to happen before it arrived.

After his release from prison, in June 1945, Nehru confessed: 'The fire is kindling in my heart'; and launched into a series of wild, inflammatory speeches which the nationalist press fanned to white heat. Some months later Wavell talked to him 'to make sure there was no misunderstanding'. He found Nehru as quiet and friendly as ever, but he seemed to have 'the state of mind of a fanatic'. Nehru admitted to Wavell that he was preaching violence – he did not see how it could be avoided. Only the day before he had openly declared: 'Revolution is inevitable.' Patel, the strong man of Congress, had spoken as threateningly: 'After the elections [which it would obviously win with a huge majority] Congress will demand an immediate and final solution.' If it were not forthcoming, then 'as sure as day follows night there will follow another struggle'. Its object would be the forcible expulsion of the British from India, which would mean wholesale massacre. Wavell, with the utmost gravity, warned Whitehall to be prepared for a Congress attempt to overthrow the British-Indian administration and set up its own government. 'I do not imagine HMG will wish to yield to force, nor can we lightly divest ourselves of our obligations to minorities.' Either the British would have to crush the revolution or 'hand over to a single party ... consisting mainly of caste Hindus and experienced in nothing but agitation'.

The trial of three INA ringleaders for waging war against the King-Emperor inflamed feeling throughout India. Even when the prisoners were finally released, vilification of the British continued. Tension rose steadily. The Viceroy felt as if he was sitting on the edge of a volcano. RIAF units mutinied and in Calcutta three days of street battles ensued, with their usual concomitants of tear-gas, bullets, brick-bats, burned vehicles and wrecked buildings. The Indian navy mutinied at Bombay and Congress boycotted the Victory Parade in Delhi.

It was towards this tempestuous scene of religious and racial passion that the three members of the Cabinet Mission, with dove-like intention, now flew. Secretary of State Pethwick Lawrence headed the Mission, Stafford Cripps and A. V. Alexander (First Lord of the Admiralty) were his wing men. The Mission had two objectives: to work out with Indian leaders a new constitution for independent India, and to form an Interim Government of Indians to govern until the constitution was ready.

Before he left, Lord Pethwick Lawrence's wife Emmeline gave him a keepsake to remind him that 'my love, my thought and my prayer will be with you every hour of the day'. The Archbishop of Canterbury wished the Mission godspeed. On landing in Delhi, Pethwick Lawrence declared: 'We bring a message of cordial friendship and goodwill.' Cripps, rather more pointedly, said: 'We have come to investigate and enquire.' Alexander, as befitted the head of the Silent Service, said nothing.

That day, 24 March 1946, the Viceroy noted: 'The three Magi have arrived.'

Other wise men, of the Anglo-American Committee, had already reached Jerusalem. There, as in Delhi, the atmosphere was highly charged. As a result of well-intentioned efforts by the new High Commissioner, Sir Alan Cunningham, to appease both Arabs and Jews, Arab workers had gone on strike, while Jewish terrorists were working overtime.

The Committee heard witnesses in the YMCA building, close to the Old City's walls. One of the first was Chaim Weizmann who, though he looked tired and ill, made a moving address. 'We appear to the Gentiles as a peculiar people,' he said, 'suspended between heaven and earth. We must explain ourselves, and everyone who does so is condemned in advance.' Richard Crossman, MP, one of the Committee's British members noted: 'He is the first witness who has frankly and openly admitted that the issue is not between right and wrong, but between the greater and the lesser injustice.'*

There was nothing so frank and open about Ben Gurion. When asked about Haganah, the Chairman of the Jewish Agency looked puzzled. Haganah? He had never heard of a military organization of that name. *Haganah* did of course mean 'defence' in Hebrew. It must be an insurance company or something of that sort. The Committee were not duped. Did Ben Gurion, a Committee member asked, agree with Dr Weizmann's condemnation of violence? Well, replied Ben Gurion, he associated himself with it, but for the Jewish Agency to help the Administration in suppressing terrorism was futile. Committee member Richard Crossman thought: 'He seems to want ... it both ways, to remain within the letter of the law as Chairman of the Jewish Agency and tolerate terror as a method of bringing pressure on the Administration. That's a doubtful policy.'

Later, when alone with Crossman, Ben Gurion was frank enough. He admitted that his main worry was that Haganah might be disbanded – at a time when 'the Yishuv was fighting its Dunkirk'.

Arab witnesses took the traditional line: unbending opposition to the Jewish National Home and total re-

* *Palestine Mission*, London and New York, 1947.

jection of the 100,000 Jewish immigrant project. As
before, they based their case on the argument – which the
most ardently pro-Zionist Committee members could not
refute – that since the tragedy of European Jewry was
due to Christian persecution, it was not for Muslim Arabs
to provide the remedy.

But it was Arab League secretary-general Abur Rahman
Azzam who most eloquently demolished the argument
that Jews and Arabs could be reconciled through recognition of their common family ties with Father Abraham.
'Our brother', Azzam Pasha told the Committee, 'has gone
to Europe and the West and come back something else
... a Russified Jew, a Polish Jew, a German Jew, an
English Jew. He has come back with a totally different
conception of things. Western and not Eastern ... he is
not the old cousin [sic]. The Zionist, the new Jew, wants
to dominate ... The Arabs simply say "No" ... we are not
going to be controlled either by great nations, small
nations or dispersed nations.'

On the way through London the Committee had called
on Ernest Bevin, who solemnly assured them: 'If you put
in a unanimous report I shall do everything to put it
into effect.' This was exactly what the Committee now
did. Unanimously, they expressly disapproved that
Palestine had ever been granted as a state to the Jews;
unanimously, they agreed that Palestine should be neither
a Jewish state nor an Arab state. No wonder Menachem
Begin called the report a shallow document. But there
was one point which pleased him, not least because it
was a victory for Jewish terrorism: the Committee were
unanimously agreed on the immediate issue of one hundred thousand Jewish immigration certificates.

The report was published in Britain and America on
30 April, with the difference that, in America, President
Truman, without so much as a word to Whitehall, announced his enthusiastic backing for it, and notably for
the hundred thousand immigrant project – a move which,
said Bevin's biographer and friend, Francis Williams,
'threw Bevin into one of the blackest rages I have ever

seen him in'. Bevin's rage was already kindled by the
murder, a few days earlier, of seven British soldiers by
the Stern Gang. With tension acute in Palestine, Bevin
protested vigorously to Washington that Truman had
acted irresponsibly.

There was anger and chagrin in Whitehall – throughout the British nation, too, as it queued for its meagre
rations, or, in the outposts of empire, kept watch and
ward over furious foreigners of whose griefs it was beginning to tire. Next day, in the Commons, Prime Minister
Attlee criticized the American president's intervention.
He would like to know, he said, if it meant that the US
were willing to help out with the enormous financial and
military involvement that the mass immigration project
entailed. Attlee refused to agree to the 100,000 before he
knew. Nor would he agree at all unless the 'private armies'
in Palestine were disbanded.

Truman, who thought the British reaction was not encouraging, immediately consulted his military leaders.
They advised him that it would be unwise to put his
money, and his men, where his mouth was. And as far
as private armies were concerned, Ben Gurion was certainly not going to disband Haganah, any more than the
Irgun and the Sternists. In fact Haganah, less than a week
after Attlee's Commons statement, informed Irgun chief
Begin : 'There is no room for difference of opinion on the
grounds for resuming operations on a large scale.' It
added that 'American friends' were trying to get the dis-
bandment condition annulled.

Attlee put the Middle East as second only after Europe
in his long list of problems. He had decided to pull
British troops out of Egypt and revise the 1936 Anglo-
Egyptian treaty. Egyptians, impatient for the talks to
start, had begun rioting. British property in Cairo and
Alexandria had suffered and two Tommies, brave, un-
questioning guardians of a moribund imperialism, had
been stoned to death. Egypt was one more knot in the
imperial tangle that the British prime minister had to
unravel – while America heckled and jostled, and Russia

glowered, ready to grab, in the offing.

Attlee badly needed Truman's help – over Palestine, to be sure, but more urgently, in the way of a loan to replace Lend-Lease, which Truman, in a blind stroke of the pen, had so abruptly ended. The outlook for Britain, said Attlee, was as black as it possibly could be. The war had used up all the resources of the British and obliged them to surrender to America much of their foreign trade. 'We'd had to sell out practically everything. We had to have the loan.'

As yet he had not got it. But if Attlee had to face Truman cap in hand, he never minced his words. On 26 May, he cabled the US president about the Anglo-American report on Palestine, saying in effect that he could give no decision on the hundred thousand immi-grants without an expert estimate of the all-round cost. This was too slow for Truman, whose primary concern, he said, 'was to relieve suffering by the admission of these hundred thousand'. He offered transportation and tem-porary housing, but Attlee was not satisfied. As obstinate as Truman, but without his largesse, he insisted on dis-cussing the Palestine problem as a whole and not in terms of the hundred thousand.

Attlee's man in India was not so inhibited by numbers. The Arab-Jewish conflict might well revolve around the obsessive figure of a hundred thousand, but Pethwick Lawrence, as mediator between Hindus and Muslims, had to think in terms of hundreds of millions. He be-lieved, moreover, that he was on a divine mission: 'I have commended myself to God for Him to fit my little piece of Himself into His great plan.' God's great plan was soon to take shape as the Cabinet Mission Plan.

Pethwick Lawrence, a charming old gentleman as Wavell called him (and, at seventy-four, a very courageous one), had to deal with more down-to-earth people than himself: his colleagues – Cripps, 'the brilliant rapier-witted improviser with strong left-wing tendencies'; Alex-ander, 'who wants cheddar cheese and English food and is so proud of the Navy'; Wavell, 'suspicious of new-fangled ideas, straightforward, blunt'. Then the Indian leaders, whom the Mission met one by one during the first week: the Congress team – its president Azad, a Muslim, over-wrought and worried, whom Jinnah had called a show boy and with whom he refused to shake hands; Gandhi, whose subtleties of mind perplexed Pethwick and whose view of Pakistan was coloured by his son Harilal, an alcoholic, who had become a Muslim in the hope that it would cure him of drink; Nehru, who did all the talk-ing for Congress; Patel, who wore his *khadi* like a Roman toga and had a Roman face, powerful and clever; the Muslim Ghaffar Khan, the 'frontier Gandhi', a tall and muscular Pathan with flashing eyes, hostile and silent. Then the Muslim League men – their leader Jinnah, cold, determined, rigid, often rude, a sick man, but im-maculate in his Savile Row suit; Liaqat Ali Khan, Jinnah's lieutenant and confidant, whom Wavell fondly called a plump and solid gentleman; Suhrawardy, Prem-ier of Bengal, (a Muslim-majority province), in the Vice-roy's opinion inefficient, conceited and crooked. The Punjab which, like Bengal, had a Muslim majority, was represented by its premier, Khizar Hyat Khan; Master Tara Singh spoke for the Sikh minority, in a husky voice which came from the back of his throat through a massive beard and was scarcely audible – not that it mattered, for he repeated himself so often that most people knew it all by heart. Dr Ambedkar was the spirited defender of the most suffering of all minorities, the Untouchables (the 'Scheduled Classes'). For yet another minority, the princely states, came the Nawab of Bhopal, Chancellor of the Chamber of Princes, modern and shrewd, but a man of tortuous ways.

The task of the Cabinet Mission, like that of the Anglo-American Committee, was to try and reconcile the ir-reconcilable. Congress wanted a united India; the Muslim League an India divided into Pakistan and Hindustan. 'Nothing on earth', cried Nehru, 'not even the UNO, is going to bring about the Pakistan that Jinnah wants'; which was the six provinces of Sind, Baluchistan, North-

West Frontier Province and Punjab in the west, and, in
the east, Assam and Bengal.

Jinnah, for his part, had said: 'No power on earth can
prevent Pakistan'; and fiery Firoz Khan Noon, a Jinnah
man, threatened that if India were united under a Hindu
Raj, a bloodbath would follow – 'the havoc which the
Muslims will play will put to shame what Genghis Khan
and Haluka did'.

Unperturbed by these outbursts, the Cabinet Mission
informed Jinnah that if he insisted on a sovereign independent Pakistan it would have to be smaller than he
hoped for, a truncated variety, with half Bengal, half of
the Punjab and most of Assam, excluded. Jinnah refused.
The unity of India, he said, was a myth. But the Mission
had another plan up its sleeve, a 'Three-Tier Plan', with
a union government at the top; beneath it a Hindu and a
Muslim federation composed respectively, at the third
tier, of Hindu-majority and Muslim-majority provinces.

Still Jinnah refused to budge. Nehru turned the plan
down flat. Cripps, whom Pethwick Lawrence likened to
the dove from Noah's Ark, flitted to and fro between the
reluctant Indian leaders, pleading, urging, arguing. His
efforts succeeded. Although the opposing parties were, as
Wavell said, poles and poles apart, they accepted, very
hesitatingly, an invitation to discuss the Three-Tier Plan.
But not in the torrid heat of Delhi. Simla was once again
given as the rendezvous.

Pethwick Lawrence opened the Simla Conference on
5 May. For two days the talks remained stationary. It was
like an *Alice in Wonderland* croquet party, thought Pethwick. 'As soon as one part of the apparatus seems all
right another part walks off.' But for the divinely inspired Secretary of State the ridiculous could not obscure
the sublime: 'We are but the instruments of Powers far
greater than ourselves, whose Will will in the end be
done.' Unfortunately, the instruments were not always as
reliable as the Powers might have wished.

Gandhi delayed an interview until his day of silence
ended. When it did, he complained that the proposed

solution was worse than Pakistan. He seemed moreover, to Wavell, to be quite unmoved by the prospect of civil war. Nehru kept launching into diatribes about vital issues and fundamental forces until Wavell suggested to him that he should not allow himself to be carried away by such things, like the Frenchman pursuing an excited mob and explaining: *'Il faut que je les suive, je suis leur chef!'* Jinnah deeply distrusted Congress, especially its Muslim representatives Azad and Ghaffar Khan. Cripps, in session, behaved like a prosecuting counsel towards his learned friend Jinnah, but was convinced that he was leading Gandhi to the altar. In Wavell's opinion, Gandhi was leading Cripps down the garden path. Cripps fell seriously ill, Alexander went sick too. Of the three Magi, only the septuagenarian Secretary of State kept his form. Three days after the conference started, he felt thrilled to be 'grappling with tremendous forces and trying ... to ride the whirlwind'. Next day, the fourth of the talks, the whirlwind blew itself out. Wavell, in a different metaphor, reported that the conference had had a death-bed reprieve but was still on the danger-list. After a 'really dreadful day' on the 11th it was quite obviously dead. 'We meet again to bury the corpse,' wrote the Viceroy. Jinnah and Nehru were there, glaring at each other from opposite sides of the grave. Jinnah, it was clear, was a sick man but, as he had said, 'I am going on even if it kills me.' Ruefully, the others realized that they would have to do the same.

The talks having failed, the Cabinet Mission, on 16 May, announced their own plan. A lengthy, detailed document, its guiding principle was stated: 'We do not accept ... a separate Muslim sovereign state as a solution to the communal problem.' Instead the Mission stuck to an improved version of their original Three-Tier Plan of an Indian Union consisting of a Hindu federation and a Muslim federation.* The princely states would eventu-

---

* Hindu-majority provinces: Madras, Bombay, United Provinces, Bihar, Central Provinces, Orissa; Muslim-majority provinces, western group: Sind, Baluchistan, North-west Frontier Province, Punjab; eastern group: Assam, Bengal.

ally form a third federation. A constitution would be framed on this basis. Until it was inaugurated, an Indian interim government would govern the country.

The Plan was an ingenious formula for the liquidation of British power in India. Winston Churchill called it an able, but melancholy document. Jinnah was at first critical – the only acceptable solution, he insisted, was Pakistan, to which the Mission's objections were based on commonplace and exploded arguments. Gandhi called it a brave and frank document. Hardly had he done so when the Mission received from him a letter in which Wavell detected a 'clever attempt of an able but unscrupulous politician to torpedo the whole plan'. When a second letter, full of misrepresentations, arrived from the Mahatma, Cripps and Pethwick Lawrence were, the Viceroy noticed, 'shaken to the core', while First Lord Alexander just sat 'boiling with indignation'.

Then Jinnah began to come round. He asked what would happen if the Muslim League accepted the Plan and Congress refused. The Viceroy gave him the answer on 4 June: 'I can give you ... my personal assurance ... that we shall go ahead with the Plan ... so far as circumstances permit, if either party accept.' Jinnah took this as a firm promise. Moreover he saw in the Plan 'the basis and the foundation of Pakistan'. He advised the Muslim League to accept it. On 6 June the League decided to do so.

Wavell, however, had no illusions. Indian politics and politicians disheartened him; the feeling that the British had lost the courage to govern depressed him. He longed for a change, and the chance was there – an invitation to take his place in London's Victory Parade. But with no victory yet in India he dared not leave. When the Muslim League announced its acceptance of the Plan, the Viceroy remarked wryly: 'Now the real battle begins.'

On 8 June, the King-Emperor stood in the Mall as the forces of his Commonwealth-Empire and their allies marched by. Exactly forty-nine years – all but two weeks – had passed since the Empire had gathered in London to fête the Empress Victoria at her Diamond Jubilee. But how things had changed since then! Britain was in no mood today to flaunt her imperial splendour, now sadly faded, in an extravagant display of pageantry – as she did in 1897, when exuberant crowds applauded the sumptuous cortège of finely apparelled personalities and proud princes, plumes nodding as they rode their spirited chargers. Today, post-war austerity characterized the celebrations. The crowds were quiet and philosophical, though they lacked none of the Londoner's usual good humour, despite the shortage of supplies. Only the day before housewives had stood in some of the longest food queues yet seen. People brought sandwiches to the Victory Parade and as soon as the procession had passed Central London became a vast picnic place, with coffee stalls massed in the sidestreets and hawkers selling peaches and apples, winkles, pies and soft drinks.

In the Mall, for one hour and forty minutes, a vast concourse of the fighting and working men and women of Britain and the Commonwealth and their allies march-ed or drove past the King-Emperor. Among the allies, the Americans had the place of honour in front; they were followed by the Chinese – the Russians, whose place they took, had shunned the proceedings. That day, Supreme Allied Commander General Eisenhower de-clared 'Though long exposed to the full fury of the attack the Empire … refused to flinch from danger or modify her defiance.'

Above the Mall there appeared a single Hurricane fighter, symbolizing the Battle of Britain. It was followed by Sunderland flying boats which had fought in the Battle of the Atlantic and patrolled and searched the seven seas; and by Lancasters which, night after night, had blasted the enemy's industry, communications and flying-bomb bases. As the aircraft flitted in and out of low cloud the heavens opened in a deluge of rain. It lasted six hours.

Today's parade, which went by the prosaic but pro-phetic code name of 'Operation Downpour', had none of the glitter and pomp of the Empress Victoria's Diamond Jubilee procession. The cavalry were on foot or riding in roaring, clattering tanks – Churchills, Cromwells, Comets, Shermans. There followed Flails and Bridge-layers, mobile offices, workshops and stores, canteens and cranes, dozers and excavators, scrapers, sweepers, ploughs and tippers and the rest of the grim panoply of modern war. The Special Forces' mini-airborne transport raised a special cheer – it included a Boot Repair Plant (Air Transportable). The marching cortège included men and women from all corners of the Empire, to be sure, but men and women in drab, functional uniforms from every branch, service and civilian, of defence and industry; a cortège of people, not of princes.

Indeed, emperors, kings and princes were notably absent from the Victory Parade. There stood beside the King-Emperor that day but a handful of 'royalties', for the most part members of minor or moribund dynasties. For as Curzon had long ago apprehended, crowns and thrones had perished since Victoria's golden days. Of the then twenty reigning monarchs, well over half had been dethroned, or worse. Dictators had ousted the emperors of Russia, Germany and Austro-Hungary, and the Caliph of Turkey, too. Emperor Hirohito, Son of Heaven, was now plain mister, and one of those who stood next to the King-Emperor that day, the young King Feisal of Iraq, was soon to be lynched by the Baghdad mob.

The British King-Emperor's people saw him not as they had seen his great-grandmother, the Queen-Empress Victoria, a semi-deity, but as a king with the common touch, as a man who had always bravely and dutifully shared their perils and privations. *The Times* called the King-Emperor the symbol of Empire feeling – which was undeniably true that day, of all days. For Empire feeling was not one of boasting and vainglory and of imperishable (as it seemed in Victoria's day) grandeur, but of rendering honour, before the King-Emperor, to the comradeship, the sacrifice, the steely strength which had achieved the greatest victory ever won by men.

Empire feeling that day derived from emotion, not logic. For neither in India's Hindu temples nor Moslem mosques, nor in Burma's Buddhist pagodas, nor for that matter in the mosques and synagogues of Palestine, did the peoples' prayers go up for the King-Emperor, as they had for Victoria, because they believed he was their lord and protector. On the contrary: in the name of three hundred million Indians, Nehru was claiming an independent republic. Jinnah, in the name of nearly a hundred million more, was bent on a sovereign state free of the King-Emperor's sway. Eire, still a reluctant member of the Commonwealth-Empire, had long ago abolished the British monarchy. Aung San spoke for Burma: 'We want independence; we don't want a governor' – which meant that Burma did not want the King-Emperor, any more than did the Jews and Arabs of Palestine.

Yet among those who saluted the King-Emperor in London's Mall that day were men from Nehru's and Jinnah's India, from Aung San's Burma, Jews and Arabs from Palestine, 'rebels' from de Valera's Eire. All had fought for the King-Emperor, along with ten million others from his Empire across the seas, men – and women – from Africa, Asia and Australasia, from islands scattered afar as Fiji and the Falklands, Malta, Mauritius, Saint Helena and Hong Kong. The British Empire was in London to salute its King-Emperor as he stood there in the heart of his war-battered capital. *Ave et valete!* Hail and farewell to the last Emperor.

The garish splendour, the pomp and pretension, the idealistic imperial dreams of Victoria's day had come to nothing. The British Empire had accomplished its mission in another, an infinitely more glorious way. It had defeated tyranny. By its lone, year-long stand against the conquering Nazi hordes, it had barred the way to the tyrant, then led the crusade which overthrew him. The Victory Parade was the British Empire's swansong. Never before had the King-Emperor stood more integrally, more really, as the symbol of Empire feeling. Never would he do so again.

As a fourteen-year-old spectator at Victoria's Diamond Jubilee, Clement Attlee had described it as the British Empire at the height of its power and prosperity. Today Attlee was Prime Minister, but of a Britain which was broke and begging her bread. Her power and her prosperity were spent. It was high time, Attlee was convinced, to dismantle the costly apparatus of empire. He hoped it could be done with goodwill, in an orderly and peaceful fashion. He hoped in vain. The coming months were to see the British Empire begin to disintegrate in a welter of abuse and bloodshed.

11

Violence 1946

Hardly had the last echoes of marching men and martial music faded from the Mall when the air was rent with explosions. The first were verbal ones and came from Ernest Bevin. At the Labour Party's conference at Bournemouth on the Wednesday following the Victory Parade, Bevin thundered out against Truman's Palestine policy. There were illegal armies in Palestine, he said (armed terrorists were filtering in, too, with the refugees). To put in one hundred thousand immigrants would cost another division and £200,000,000, and this was more than Bevin was prepared to ask of a Britain already crippled with debt and taxation. People ridiculed Bevin for this statement, yet he was only taking the same line as Truman, who so far had refused to shell out a dime, let alone a division, for the Palestine business.

Still boiling with rage against America, Bevin's firing became wild. Americans were pushing for the transfer of Jews to Palestine, he accused, because they were not wanted in New York. This tirade hurt Truman, then fighting hard to ease the US immigration laws. And it so infuriated Americans that they pilloried Bevin, the King-Emperor's nominee, with Hitler as an anti-Semitic criminal. Yet it was a Jewish American journalist, Maurice J. Goldbloom, who shrewdly observed that one reason for American anger was that Bevin's outburst 'contained some uncomfortable grains of truth'.

At this stage Bevin was shooting more at the Americans than at the Jews. Once he laid down his gun and turned to Palestine, he became lucid. He understood, he said, that the Jews wanted not merely a Home, but a Palestinian state. That is what he would strive to achieve, but it would need patience and work. He believed that Palestine Jews never had a better chance for statesmanship.

Patience and statesmanship had no appeal for the desperadoes of the Yishuv. For them, violence was the cure-all, the quickest and surest way to rid Palestine of British rule and Arab domination. The terrorists believed in winning a Jewish state by conquest. Or, as *The Times* more harshly put it, the 'sinister elements' of the Yishuv, gripped 'in an atavistic tradition of Eastern European anarchy and terrorism', were 'adopting Hitler's own plan to resolve racial issues by violence'.

The Jewish 'Resistance' resumed its war. Around midnight on 16 June, Stern Gang men blasted their way into the railway workshops at Haifa and set them ablaze. Haganah had a picnic, though a costly one, that night, blowing up eleven bridges as well as, accidentally, fourteen of their own men.

This was a bitter time for Jew and Briton. There were few British soldiers who did not feel sympathy for the suffering and the aspirations of the Jews. They could even admire the careful, often brilliant planning of the terrorists and their daring and courage in action. It was their 'dirty tricks' which angered both soldiers and police. That night, as often, the terrorists wore British uniforms – an artifice for which the long-suffering Tommies had but a single word: treachery. It turned their sympathy into hatred and worse, a desire for revenge.

Two days later, at the officers' club in Tel Aviv's Yarkon Street – a club created by Jews to provide hospitality to the British – Irgun men kidnapped five officers at gun point. Ben Gurion, then in London, expressed his horror and grief; Moshe Shertok, the Agency's political chief, denounced the kidnapping as 'futile'. But Irgun chief Begin soon proved that terrorism paid. The British, he reckoned, knew very well that if they executed Ashbel and Chimchon (condemned for the Sarafand raid) the Irgun would hang their British hostages. He was right. By the beginning of July, Shimchon and Ashbel received a reprieve. (Ashbel's, as it turned out, was a brief one). The British officers were thereupon released.

When British security men discovered a terrorist list of potential hostages, big fish the rebels called them, Prime Minister Attlee decided to take drastic action. In the early hours of 29 June, the Jewish Sabbath, British troops occupied the Jewish Agency building in Jerusalem. Top men of the Agency, known to be implicated in Haganah's operations, were arrested. One they did not catch was Chairman Ben Gurion, who had slipped off to Paris.

Throughout the day, Kol Israel (the Haganah radio) kept repeating: 'The Jewish people will fight back. Out with the unclean sons of Titus ... Down with the Nazi-British regime.' That day the head of the 'Nazi-British regime', High Commissioner Sir Alan Cunningham, also spoke. His sweet reasonableness would have made a Nazi blush. He reassured Palestinians: 'It is not the intention to proscribe or close the Agency.'

Attlee's drastic action only brought him more brick-bats. The Chief Rabbi, Dr Herzog, complained that the arrests, coming on the Jewish Sabbath, were a shameful affront to Jewish religious sentiment. However the terrorists themselves were not above killing British soldiers on the Sabbath. The Chief Rabbi movingly alluded to 'the root cause of Israel's seemingly endless tragedy – its homelessness'. Chaim Weizmann similarly admonished Britain. 'The remnant of the Jewish people,' he said, 'still languish behind barbed wire.' Britain was entirely to blame for Jewish terrorism, said the *Washington Post*, because of her dilatory, evasive and bankrupt policy.

Unfortunately Britain had no ready answer to the critics. In the Commons, Attlee cried: 'We shall never yield to violence!' But his appeal to Truman for moral support fell flat. Truman merely hoped that things would 'soon return to normal'. His lack of realism was stunning. For the Palestine fuse was sizzling to its end. The situation was about to explode sky high.

For the Irgun's 'Operation Chick' against the British HQ, situated in a wing of Jerusalem's King David Hotel, the planning was as usual meticulous. At about midday on 22 July, when work in the offices was in full swing with complete staffs, a party of 'Arabs' in flowing Bedouin robes entered the hotel kitchens with a load of milk churns – which contained not milk, but TNT. The Irgun, who affected a horror for killing innocent people, had been careful to warn the hotel beforehand. But they had not been careful enough. Begin claimed that the hotel switchboard operator was warned twenty-seven minutes ahead. The hotel told a different story: their civilian operator, warned one minute before the explosion, had time only to tell the man standing beside him. No warning was received at the military switchboard.

The explosion rent the south wing of the King David Hotel from basement to roof, six storeys of stone, concrete and steel. A BBC report said 'The entire wing was cut off as with a knife'. A huge blood patch on a white wall fifty yards away showed where one victim had been blasted to death. Other dead and injured lay buried beneath the twisted masonry while, to the clatter of pneumatic drills, rescue work continued for several days.

Out of the debris were dragged ninety-one dead, British, Jewish and Arab, of the Administration's staff. Of them its Chief Secretary, Sir John Shaw, said 'Their only crime was devoted, unselfish and impartial service to Palestine and its people ... They have been rewarded by cold-blooded mass-murder.'

The Jewish Agency and Va'ad Leumi, the Jewish National Council, expressed horror at the 'dastardly crime perpetrated by a gang of desperadoes'. From Paris, Ben Gurion vociferated: 'Irgun is an enemy of the Jewish people'. Haganah, however, was privy to the entire operation.

In the heat and horror of the moment, General Barker, the army commander, expressed his 'contempt and disgust'. He prohibited British troops from all contact, aiming, as he said, 'to punish the Jews in the manner the race dislikes most: by hitting them in the pocket'.

It was puerile stuff, but a bagatelle compared with what Zionist propaganda had been spewing forth for years against the 'Nazi British, the unclean sons of Titus'. Barker's order generated further odium against the British. It was apparently a greater sin to be anti-Semitic than anti-British. Bewildered Britons felt somewhat galled as they reflected, with the Archbishop of York (who had joined the fray), that 'if we had not stood alone against Hitler, there would be no Jews in Palestine or anywhere else'.

Behind this sordid slanging match there remained, practically unalleviated, the stark tragedy of European Jewry with its concomitant, Jewish terrorism. In the House of Lords, Lord Rothschild, himself no Zionist, succinctly described how tragedy and terrorism were connected. First, Jews had been persecuted in almost every country for centuries; second, almost all the young Jews in Palestine had had relations who had been tortured or gassed to death by Hitler. How many of their lordships, asked the noble lord, were in the same position as himself, 'of having an aunt, whom he dearly loved, clubbed to death by the SS?'

Ernest Bevin, who was considered one of Britain's greatest foreign secretaries, was anathema to the Jews. He was the callous monster frustrating their fanatical desire for a Jewish state, where Jews would be free at last from persecution.

Attlee and Bevin, still piously hoping that the two peoples, cousins after all, would hit it off, accepted an Anglo-US Plan for a Palestine Federation. But for Truman it represented, as *The Times* said, 'a dilemma whose horns have been goring the President for months'. The horn which hurt most was the powerful and vociferous US Jewish electorate, who were gunning for an all-Jewish state. Truman declined formal support for the Plan.

Meanwhile the Jewish Agency, gathered in Paris about its chairman Ben Gurion, came up with a plan of their own – for partition. They now had no further need of Britain, but looked instead to American Zionism and its militant leader, Rabbi Abba Silver, to make their dream of statehood come true.

On the eve of the King David Hotel disaster, the hard-pressed British had been shaken by another event, unique in their history. Bread was rationed.

At the beginning of 1946, Attlee had warned Truman of the danger of famine in Europe and Asia, and of the heavy sacrifices he intended to ask of the British people, some of whose food supplies he felt bound to divert to other more needy areas. The British, wrote Attlee hopefully, would feel encouraged by the knowledge that other countries were doing the same. Truman reacted positively to what he called 'the vivid picture of ... hardship endured by the British' – who, in April, turned over 200,000 tons of their wheat supplies to other hungry people and saw their 2lb loaf consequently reduced in size. By mid 1946 Bevin felt moved to tell the United Nations Assembly that there were countries still 'living in plenty and shirking the food crisis'; what riled him most was that some of the bitterest criticism of Britain was coming 'from the mouths we feed' – which included not only Palestine, but the immigrants on the way there. Another case was Germany: Britain had sent 400,000 tons of her own wheat supplies to her ex-enemies. For her pains, she herself was now on the bread-line.

Other sinister portents hovered over the home front. The fishing industry was uneasy; coal mines were producing fitfully – a shortage of five million tons was forecast for the coming winter. Animal feeding stuffs were scarce and the meagre ration of meat, milk and eggs (one a week) was threatened. Storms meanwhile had played havoc with the harvest.

In this moment of gloom, however, a possibility occurred of injecting new life into Britain's war-impoverished economy – the war had cost her more than £4,000,000,000, a much higher contribution per head than America's. On 13 July, the US Congress (despite the opposition of US Zionists) voted a 3,750 million dollar loan for Britain. As Attlee said, Britain had to have that loan. Truman had brought a kind of Pearl Harbour to Britain, cancelling Lend-Lease at the very moment that the financial experts were negotiating in London. One, Assistant State Secretary Clayton, heard the news in a Cambridge tea-shop; the other US Treasury official, Collado, was told by his week-end hosts. 'It made quite an impossible situation,' commented Attlee.

It took Britain months of hard bargaining to get the loan. Rabbi Silver, the Zionist leader (and Republican representative), wanted to apply pressure to Britain on Palestine by having the loan shelved. Congress debated it hotly. Another Republican, Mrs Bolton, said: 'Do you know what a blitz costs? Have you gone without all the things that make living a pleasure ... day after day, year after year? Have you seen a long war that threatened your very existence end, only to be told ... that you must just pull in your belts another notch? ... You cannot say that Britain has not put everything she has and was and is into this war.' The closing speech of Mr Speaker Rayburn was loudly cheered. 'God pity us', he said, 'when we have no ally across the Atlantic, and God pity them, too.' So Britain got her loan – 'a kind of crutch', *The Times* called it, 'during convalescence'.

On 22 July, the day that the King David Hotel atrocity blew sky-high the slim remaining hopes of Anglo-Jewish understanding, Viceroy Wavell took a step which was to rock India with a chain of communal explosions. He intended, needless to say, exactly the contrary: he hoped to create a coalition of the Congress and the Muslim League. Wavell wrote to Nehru and Jinnah with proposals for an interim government, to act while the final negotiations for India's independence were being completed. Wavell proposed a cabinet of six Congress, five Muslim League and three other Indian ministers. Jinnah's reaction was immediate: 'Your proposal destroys the principle of parity.'

Wavell had, indeed, promised the Muslim League parity with Congress in the future Interim Government. He had also assured Jinnah that if Congress did not accept the Cabinet Mission Plan (which included an Interim Government) he would 'go ahead' with the Muslim League. Congress had not accepted, but they had informed the Viceroy that the Plan and the interim government 'hung together'; they would never accept one without the other. On 16 June Wavell had made a last attempt 'to make the children play together'. He would, he told them, form a government with any party who accepted the Plan.

Congress now made a complete volte-face: they accepted the Plan – with reservations – but refused to join the interim government. The Viceroy was trapped: he could not now go ahead with Jinnah. A sorry business he called it; Congress had the ability 'to twist words and phrases'. Their sinister manœuvring caused First Lord Alexander to explode with wrath. He had never, he said, seen a more deplorable exhibition during his political career. Wavell, in a letter to the King-Emperor, told him of 'the quibblings, hagglings tergiversations and small-mindedness of Indian political leaders, especially Congress'. He was now left with 'one rather sickly infant, the Constitutional Assembly ... and one still-born babe, the interim government'.

Jinnah made a wounding thrust at the Viceroy: 'You have chosen to go back on your pledged word,' he accused him. And Jinnah quickly realized what Congress had meant by accepting the Plan with reservations. Completely disregarding its recommendations on the grouping of provinces – what Jinnah had called the basis and the foundation of Pakistan – Nehru declared: 'There will be no grouping.'

Jinnah felt himself betrayed. At a meeting in Bombay on 29 July, the Muslim League decided to withdraw its acceptance of the Plan and 'to achieve Pakistan ... to get rid of the present slavery under the British and ... Hindu domination'. Jinnah compared 'the reason, justice, honesty and fair play' of the League with 'the perfidious dealings of Congress'. And he declared: 'Never have we ... done anything except by constitutional means ... But ... this day we bid good-bye to constitutional methods.' It was decided to go over to Direct Action. 16 August was fixed for Direct Action Day. As the meeting ended, Muslims who had been honoured by the King-Emperor, veteran statesmen and soldiers, mounted the stage and publicly renounced their titles.

Now that Jinnah and the League had dropped the Plan, the Viceroy asked Nehru to form an interim government – with Jinnah's cooperation if he could get it. He could not. So Nehru was left alone to form a Congress government. The manœuvre had brilliantly succeeded.

Meanwhile the stage was being set for the holocaust. In Calcutta, second city after London of the British Empire, Chief Minister Suhrawardy had declared 16 August a public holiday – a dangerous if not criminal decision, considering the tension between the Hindu and Muslim communities. The 16th broke warm and sticky – typical monsoon weather. To Major Livermore, conning the city through his binoculars from the roof of Fort William's Dalhousie Block, there seemed to be a curious stillness in the air. The Maidan* was deserted and the city's main thoroughfare, Chowringhee, was dead. Towards noon, people began converging on the Ochterlony Memorial, where Suhrawardy was due to speak at 3 pm.

Communal incidents were at first sporadic, but by 2 pm the York and Lancaster Regiment were ordered out to help the police to break up Hindu-Muslim brawls. An hour later, Suhrawardy began to harangue an immense crowd on whose fringe there gathered growing numbers of dreaded goondas.† Suhrawardy's speech over, the goondas made straight for the town centre where they set to, looting and burning Hindu shops. When Livermore's battalion headed along Upper Circular Road that afternoon, panic-stricken crowds were fleeing south out of the city. By midnight, the centre of the Empire's second city looked as if 'an armoured division had swept through on the tail of a heavy bombardment'. Streets were gaunt with the charred embers of looted shops and flooded by water gushing from hydrant cocks which the mob had opened to impede the firefighters. All night long rioters, armed with guns and swords, iron bars and loaded

* Open park.
† Hooligan, assassin.

sticks, charged hither and thither murdering, raping, looting, burning. 'It was unbridled savagery' commented General Tuker. His meagre forces were as yet unable to prevent the butchery, which continued with unabated fury throughout the morning of the 17th. From Garden Reach, Kidderpore, Metia Bruz and Beliagatia – residential quarters – and from the *bustees* (slums) along the banks of the Hooghli River, came the sickening sound of killing, while 'fire-bugs' fed the flames with kerosene-soaked sacking. Overhead hung a sullen pall of smoke; bloated bodies floated in the flooded streets, others were wrapped in sacks or stuffed into dustbins. The Sobha-bazar Market was strewn with dead; fifteen horribly muti-lated corpses lay huddled in a single room, twelve in another. Over a hundred bodies had to be cleared from a cross-roads before the army trucks could pass; a little further on a hundred more marked another fearful mass-acre.

By the 18th the mob had spent its fury and the Calcutta garrison had regained control. There remained the hide-ous business of clearing the streets. 'Operation Grisly', as it was called, was assigned mainly to British officers and soldier volunteers. Clad in gas clothing and 'stench-masks', they were aided by Doms, a Hindu caste who would handle corpses. The Doms went about their foul task uncomplainingly – with the nose-pad of their stench-mask clapped to their foreheads.

An unearthly sight met Major Livermore and his 'Grisly' men as they stumped the streets of Calcutta city: piles of garbage and rotting humanity; corpses stacked in handcarts, with arms and legs protruding stiffly, like broken dolls; bodies which burst into a sickening mass as they were loaded on to the trucks, others so swollen that they needed an outsize grave. All night long the ghastly work went on, while other soldiers dug desperately at improvised cemeteries – at one they buried seven hun-dred corpses that night.

Their macabre task achieved, the soldiers were drop-ping with exhaustion. Despite decontamination treatment they stank so much that their comrades recoiled in disgust; for two days the men of the death-squad could eat nothing – only drink neat gin and smoke. All this they did to stave off pestilence and hide the shame of Calcutta, the King-Emperor's second biggest city, where four thousand of his subjects had been foully massacred.

The Great Calcutta Killing left Gandhi angry, but philosophical. To the shocked Viceroy he exclaimed, thumping the table: 'If India wants her blood-bath, she shall have it.' It was in this atmosphere that his disciple Nehru, his uncrowned king and prime minister as Gandhi called him, and 'the only Englishman in my camp', was sworn in, on 2 September 1946, as head of the interim government. 'May we prove worthy servants of the Indian people,' bravely declared Nehru as the Indian people returned anew to the slaughter. This time it was the streets of Bombay and Ahmedabad that flowed with blood.

The Burmese, to whom long ago Britain had promised political progress *pari passu* with India, were jealously watching India's rapid, if bloody, advance towards independence. The Burmans themselves had been granted no such favour as an interim government. They felt that Britain was neglecting them: Burma, in short, was seething with discontent. His Majesty's government had so far failed to remedy Burma's crying economic grievances, as the Government's chief secretary, F. S. V. Donnison, called them. Privately he opined that 'the Burmese are jaded, discouraged and cynical'.

Two terrible campaigns had been fought across the Golden Land. Towns had been devastated, the rich countryside ravaged, communications disrupted. Rangoon, once one of the British Empire's proud capitals, was now a derelict agglomeration of shabby buildings, eaten with grime and decay. The streets were unlit at night and littered with garbage and 'banana currency' (Japanese bank-notes). In the open spaces, homeless Burmans were squatting in *kwetthits*, shacks made of bamboo poles and matting which afforded but primitive, unhygienic shelter. Government House, in all its faded Victorian glory – it had been mistaken, in a recent quiz, for the Railway Orphanage at Woking – was still intact. But at the Gymkhana Club grounds, cricket would never again be played.

British officials and businessmen had come to Rangoon on 'Operation Shylock' – the rehabilitation of Burma's economy. They were no longer called *Thakin*, 'Master'; that title was now used only for the Burmese nationalists, led by Aung San, who were in the process of booting the British out of Burma. The British ex-masters no longer lived in cool and comfortable villas along the Prome Road. Some slept on the floor in Lloyds Bank, with boxes as tables. Others were lodged in Fytche Flats, a three-storey block with no fittings or furniture, no hot water either, but with electric light – shed by naked bulbs. The 'inmates' called it Belsen.

The rehabilitation of Burma was the worthy aim of the British Government. But the Golden Land remained torn by poverty, lawlessness and chaos. During sing-songs – one of the few distractions at 'Belsen' – frustrated, middle-aged British officials and businessmen took delight in singing, to the tune of 'Waltzing Matilda':

> Rehabilitating Burma, rehabilitating Burma,
> Who'll come rehabilitating Burma with me?
> And he sang as he sighed and filled up forms in triplicate
> Who'll come rehabilitating Burma with me?

It was clear that the British also, like the Burmans, were 'jaded, cynical and discouraged'.

After nearly a year's shilly-shallying by its old-guard Executive Council under Governor Dorman-Smith, Burma had become a bubbling cauldron. With the arrival, on 30 August 1946 of the new Governor, Sir Hubert Rance, the lid blew off. Rance promised Burma self-government 'like the Dominions and Britain'. Whitehall had at last woken up.

But Aung San and his AFPFL were taking no chances; they, too, meant to have a hand in the independence business. Their peaceful but paralysing coercion began on 2 September with a police strike. The PVO, Aung San's so-called social workers, stepped in to keep the peace. They appealed – successfully – to Rangoon's underworld to take it easy during the strike. Strikers, camping in hundreds on the steps of the golden-spired Shwe Dagon pagoda were fed by the public. By the middle of September, other government workers were out. But tempers remained cool, and though smiling pickets squatted at the main entrance of buildings, they did not stop anyone going round to the back-door. Paralysis, however, was setting in. When British Income Tax Commissioner S. Hildersley asked a Government House official how things were going, he was told: 'Going's the word.'

First to go was the Executive Council, on 22 September, a happy day for Aung San in more ways than one – his wife Daw Khin Kyi presented him with a daughter, their fourth child. Next day, a general strike completed Burma's paralysis. The AFPFL had forced HMG against the wall. Eleven months earlier, Governor Dorman-Smith had refused them a majority of seats on the Executive Council. But here was Governor Rance telling them, on 26 September, that their demand was approved.

Aung San's great victory was marred by tragedy. That day his new-born daughter died. Pathetically, he said: 'To bring forth an innocent child so that she may die after a few days is so sad and futile.' Then he plunged back into the struggle. Until now he had been in opposition. 'Imperialism's Day of Judgment is coming,' he had cried recently, and quoted Abraham Lincoln: 'No nation has the right to rule another.' Now he was in power, but not altogether sure of himself. He learned, under the Japanese, to be careful and wary. He now wondered how he would get on with the British.

Aung San had a good friend in Governor Rance, whom

the Burmans loved. Rance now told them that the new Council inspired 'a vision of Burma as we all want to see her, a united country'. The Council, he said, was a judicious blending of youth and experience. Aung San, as its Deputy Chairman, was now virtually prime minister. He represented youth – he was not yet thirty-two. His political rival, forty-five-year-old U Saw, the pre-war prime minister, represented experience.

Cynics thought that the inclusion of U Saw in the present Executive Council would lead to a break-up between the two rivals. They were right, but they never expected that it would be so violent. U Saw did not spare his contempt for his youthful rival; he was bumptious and self-confident, dressed in Western clothes and spoke fluent English. He cultivated a circle of British friends, among whom was a dark, stocky Welshman, a captain in the REME who was attached to the Rangoon police – as a small-arms expert.

While the Burmese sky was far from clear, dark clouds hung over India. When Nehru's Congress government took office on 2 September, Gandhi consoled India's hundred million-odd Muslims: they were the Hindus' brothers, even if not represented in the government. Muslims, however, did not get that all-India brotherhood feeling; black flags, millions of them, appeared over Muslim homes throughout India. The Muslims were playing Gandhi at his own game, encouraged by the Muslim League, to show their 'silent contempt' for the Hindu government.

Silent contempt was a welcome change from slaughter, but it was not to last for long. Depressing reports of communal tension in the Punjab were arriving in the Viceroy's office and Gandhi now opined that brotherly Hindus and Muslims were nearing civil war.

Starkly impressed by the horrors of Calcutta, Viceroy Wavell was determined to make another attempt to get Jinnah into a coalition government. Jinnah himself was willing; Gandhi and Nehru quite evidently were not. A talk with Gandhi convinced the Viceroy that the Mahatma was 'an unscrupulous old hypocrite; he would shrink from no violence and blood-letting to achieve his ends'. When Nehru insinuated that the Viceroy was playing the classic game of divide and rule, Wavell wearily answered that the British were trying on the contrary to unite and quit.

By 15 October, Wavell's efforts at last succeeded. A coalition government was announced. 'I wonder,' thought the Viceroy, 'whether I can induce them to work together.' He was frankly doubtful.

The omens were not good. The day before the announcement, a fresh bout of killings began in the Noakhali district, in East Bengal, some 200 miles from Calcutta.

Three hundred of the King-Emperor's innocent subjects were foully slaughtered in these Noakhali killings, a deplorable death roll, but a comparatively low one, considering the bestial passions unleashed and the paucity of the Emperor's forces available to restore order. Unfortunately, the Hindu press, in a bout of hysteria, magnified the calamities of its own people, and Hindus fleeing north into Bihar State, athwart the Ganges upstream from Noakhali, inflamed Hindu vengeance with their pitiful tales. In Bihar, Hindus outnumbered Muslims by thirty-two millions to five.

On 25 October, the day that saw Viceroy Wavell's doubtful realization of a Hindu-Muslim *entente*, with the swearing in of his coalition government, the vengeful Hindus of Bihar observed 'Noakhali Day' to commemorate their slain brethren. It sufficed to touch off the explosion. For a week, Chapra became the scene of murder and arson. A hundred Muslim houses were burnt down, the occupants perishing in the flames. Fifty more were burnt at neighbouring Paigambarpur. Women wept for their children. One mother had seen her baby cut in two. Another gave all her savings so that her children might be spared; they were then murdered before her eyes. Infants were done to death on their mother's knees, then flung into the village well, already nearly choked with dead. Yet Muslims fleeing the Hindu fury were helped by other Hindus to board the train. Pyarelal, Gandhi's secretary, who was there, thought: 'Man is a strange mixture of the brute and the angel.'

A week later, at Bihar Sharif, the 'Bihar butchery' began in earnest. Under the British Raj, the Emperor's Hindu subjects had lived in peace and amity with their Muslim neighbours. Now, on the eve of independence, they suddenly turned on them in an orgy of killing. As in Noakhali, neither old nor young were spared, and once again it was the sparse patrols of the British-led Indian army which came to the rescue. They included units of the Madras Regiment and the Gurkhas–Hindus, who faced unflinchingly their barbaric Hindu brethren.

Gurkhas led by Colonel Venning and Colonel Murray found, at Bikatpur, foully mutilated women and children; at a burning village nearby, women, children and a few old men, had been stripped naked and burnt alive. At Nimi, a small patrol drove off a frenzied mob and rescued hundreds of Muslims, escorting them through the night while the mob, a dark mass of stealthy, dimly seen figures, continued to harry them. Throughout that night and the following day patrols scoured the district. One found two hundred Muslims dead among the ashes of Kanchipur village. Near Barkandi, a single platoon scattered a mob of five thousand as they massed to attack.

Night fell again, and once more patrols had the nerve-wracking job of escorting refugees across unknown country while they could hear the ghoulish cries of mobs as they revelled in the slaughter. Twelve dauntless sepoys of the Madras Regiment, finding their road blocked by a yelling mob hundreds strong, fixed bayonets and advanced. The mob fled.

The killing reached its bloodiest on 6 November. Fifteen thousand Hindus, lusting for Muslim blood, ransacked Tehara, burning their victims alive or butchering them with knives and spears. Colonel Venning, leading his Gurkhas towards the village of Nagar Nahasa, could hear the wild cries of the mob as it closed in on the village, determined to kill every Muslim it could find. The Gurkhas repulsed 'the enemy' – their Hindu co-religionists – and saved the Muslims of Nagar Nahasa. Neighbouring villages were less fortunate: as they made their way across country to the safety of the Gurkhas they were intercepted and wiped out. The Bihar Hindus had exacted a high price to avenge their three hundred brethren murdered at Noakhali. They had slain nearly seven thousand Muslims.

In the evening of that day of wanton slaughter, 6 November, the fairground beside the Ganges at Garhmukteswar, five hundred miles up-stream, near Delhi, was thronged with Hindu pilgrims, who had come for the ritual cleansing in the holy river. Hundreds of Muslims were there too, to join in the fun of the fair. Then, as a Muslim Wall of Death rider spiralled crazily, he shouted some harmless jibe at a woman of the Hindu Jat people. Instantly there went up a terrible cry from the Jats and the Wall of Death became an inferno of killing. Jats rushed out and fell upon Muslim stallholders, spearing and strangling them, sparing no one, not even pregnant women, whom the infuriated Jats ripped up, then, tearing the babies from their wombs, bashed their brains out. Women and girls were seized and raped, their legs torn asunder – while Jat women urged their men on to further bestialities.

Nothing effective was done to stay the slaughter: the police superintendent was a Hindu and his men looked on as the killing continued into the next day, when Jats sacked and burnt Garhmukteswar's Muslim quarter. They rushed howling, slaying, looting through the narrow streets, between the crumbling red-brick walls, up the hill to the hospital. There they murdered the doctor and his Muslim patients. The doctor's wife was spared the butcher's knife only to be raped and paraded naked round the town.

How could Nehru feel so exhilarated (as he said) with India's five thousand-year-old civilization, after the bestial killings of Calcutta and Noakhali, of Bihar and Gar-hmukteswar? How was it possible that the blood-crazed murderers and their pitiful victims could belong to what the King-Emperor called his world-wide family? They were his subjects. 'I think', the King-Emperor had said recently, 'of men and women of every race and creed within the Empire', who were living 'in the ways of peace' and whose children were 'freed from unnatural fears'.

Certainly, Britannia had done more in 150 years than Mother India in 5,000 to unite her people and enable them to live at peace with themselves. But now that India, with her own Indian government, of which Nehru was the 'exhilarated' head, was on the verge of independence, the King-Emperor's sway was fatally weakening. As Viceroy Wavell noted on 6 November – the day of great slaughter – 'we have now the responsibility without the power, whereas the Indian provincial ministries have the power, but little or no sense of responsibility'.

What a terrible come-down since Empress Victoria's time! On the day of her acclamation, not seventy years ago, her poet-Viceroy Lord Lytton had reminded her grateful subjects that it was to English statesmen that India owed her progress and civilization. Bold as his claim was, it was true. The 'intestine broils', the strife and anarchy under Tamerlane's dynasty and the Mog-huls were over. Victoria's goodwill, the Viceroy had said, was India's most cherished possession. Princes and people were secure in the protection of the imperial power; all races and creeds could live in peace. The Empress, the Viceroy had concluded, regarded India as a glorious in-heritance to be handed on to her descendants.

Yet here was today's Viceroy admitting that Britain no longer had the power – or even the will – to control events, as events had so grimly shown. Of the 'glorious inheritance' the Viceroy had recently written to the King-Emperor that 'the orderly withdrawal from our rule in India without a rebellion or civil war' would be (as Wellington had said about Waterloo) 'a near-run thing'.

India was on the verge of an unimaginable holocaust.

Her leaders were losing their grip. Both Nehru and Jinnah were clearly heading for a nervous breakdown. The Viceroy, too, was feeling the strain: he slept badly and suffered from migraine and violent nosebleeds. The Indian government, supposedly a Hindu-Muslim coalition, was divided against itself. The Cabinet Mission's plan for the grouping of provinces – what Jinnah had called the foundation and the basis of Pakistan – was still a bone of contention. The Constituent Assembly, too. Nehru wanted it summoned: Jinnah said it would be a disaster. The Viceroy told Jinnah that his best course was to come into the Constituent Assembly, then negotiate. His Excellency then summoned the Constituent Assembly for 9 December. Jinnah immediately ordered Muslim Leaguers not to participate – thus dealing a deathblow to the Cabinet Mission Plan, and creating a deadlock: without agreement between the two parties the Constituent Assembly could not form a new constitution for India. The alternative was civil war.

As Jinnah remarked: 'It is a tradition of the British nation that they only wake up when there is something dangerous.' His Majesty's Government now woke up. It invited these three distraught men, the Viceroy, Nehru and Jinnah, plus Liaquat Ali Khan (Jinnah's number two) and Baldev Singh, the Sikh leader, to talks in London. Jinnah accepted. Nehru refused, but relented when Premier Attlee sent a personal appeal. Then Jinnah backed out, as if he felt that he too deserved a prime-ministerial appeal. Liaquat Ali finally persuaded Jinnah to go.

The talks began on 3 December. Wavell took care to warn the Cabinet beforehand that the aim of Congress was 'power, and to get rid of British influence as soon as possible'. Then they would deal with both Muslims and Princes, 'the former by bribery, blackmail, propaganda and if necessary force; the latter by stirring up their people against them'. Gandhi would remain in the background; he felt that his life's work of driving the British from India was almost accomplished, and he knew that non-violence, a weapon for the weak against the strong, would now be replaced by more direct weapons.

After two days of fruitless talking, the Indian leaders lunched with the King-Emperor at Buckingham Palace. If, in nine years on the imperial throne, the Emperor had failed to get to India, India's leaders had at last come to him. Unfortunately, their visit had created a tense atmosphere. In the hope of easing it, the luncheon was attended by the Queen-Empress and by Queen Mary, whose husband, King-Emperor George v, had, on his visit to India over forty years ago, told the great Gokhale: 'I have never seen a happier people.' The young princesses, Elizabeth and Margaret, were there too, to liven things up. But it was a sticky luncheon for the King-Emperor. He sat between Nehru and Jinnah, knowing full well that, failing an agreement between them, then 'the only alternative is civil war, which we will be powerless to prevent'. Nehru was 'very uncommunicative'; Jinnah 'told me a great deal'. The King-Emperor wisely decided that the moment was most unpropitious to make the little speech that he had prepared. So he held his peace. 'The leaders of the two parties', he concluded, 'will never agree.'

He was right. The only party to the talks which made any concession at all was His Majesty's own Government, who made a ponderously worded announcement to the effect that it would never agree to a constitution being imposed on an unwilling section of the Indian people. It was a tacit admission of Pakistan.

Two days later, the King-Emperor told Attlee how worried he was. He was haunted by the fear of civil war in his Indian Empire: 'We have not got enough troops or authority to keep order' – a lamentable lapse since Empress Victoria's viceroy had spoken of the strong hand of the imperial power, which was there 'to protect and to guide'. Commenting on his viceroy's plans to evacuate India, the King-Emperor objected that 'we cannot do so without leaving India with a workable constitution'.

The Constituent Assembly met in Delhi next day. Nehru, who had returned there hot-foot from the King-

Emperor's presence in London, demanded that India be an independent, sovereign republic, and added that 'we are not going to have an external monarchy'. Two days later, on 15 December, at Benares, he drove the nail home: 'We have now altogether stopped looking to London ... We cannot and will not tolerate outside interference.'

Jinnah had stayed on in London, his old haunt, where he had so many memories. The day after Nehru had rooted for an Indian republic, Jinnah, in London's Kingsway Hall, cried, amidst shouts of *'Pakistan Zindabad'* ('Long live Pakistan!'): 'We want a separate state of our own [where] we can live according to our notions ... Give Muslims their homeland, and give Hindus Hindustan.'

The Viceroy had stayed on too, to do some Christmas shopping and to get approval for his future plans from the Cabinet. When finally he took leave of the Prime Minister, he noticed that he was 'not at all gracious'. Wavell wondered: 'Am I wise to go back?' then dismissed the thought. 'Q' (Queenie, Lady Wavell) and the family, he knew, were longing to see him. What he did not know was that Attlee had decided to sack him.

The Prime Minister was convinced that Wavell had shot his bolt. He was a great man and 'a good viceroy in many ways', Attlee agreed, but 'a curious, silent bird'. Silent people, Attlee considered, 'don't get on very well with Indians, who are loquacious'. Attlee 'looked all around for someone who, besides having the right qualifications, could out-talk an Indian'. Then he had an inspiration: Lord Louis Mountbatten, cousin of the King-Emperor and, like him, a great-grandson of Empress Victoria.

Three days before his ungracious farewell to Wavell, Attlee had revealed his inspiration to the King-Emperor. 'Rather unexpectedly', said Attlee later, 'the King-Emperor warmly approved – not everyone would let a member of the Royal Family go and take a risky job ...' Attlee laid six to four against Mountbatten's succeeding. But he had weighed him up as 'an extremely lively, exciting personality. He had an extraordinary capacity for getting on with people. He was also blessed with a very unusual wife.'

The following day (hardly twenty-four hours before saying good-bye to Wavell) Attlee broached the idea to Mountbatten himself. 'Bit of a shock for him,' he admitted – the Admiral who, as 'Supremo', South-East Asia Command, had been for so long high and dry, was longing to go to sea again. But, as Attlee said, he very patriotically agreed to take on the job – on his own conditions, the essential one of which was that his role as Viceroy would be not to prolong the British Raj, but to end it, and that within a fixed time limit.

Attlee was forcing the pace. Hardly had he asked Mountbatten to dismantle the Indian Empire when, on 20 December, in the House of Commons, he rattled off, as Churchill put it, his plans for Burma, that 'the Burmese should attain self-government by the quickest and most convenient means possible'. Attlee hoped that Burma would remain in the Commonwealth but there was to be no coercion: 'We do not desire . . . within the Commonwealth and Empire any unwilling people.'

Many (including the King-Emperor) thought that Attlee was going too fast. Churchill protested at his 'appalling haste' – there was only one word for it: scuttle. 'The British Empire', he jibed, 'is running off almost as fast as the American loan.' He deplored the 'steady and remorseless process of divesting ourselves of what has been gained by so many generations of toil, administration and sacrifice'. Why, it was hardly a year since the superb exertions of the British 14th Army, the 'enormous sacrifices in life and treasure . . . in British and Indian blood', had liberated Burma from the Japanese. But Churchill's own superb exertions in defence of imperialism could not deflect Attlee. 'You can't put the clock back,' said the Prime Minister. 'We have not been going too fast, but too slow.' He had invited the Burmese leaders to London shortly after Christmas.

Britain's second post-war Christmas was celebrated, no less than the first, under the sign of austerity. Power failures and fuel cuts, on top of a spell of bitterly cold weather and pea-soup fogs, had Britons shivering or groping sightless in the murk. Their meagre rations of food and household goods dulled the joy of living: meat was limited to 1s 2d worth – about 25 cents – a week, and bacon had just been cut to 2 ounces – 60 grammes; there was no end in sight to clothes rationing, and sheets and blankets were about to go on the ration. On Christmas Eve, London housewives queued for more than two hours for bread and food – all this on the eve of the seventieth anniversary (1 January) of Victoria's acclamation as first Empress, when Britain had so proudly displayed her wealth and splendour to the world.

And now Victoria's great-grandson was making his last Christmas broadcast as King-Emperor. He was thinking, he said, of 'that world-wide family of the British Commonwealth and Empire ... composed of so many races, dwelling in so many climes'. His voice was grave. 'We have survived the greatest upheaval in human history,' he said. 'We cannot expect a world so grievously wounded to recover quickly.' And paraphrasing blind old Zacharias as he prophesied 'Blessed be the Lord God of Israel,' the King-Emperor also ventured a prophecy: 'In His own good time God will lead our feet into the way of peace.'

12

'An old, run-down country' 1947

It was a tragedy that the Jews and the British, whose common source of strength and wisdom is the Bible, should now be involved in such a bitter quarrel. Hardly had the King-Emperor uttered his prayer for peace, when the Jewish terrorists struck.

Although Irgun's destruction of the King David Hotel had outraged the feelings of Palestine Jews – one newspaper called it malignity and madness, another criminal and lunatic – the terrorists did not relent. They continued to concentrate on robbing banks and assassination. Their victims included Jewish policemen – 'collaborators'. One was shot dead as he queued for a bus; most were stealthily murdered. Soldiers and police, on duty and off, were sniped at or machine-gunned in the streets; others were blown to pieces in bomb-traps, set, as *The Times* said, with bloodthirsty and cunning skill.

The terrorists threatened to carry their war to Britain, to wreck buildings and assassinate leading men. When the King-Emperor opened Parliament on 12 November, Scotland Yard detectives, armed for the occasion, provided special protection for him. (His normal bodyguard was one unarmed, bowler-hatted detective.)*

While terrorism continued unabated, there continued also to pour into Palestine boat-loads of 'illegal' immigrants which the Royal Navy guided safely into port. When eight hundred illegal immigrants were shipwrecked in the Dodecanese, the RAF dropped food and clothing and, in a very hazardous sea, hundreds of marooned immigrants were taken off in the British destroyer *Chevron*. (A few weeks earlier terrorists had tried to sink her.)

Up to mid-August, the British had accepted immigrants

---

* The King-Emperor made no mention of Palestine in his speech from the throne. Nor, strangely enough, is there, in Sir John Wheeler-Bennett's eight-hundred-page biography of King George VI), a single allusion to the Palestine troubles.

far in excess of the monthly quota of 1,500. Then they decided to switch the excess to internment camps in Cyprus. The *Maapilim*, instead of gaining the Promised Land, found themselves once more behind the barbed wire of a concentration camp with – bitterest irony – German prisoners released from a neighbouring camp staring at them from outside. Zionist propaganda depicted these camps as no better than Nazi death camps. The difference was that foreign medical and social helpers were admitted; so was the press. Accusations varied, but *The Times*, with its habitual cool, reported that conditions were no worse than in a military camp: Nissen huts with twelve per hut, cookhouses, amusement halls, a clinic with ninety-six beds, with four hundred more, reserved for serious cases, at Nicosia hospitals. Schools and courses of instruction took care of the children, for whom there was also a special clinic. Hundreds of marriages took place, and during the first year three hundred babies were born. There was only one drawback: all the new-born were British subjects.

By the end of 1946, the Irgun and the Stern Gang had assassinated 373 people. Weizmann understood the young Jews' violence – but they were wrong. 'Jews', he told the Zionist Conference, 'came to Palestine to build, not to destroy.' To American Zionist leaders Rabbi Silver and Emmanuel Neumann, who had incited Palestine Jews to revolt, with 'the full political and moral support' of American Jewry, Weizmann retorted: 'Moral and political support is very little when you send other people to the barricades to face tanks and guns.' The new settlements in the Negev were better than a hundred speeches 'made in New York, while the proposed resistance is to be made in Tel Aviv or Jerusalem'.

'Demagogue!' shouted Neumann and a tense hush followed while the veteran, half-blind leader pondered his reply. Then, with intense emotion, he exclaimed: 'I – a demagogue! I who have borne all the ills and travails of this movement … In every house and stable in Nahalal, in every little workshop in Tel Aviv or Haifa, there is a drop of my blood ... If you think of bringing redemption nearer by un-Jewish methods ... then you commit idolatry ... Zion shall be redeemed by judgement – and not by any other means.'

Congress thereupon rose and sang *'Hatikvah'*, as their aged leader groped his way out of the hall – and off the Zionist stage for ever. By an overwhelming majority, a resolution was adopted 'opposing and condemning acts of murder and bloodshed of innocent people as a means of political struggle ... the terrorist acts of certain groups in Palestine ... distort the true character of the Yishuv ... and do not advance, but rather injure its just struggle'. Yet the savagery continued.

On the first day of 1947, an Irgun terrorist, Dov Gruner, was sentenced to death. He had been captured, with half his jaw shot away, during an attack on Ramat Gan police station. Dov had proved himself a good and brave man fighting during the war in the Jewish Brigade, for the British. Then he turned against them and became a terrorist – 'crazed', as Professor Brodetsky, leading British Jew, said of men like Dov, 'by the sufferings of their nearest and dearest and the obstacles put in the paths of their relatives to join them in Palestine'. However, added the professor, 'their acts are criminal and must be condemned'.

Dov Gruner, when he was condemned, expressed most vehemently the opposite conviction. It was the duty, he maintained, of every Jewish citizen to fight the British 'oppressors'. 'There is no force in this world', he cried, 'that can break the link between the people of Israel and their one and only country.' Dov Gruner was due to die on 29 January. He would be the first prisoner to be executed in Palestine since 1938, if the sentence was carried out, for despite all the terrorism and all the bloodshed, no executions had yet occurred.

Now a cry went up from both sides, British and Jewish (including that implacable critic of British Policy, Rabbi Silver) appealing to the Irgun to lay off terrorism. But the Irgun broadcast on 15 January, rejecting the appeal. They might have done otherwise had they known that Premier Attlee had already told Baldwin, head of the US Action Committee (who passed it on to Truman), that 'it was no longer a question of whether there should or should not be a Jewish State ... but when it should be created, what form it should take and what its boundaries should be'.

When, on 25 January, Dov Gruner's sentence was confirmed, the Irgun took preliminary steps to execute their threat of 'blood'. On 27 January, British businessman H. A. Collins was just finishing tea in his home when he had the rather strange experience, as he called it, of facing the automatic weapons of his three kidnappers. Judge Ralph Windham's experience was even stranger: he was hustled off, complete in wig and gown, from the seat of Justice in a Tel Aviv court.

Terrorist chief Begin always claimed that Irgun's prisoners were well treated. Even Collins admitted: 'I was treated – according to their ideas – extremely well.' That is, chloroform was poured all over him; he was struck on the head by a pick-axe handle; he was thrust into a sack, dragged across rough ground, then cast into a cellar where he remained, gagged, bound and blindfolded for twenty-four hours. Though his head wound was expertly stitched up, the chloroform burns prevented him from eating. They had, according to Mrs Collins, disastrous effects on his health and caused his death fourteen years later.

Appeals to the terrorists were now intensified. The Chief Rabbi, Jewish Agency Chairman Ben Gurion and its Political Department Chief, Mrs Golda Meyerson, added theirs. David Remez, chairman of Va'ad Leumi, the National Jewish Council, wanted to use force to protect Jewish citizens against the terrorists' methods of murder and extortion, of coercing teachers and pupils, of threatening police and truck drivers. High Commissioner Cunningham stayed Dov Gruner's execution, due on 29 January, but promised martial law if the Irgun's two hostages were not returned. In the Commons, Oliver

Stanley – with little regard for the hostages – attacked the Government for making terms with criminals. Winston Churchill asked, why stay in Palestine, which cost the British taxpayer £30 million a year and held down one hundred thousand soldiers? Clear out, he urged, and Britain would thus be divested of 'a responsibility which is covering us with blood and shame'.

Collins and Windham were released; the High Commissioner had scored a point. But when he demanded of the Va'ad Leumi and the Jewish Agency to back him in suppressing terrorism, to recognize 'the ordinary legal and moral duty to cooperate against crime which belongs to citizens ... of any civilized state', both refused.

The Burmese were aspiring as fervently to win back the Golden Land from the British as the Jews were to redeem the Promised Land. Burma, however, though devastated by war, was mercifully spared the communal and the refugee problems which so bloodied and embittered the Jewish and the Indian struggle for independence. Burma's way was not the way of violence, although she did carry, sheathed like a kind of side-arm, the weapon of violence. Thus discreetly armed – with the threat of rebellion should their efforts fail – Burma's leaders had been calmly and fruitfully negotiating in London, since 13 January, with His Majesty's Government.

Although Premier Attlee had greeted them with the assurance that there was real goodwill and sympathy for Burma and that it was for her alone to choose her future, the Burmese were at first very suspicious. 'They could not believe', Attlee said, 'that we were prepared to abide by the choice of the Burmese people.' As the talks progressed, Aung San and his colleagues – 'we are just a lot of raw lads', one of them confessed – gained confidence. On 27 January 1947, in the Cabinet Room at No. 10 Downing Street, which the men from tropical Rangoon found pleasantly warm after the freezing cold outside, Attlee and Aung San signed an agreement. Although Churchill later called it a dismal transaction, it assured smooth and rapid progress towards a free and independent Burma. After the signature came a note: U Saw was unable to associate himself 'with these conclusions'.

Apart from U Saw, whom he regarded as one who would 'smile and smile and be a villain', Attlee found the Burmese 'a nice lot of lads'. He had them down to lunch at Chequers.* It was a friendly affair but, as the Prime Minister said later: 'My wife little thought that she was entertaining a prospective murderer and his victims.'

Aung San returned to Rangoon in triumph. He told the Burmese 'the road to freedom is open'. Britain had agreed to a Burmese Interim Government pending the election of a Constituent Assembly, which would write Burma's new constitution. It would also decide whether Burma would stay in the Commonwealth-Empire or not. Either way, said Aung San, 'I want Burma to be a real and sincere friend of Great Britain.'

This was not exactly the sentiment motivating the Jewish freedom-fighters at this moment. Their authorities had rejected the High Commissioner's plea to back him against terrorism. And now the terrorists declared: 'We open the fight against the oppressors' – who themselves prepared for the worst.

Early in February 1947, the Palestine Government announced 'Operation Polly'. Nine-year-old Michael Blaze, back for lunch from Jerusalem's English school, asked his mother, Nora: 'What does evacuation mean?' She, 'in trepidation', switched on the radio. All British women and children, came the dreaded announcement, were to leave immediately. Next day they were escorted out of Jerusalem, through streets lined with grinning, jeering Jews. 'We stuck up our chins and looked straight ahead,' said Nora Blaze.

The 'emigrants' were lodged temporarily in Sarafand Camp – at forty to a Nissen hut, their lot was much tougher than that of the Jewish immigrants interned in Cyprus. Then the train took them off to Egypt. Near

* The Prime Minister's official country residence.

Gaza, Arab children flung stones at the windows. 'Nobody loved us any more,' reflected Nora Blaze sadly. A missionary in the carriage tried to console her: it was all prophesied in the Bible, he said, and read from the 114th Psalm that 'when Israel went out of Egypt ... Judah was his sanctuary ... The sea saw it and fled: Jordan was driven back.' But, added this aspiring prophet, in the fullness of time 'a great power from the north' would take Palestine from the Jews.

For over a month, the British families lived in a disused army camp at Maadi, near Cairo – a sandy slum in comparison to the Cyprus camps where those other unfortunates, the *Maapilim*, were interned. At Maadi, the British mothers and their children shuffled across what seemed like miles of sand to the canteen – or the latrines. At night the sweeping searchlights would point the way, hover politely, then light the way back. The canteen staff, German prisoners of war, were unsympathetic. 'It serves you right, you should have let us finish the job,' they told the British women. 'We were shocked into silence,' said Nora Blaze, with the awful thought that her Jewish friends in Palestine would have gone to the gas chambers had these men of Rommel's Afrika Korps not been defeated. But all that belonged to the past, as did the sweet influences of Palestine life, the cyclamen on the hillsides, the sky as blue as larkspurs, the clean, flower-scented air. The Rose of Sharon was budding in Nora Blaze's Jerusalem garden as she and Michael sailed slowly up the Mersey towards Liverpool, under a leaden sky, to the rigours of rationing and fuel shortages, to the chilly gloom of an English winter.

The British army and officials left behind now withdrew into security zones – government ghettoes, as Menachem Begin contemptuously called them, but more frivolously known in the Yishuv as 'Bevingrads'. Amram Darai, convicted terrorist, told his British captors: 'You have turned the country into a gaol and now have to lock yourselves up inside it.'

Humiliating – and boring – as the situation was for the

'oppressors', they occasionally managed to get a laugh from it. When S. H. Shaw, government geologist, after parting from his family, returned to his empty home behind the barbed wire, he switched on the radio, to hear the strains of 'Don't fence me in'. Raymond Knight of the RAF, deep in thought as he walked past a police post, tripped over some barbed wire to finish up at the feet of a sentry, gazing down the barrel of a Sten gun. 'Pass friend,' said the sentry. 'No terrorist would have sworn as you did.' But many were the soldiers and police who thought, as one of them said, 'that our job was tragic and useless, that we were doing somebody else's dirty work'. Some felt like the Tommy who wrote home: 'Dear Mum, I am in Bethlehem where Christ was born, but I wish to Christ I was in Wigan where I was born.'

The *Maapilim*, the 'illegal' immigrants, kept up their heroic assault in their rickety, leaky ships. One truck-load of 'illegals' attempting to get inland was held up by a solitary British police constable, John Symondson. He was eighteen. He covered the escort of three Haganah men with his Tommy-gun and took their weapons. 'They were scared,' said Symondson – and so was he. 'I was in a mess; I had three healthy men more than a mile from help with night falling.' He also had thirty 'illegals' sitting in the truck, in utter silence – the total silence was uncanny. 'All wrong-doers', said Symondson, 'could wring your heart with their tales of concentration camps.' But this time the proof was there. The 'unbelievably pathetic' *Maapilim* showed him the ghastly tattooed marks on their arms. Though, as a police constable, he felt a strong sense of duty, he knew instinctively that he must let them go. He showed them a route across the hills which would avoid the next police post. The immigrant problem, thought the youthful police constable, was difficult to come to terms with. Political theory was one thing, meeting the 'illegals' face to face another. He could not bring himself 'to carry on the Nazis' work'.

Ernest Bevin was at this time trying – vainly – to finish off the Palestine problem. The London talks had been resumed on 27 January. To add to his difficulties, Bevin, exhausted and over-burdened ('everyone is kicking us around' he had recently told Wavell), had heard that very day from the Egyptians that they had decided to abandon the talks with Britain about the future of the 1936 Treaty. The main trouble was the Sudan. Egypt wanted it; Britain refused to sign it away, with its hopes of independence, to Egypt. So Egypt decided to put her claim to the UN.

The Jews, meanwhile, had refused to show up at the London talks. Instead, they held informal meetings with Bevin, while the Arab team, now under Mufti Haj Amin's remote but personal control, met formally, as they had done in 1939, in St James's Palace. Their case was similarly formal: since 1918 Palestine's Jewish population had increased, through immigration – legal and illegal – from seven to thirty-three per cent, Jewish land purchases from one to thirty per cent. The Jews' modest claim for a spiritual home had been inflated to one for a Jewish state, which they were trying to achieve by terrorism. A Jewish state, said the Arabs, would mean a running sore, a source of permanent trouble in the Middle East. The sons of the prophet did not err in their soothsaying.

Bevin, and the new pro-Zionist colonial secretary, Creech-Jones, talked with the Jews, led by Ben Gurion, in a room in the Colonial Office. The atmosphere was depressing; power cuts left them conversing darkly by candlelight and the massive, slouching Bevin, his heart failing, had to take a stimulant, amyl nitrate, and be carried in a sedan chair. He seemed to Dr Abba Ebban 'to symbolize the policy of a tired nation, weary of responsibilities beyond its power'.

On 18 February, after explaining to the House of Commons that His Majesty's Government had no power to award Palestine either to the Jews or to the Arabs, or to partition it, Bevin concluded: 'The only course open to us is to submit the problem to the judgement of the United Nations.' Later, Premier Attlee, in more relaxed fashion, explained: 'It was no good our holding the baby any longer with everybody gunning for us. The only thing was to pass the problem to the UN and agree to do what they said.'

The day before Bevin presented his conclusions to Parliament, the King-Emperor had arrived in Cape Town on an official visit. But neither the summer sunshine, nor the majestic back-drop of Table Mountain, straight and solid above the lovely sweep of Table Bay, nor the immense crowd's rousing welcome, could distract him more than momentarily from the leaden, depressing cares of state. With Britain at the nadir of her fortunes, he had telegraphed, on the eve of his arrival, to his prime minister, expressing 'the sympathy of the King and Queen with the people in their hardships' – which were as grim as any they had endured during the war.

A chronic coal shortage had thrown nearly two millions out of work in four days. The Austin car factory had closed down, sacking 15,000; 245 cotton firms stopped production; 2,000 dockers struck in London docks. Drastic electricity cuts left domestic users without current for five hours a day. Emmanuel Shinwell, Minister of Fuel and Power, declared that complete disaster was possible within ten days. The Prime Minister warned the nation of an 'emergency of the utmost gravity'. And Anthony Eden, Churchill's right arm, declared that this was Britain's greatest industrial crisis for twenty years – an opinion which the London correspondent of the *New York Times* underlined. Britain, he said, was an old, rundown country. Exactly fifty years earlier, his newspaper had believed that Britain seemed 'plainly destined to dominate this planet'.

The coldest winter for years was paralysing Britain in its icy grip. Gales and fog, ice and snow, slowed or stopped movements of vital coal; roads were blocked, railway points frozen solid, trains buried deep in snow. True, winter sports were in full swing on Hampstead Heath; excellent skating could be had on the Norfolk Broads; and even *The Times* consoled itself that the

Continent was no longer isolated: the French coast, it reported, was visible for the first time in five weeks. But the day that the King-Emperor, in the tropical uniform of Admiral of the Fleet, set foot on South African soil, most Britons were shivering in 10°C below zero. Two and a half millions of them were now out of work. The King-Emperor wrote to his mother, Queen Mary: 'I am very worried over the extra privations which all of you at home are having to put up with in that ghastly cold weather ... I wish I was with you.'

Other anxieties weighed on the King-Emperor. There was the failure of his Foreign Secretary to solve the burning problem of Palestine; then, his 'world-wide family' was beginning to break up. Both India and Burma (which accounted, in population, for more than two thirds of it) had declared their intention of becoming independent republics – and how could a republic have a king? In South Africa itself there were strong republican feelings among Afrikaners, descendants of the Boers who had fought with such spirit against Empress Victoria's soldiers. The very day of the King-Emperor's arrival, Dr François Malan, inveterate republican and now leader of His Majesty's Opposition in South Africa's Parliament, snubbed the King of South Africa by absenting himself from the presentation of loyal addresses. But the Doctor and his republicans were there when the King of South Africa, for the first time in the country's history, opened Parliament. The King-Emperor was a stickler for ceremonial, but he detested it stiff and starchy. Ease and dignity were his criterion. Playing on the home ground, however, was one thing, playing away was another. The local officials could not always be depended upon to achieve the desired effect. They were sometimes over-anxious, under-rehearsed and did not know the ropes. This was the background to a fleeting crisis as the King and Queen of South Africa left the Parliament building. They were not the first to emerge. I was.

Before me, the red carpet stretched away down a long flight of stone steps lined with rigid, silent soldiers and,

beyond them, a vast, multicoloured crowd. It was vital
to maintain my distance of some three yards ahead of
the King and Queen, otherwise I should find myself des-
cending the steps alone. Without a rear mirror it was
going to be difficult. I advanced stiffly a few paces. Suddenly, the band struck up an air which I did not immediately recognize as *'Die Stem'*, the South African anthem.
Above the thump of drums and blast of trumpets, I
heard the King-Emperor shouting: 'For God's sake, stop!'
I froze to a standstill, but the anthem is a long one and,
as it ended, the royal patience began to run out. 'Go on,
for God's sake!' I heard King George vi shout again.
A few paces forward, then another order, 'Stop', and a few
seconds later, 'Go on'. Jerkily, it seemed, we at last reached
the steps; from then on the let-down went normally. The
contretemps, though nerve-racking, probably went unnoticed. To one seasoned observer,* the solemn proceedings seemed to link up across the oceans and the
centuries with the far-away English Model Parliament of
1295.

Back in the Mother of Parliaments, Bevin, on 25 February, reviewed with some bitterness the failure of his Palestine policy. As he had previously admitted, the mandate
was unworkable, the obligations undertaken by Britain
to both sides were irreconcilable. The mandate contained
contradictory promises: it provided for thousands of
Jewish immigrants while saying that they were not to
disturb 'the people in possession', the Arabs. All along
he had tried to obtain Arab goodwill. Then, he said,
after a meeting with the Jews: 'There was a feeling ...
that I had the right approach at last.' But – and he felt
intensely about it – 'the whole thing was spoilt' by being
dragged into the arena of American domestic politics,
where Democrat Truman and Republican Dewey were
vying for the Jewish vote. 'In international affairs,' complained the British Foreign Secretary, internationally re-

* Dermot Morrah, in *The Royal Family in South Africa* (London, 1947).

nowned for his firm, straight dealing, 'I cannot settle things if my problem is made the subject of local elections.' Palestine, he was convinced, must have independence, 'the mandatory power could not go on for ever'. He had therefore asked UNO to recommend a solution. On 4 March, Britain sent an urgent note requesting UNO to set up a special committee on Palestine – UNSCOP. Its first meeting was set for 28 April. The last phase in the fight for a Jewish state was imminent.

For India, too, there had just begun the momentous final chapter. On 20 February, the day before the King of South Africa opened Parliament in Cape Town, his British prime minister, Attlee, told Parliament that it was His Majesty's Government's 'definite intention to ... effect the transference of power into Indian hands by a date not later than June 1948'. Viceroy Wavell, the Premier said (untruthfully), had asked to resign. Mountbatten would replace him.

In the debate which followed in the Commons, Sir Stafford Cripps, author of two unsuccessful attempts to hand back India to the Indians, upheld the Government's dramatic move. The British, he said, in their long association with India, had done much to inspire Indians to go forward to the inevitable stage of self-government. The gradual grant of extended powers to Indians had encouraged them to ask for more: *'l'appetit vient en mangeant'* – 'appetite comes with eating'. Winston Churchill passionately denounced the handover; the brief time-limit would not be used to melt Hindu and Muslim hearts, but to prepare for civil war. He spoke of melancholy transactions which would 'darken, aye redden, the coming years'. Contrasting 'little Palestine' with 'mighty India', he said that two bottles of medicine had been sent to the wrong patients; Palestine's medicine was four times stronger (in troops) than India's. With grief he watched 'the clattering down of the British Empire with all its glories', a calamity which bore 'the taint and smear of shame'. Premier Attlee, unperturbed by the great Churchill's imperial oratory, replied that Churchill was fifty years out of date. 'We have done a great work in India,' he claimed. It was time that Indians shouldered their own responsibilities. Mountbatten's mission was one of fulfilment, not betrayal.

Viceroy Mountbatten reached Delhi on 23 March. During a heart-to-heart talk with ex-Viceroy Wavell, he declared his intention of writing that very day to Gandhi and Jinnah. 'One more viceroy', Wavell commented sceptically, 'who hopes to reconcile these intractable personalities.' A few days later the ex-Viceroy, recalling his politician-friend 'Rab' Butler's words 'Politics is a dirty business', wrote *finis* to his viceroyalty: 'I am glad I have finished with politics.'

Mountbatten found India in a most unsettled state. Muslim squatters in Assam, from across the Bengal border, were constantly clashing with the police; a police mutiny in Bihar had led to further bloodshed in that already violence-ridden province: communal violence was erupting in the North-West Frontier Province and in Bombay, Calcutta and even in Delhi itself. Worst of all, the Punjab was aflame. That province so beloved of the British Raj (from which it recruited its finest soldiers) had seen, during March, its great cities sullied with the stench of blood and burning: Lahore and Amritsar, Multan, Rawalpindi and Jullundur – nostalgic-sounding names to generations of British sahibs.

About fifteen miles from Jullundur there lived, in a tiny village, Khanpur Dhadah, a seventeen-year old Hindu boy, Kanda. On 8 March, he watched aghast as the Lahore train stood at No. 1 platform at Jullundur Station. 'Out came the few lucky ones, sickened, unshaven and unwashed, with tales of woe on their lips.' Some had lost their wives, others their young daughters, seized by burly, lusting Muslims. Another train pulled in, full – of dead. Kanda beheld a sight so ghastly that he would never forget it: an old man, bearded and in tattered clothes, moaning as he dragged a hand-cart in which lay the dismembered body of his own son. Kanda was a scout and did his 'sincere bit' of rescue work. One day he decided to visit his family – normally a one and a half hour run on his bicycle (nicknamed 'Chalo' – 'Let's go!'). But this time, for safety, he took the bus, whose passengers were a mixture of Hindus, Sikhs and Muslims. Near Khurla Kingra they were held up by a mob of two hundred Muslims. Kanda felt really terrified – he was 'attuned to the Almighty', expecting to die. Two Muslim passengers, Bismilla Khan and Attar Khan, reassured the Hindus, whom they would protect, they said, with their lives. Luckily the mob, mostly sturdy Muslim youths, were persuaded to let the bus go.

Into Kanda's village there poured a stream of Hindu refugees, with unspeakable tales of Muslim brutality. They told of infants who had been snatched from their mothers, hurled into the air, then caught on the spears of the mob. The feet of children were hacked off – then, with the shoes still on, handed back to their parents. The mob, as Kanda put it, 'forced the ladies nude, took intercourse with them and sometimes severed the top of their breasts'.

Nehru, visiting the Punjab, admitted that he had seen behaviour by human beings which would degrade a brute and pleaded: 'Let people struggle for their political aim ... as human beings, with a measure of dignity.'

The new Viceroy, too, had heard stories of unimaginable sadism, of families roped together, drenched with oil and burnt alive – British subjects, members of the world-wide family of his cousin, the King-Emperor, who had entrusted him with their protection. A week after his arrival, the Viceroy wrote to the King-Emperor: 'The scene here is one of unrelieved gloom ... I can see little common ground on which to build any agreed solution for the future of India ... Unless I act quickly I may well find a civil war on my hands.'

Mountbatten did act quickly. No sooner was the letter written than he got down to talks with Gandhi, Nehru and Jinnah.

*   *   *

By this time the King-Emperor had trekked across South Africa to Pretoria, the administrative capital. He had come most of the way in his splendid, air-conditioned White Train. Out of it he would step, with the Queen and the princesses, in the cool of the morning to embark on his arduous day's schedule; in the evening he would climb back into the train to relax, dine with his entourage and sleep. For thirty-five nights he was railborne, either speeding through the night or drawn up in a special siding. As the White Train glided across the veldt, or serpentined through rugged mountain ranges, the events of his great-grandmother's reign as Empress often caught up with him. On the way over the Outeniqua Range, a gnarled old Boer, Henry Dreyer, galloped alongside the train until, at Power, it stopped. Breathless, Dreyer explained to the King-Emperor that, although he had fought against Victoria, now that he had seen the King of South Africa in the flesh, he was through with being a republican.

The royal couple were hailed in the toughest republican strongholds, like Bloemfontein, Stellenbosch and Paarl. I was with the King at Paarl when, tanned and bareheaded, his profile as fine as if etched on a postage stamp, he received a stiffly spoken but loyal address. In the middle of it a sudden gust of wind stirred the branches of oak trees overhanging the royal daïs and sent a shower of acorns bouncing off the King's bare head and the Queen's hat while royalists, led by the Royal Family, and republicans dissolved into fits of laughter.

The White Train, as it crossed the veldt, slowed down at wayside halts where Africans, who had waited for the King all day, chanted their haunting songs in the limpid evening air. Sometimes the train stopped and the King and Queen and their daughters got out on the platform. Wearing relaxed clothes like the rest of us, they were not always recognized. At one such halt a South African police officer was overheard explaining to a group of piccaninnies: 'That is Mr King and next Mrs King; then behind them, Princess Elizabeth King and Princess

Margaret King.'

The King came to Grahamstown. There for the first time the descendant of the Great White Queen heard the native greeting 'A Sozizwe!' – 'Father of Nations!' He was in Basutoland for the anniversary of the day when the great chief Moshesh had placed his newly founded nation under Victoria's protection. It was now her great-grandson's turn to thank the Basutos for coming 'to my assistance when I was beset by many and powerful enemies'.

As the King of South Africa drove into Ladysmith, his South African premier, Jan Smuts, sat beside him. The old Boer leader pointed to the surrounding hills where, only forty-seven years before, his artillery had shelled the Queen-Empress's besieged garrison.

In Zululand where, at Isandhlwana, a thousand of Victoria's soldiers had been slain in half an hour by Chief Cetewayo's impis, an aged warrior who had taken part in that carnage now acclaimed the Great White King, as 'the lion whose roaring silences the rest of creation'.

In Swaziland, a thousand warriors, their gleaming black bodies girdled with leopard-skins, their heads adorned with swaying black feathers, assegais held aloft, surged towards the Great White King in 'the dance of the impenetrable mystery'. Here, on the African high veldt, Victoria's one-time recalcitrant children had settled contentedly within the circle of the world-wide family that she had founded.

So, it seemed, had her erstwhile 'presumptuous little foes', the Boers. At Pretoria, a thousand Outstryders, veteran Boers, now saluted the ruling scion of the British Imperial Family. Some of those fine old bronzed, wrinkled men were so moved that they knelt, tears streaming, and kissed the hand of the King of South Africa.

Less gracious, but warm and massive, was the affection shown by the dense black throng of Africans who lined the route as the King, the Queen and the princesses, in their sleek open Daimler, drove through the mining towns of the Rand. I was up front next to the chauffeur, a pink-faced, sandy-haired South African new to the job of driving royalty.

For all in that Daimler it was to be a rough ride. Exhausted by his travels and the cares of state, the King's nerves were on edge. He immediately took over the driving, from the back seat, uttering a series of cross and contradictory orders. Before long the well-intentioned chauffeur was badly rattled. The Queen was trying to calm the King; the princesses were trying to make light of things, which got worse and worse until I thought to myself 'If we go on like this there's going to be an accident.'

Then it happened – not an accident, but something which at that moment looked far more sinister. A black man, wiry and of medium build, shot out of the swarm of sweating, shouting Africans and sprinted with terrifying speed and purpose towards the royal Daimler. He clutched something in one hand and before the police could stop him had with the other grabbed hold of the car so tightly that the knuckles of his black hand showed white. While the Queen landed several deft blows on the man with her parasol, the King shouted to the chauffeur to accelerate. The assailant loosed his grip and I saw him fall into the road, where he was seized by the police and dragged away.

When the King returned to Government House, Pretoria, where he was staying, a message from the police awaited him. It said that the mysterious assailant was harmless. The object in his hand was a 10/- (ten shilling) note; he wanted to give it to Princess Elizabeth as a present for her twenty-first birthday, due in a few days. The King told me 'Find out how he is. I hope he was not too badly hurt.' Then he continued 'I am sorry about today. I was very tired.'

There was something so pathetic about the way he said it that I felt like putting my arm around the King-Emperor and saying 'Don't worry. It's O.K. Forget it.' Instead I just mumbled respectfully 'Thank you, Sir.'

These loyal feelings, and his own anxious feelings for

his people in frozen, far-off Britain, now broke like converging waves on the King-Emperor, overwhelming him
with emotion. 'Lord, our Heavenly Father', he had prayed
together with South Africans during a service of the austere Dutch Reformed Church, 'look down with com-
passion ... upon our brethren in Britain and lighten the
burden of these rigorous days.'

His British prime minister, Attlee, had rallied the
nation. 'Before the war we were rich,' he told them. 'We
owned money and railways and so forth abroad ... We
sold these in order to help win the war.' Some people
abroad were 'suggesting that the day of this country is
over'. Attlee answered them: 'The British people are
never daunted by their difficulties' – which at this
moment were dramatic.

Winter had renewed its onslaught. Gales, blizzards,
frost and floods had paralysed industry, disjointed public
life and produced an agricultural crisis unparalleled in
British history. The Thames had burst its banks; it was
three miles wide at Chertsey; Reading had its worst flood
disaster for three hundred years; the fertile Fenlands were
flooded. In the north, snow-drifts had created the biggest
road transport hold-up in history, and passengers in a
Glasgow train were marooned for five days in the snow.

Such bad tidings of his own people left the King-
Emperor torn between his duty towards them and his
South African people. The tour, as the Queen-Empress
Elizabeth wrote, was 'doubly hard for Bertie, who feels
he should be at home'.

The tour, nevertheless, continued. In Pretoria, the
King-Emperor called President Kruger, Queen Victoria's
enemy, 'that great patriot'. His Majesty paid homage at
Cecil Rhodes's lonely grave among the huge granite
boulders of the Matopo Hills, and told Rhodesians
'Southern Rhodesia has a great future ...', little dreaming that this future would evolve along the lines of the
rebellious American colonies of his ancestor, George III.

The Paramount Chief of the Barotse, a water people
dwelling beside the Zambezi, arrived in the royal barge,

paddled by a crew of cabinet ministers. Clumsy paddling, he explained, could result in a minister being thrown overboard to the crocodiles. 'That gives me ideas,' mused King George, who told his Barotse liegeman: 'I am pleased to meet you near the place where your father first accepted the protection of Queen Victoria.' To the Mashonas and Matabeles, not long ago the terrorized vassals of the great chief Mzilikatzi, 'Pathway of Blood', and of Lobengula, to whose kraal Rhodes had ridden alone and unarmed, the Great White King now said: 'We take with us very happy memories of ... this pleasant land.' In Bechuanaland, Chief Batoen glittered in the scarlet Dragoon Guards uniform presented to his grandfather by Queen Victoria; Chief Tshekedi rivalled him in glory, attired in Royal Horse Guards blue which the bountiful Empress had bestowed upon his father, Khama. Her patronage had paid off handsomely; her great-grandson now thanked the chiefs for Bechuanaland's 'magnificent response during the recent times of great danger to our Empire'.

Back in Cape Town, the time had come to say '*Tot Seins*'.* There were moving speeches, the first of which came, on her twenty-first birthday, from Princess Elizabeth, heir to the Imperial Crown, which she would never inherit. Her simple, sincere dedication stirred all hearts: 'I declare that my whole life ... shall be devoted to ... the service of our great Imperial Commonwealth to which we all belong.' It was a declaration above all of faith in the future. For, as things stood, four hundred million Indians and seventeen million Burmese had, through their leaders, already declared their intention, as independent republics, of no longer belonging. Ireland belonged only reluctantly, and Palestine continued to struggle desperately not to belong.

The King-Emperor wrote to Smuts that he felt his visit had been worthwhile if it had altered the conception of monarchy of some South Africans. There was no doubt that it had; the victory of the shy King, generously

* Afrikaans for 'farewell'.

aided by the Queen, over doubting, sometimes hostile South African hearts, was complete. But it did not last.

Certainly South Africa and Rhodesia proved to be lands where past imperial nightmares had melted in the sunshine of kindly reminiscence and the past glory of imperial Victoriana. But they would prove, too, to be lands where future imperial dreams were soon to be shattered.

13

Mountbatten Zindabad!

The warm imperial glow left by the South African tour was being fast dissipated elsewhere in the Imperial Commonwealth. India, for one thing, was on the verge of civil war. It was vital that Viceroy Mountbatten should act quickly. To his pressing invitation Gandhi replied: 'I dare not resist your kind call'; and, breaking off his pilgrimage through ravaged Bihar, he presented himself, as ever in loincloth and sandals, at Viceroy's House on the last day of March. Mountbatten, unlike Wavell, was deeply impressed by Gandhi, both as saint and politician. Very wisely, however, he decided not to negotiate directly with the Mahatma as everyone before him had done.

After the first talk, when they chatted, relaxed, about old times, Mountbatten felt that 'he had progressed along the path of friendship'. Next day, Gandhi came up unexpectedly with his own solution of the Indian problem: he wanted Jinnah to head a new Interim Government. Surprised, Mountbatten asked how Jinnah would react, and Gandhi replied: 'Doubtless he will say: "There he goes again, that cunning old Gandhi", but in fact I am quite sincere.' Congress, however, did not agree with Gandhi's plan, and that was the end of it.

Gandhi had another plan. Would the Viceroy, he asked the astounded Mountbatten, be prepared to devote his life, as Charlie Andrews, missionary, pacifist and Gandhi's 'blood brother', had done, to the Indian cause – not as Viceroy, but as Head of an Indian State, paid for by the Government? Discreetly, the dashing Admiral-Viceroy replied that he hoped Gandhi would not insist.

Gandhi, apostle of non-violence, said another strange thing to the Viceroy: he would prefer to see a united India involved in a blood-bath rather than accept partition. It was an extraordinary statement: Gandhi, after all he had seen of the devastation and misery left by the blood-baths of Calcutta, Noakhali and Bihar, was still ready for more. His disciple Nehru was scathing about the Mahatma's on-the-spot attempts to soothe communal strife, instead of going to the root of the trouble. Yet Nehru adulated his master: 'This little man ... is a colossus before whom others ... are small of stature. In this world of uttermost violence ... in an acquisitive society madly searching ... for new luxuries, he takes to his loincloth and his mud hut.'

Mountbatten was struck by Nehru's sincerity. Together they discussed the problem of partitioning Bengal and the Punjab. They talked about Jinnah. Nehru thought him a very remarkable man and admitted the success of his policy; the Viceroy himself was convinced that Jinnah was the key to the whole situation. At their first meeting, the Muslim leader was in a most frigid, haughty and disdainful frame of mind. The Viceroy used all his persuasion to try and get Jinnah to accept the Cabinet Mission's plan for an Indian Union, but to no avail, Jinnah refused to be deflected from his aim of creating a Muslim state. He distrusted Congress, as did his right-hand man, Liaquat Ali Khan, who told the Viceroy that, if the Muslim League were awarded only the Sind Desert, it would be better than to continue in bondage to the Congress. Jinnah was equally emphatic. He insisted that only a 'surgical operation' could do the trick; India and the Indian Army must be cut in half, so that he could create Pakistan out of the half which belonged to the Muslims.

Jinnah wanted a 'viable' Pakistan, not what he had once called a 'moth-eaten' one, with only half of Bengal and of the Punjab. He pleaded with the Viceroy to preserve the unity of these two provinces, even at the expense of their remaining independent. The two men argued back and forth, Mountbatten insisting that, if partition were applied to the rest of India, it must in all logic be applied to Bengal and the Punjab.* 'If you persist in chasing me with your ruthless logic,' protested the visionary Muslim leader, 'we shall get nowhere.' The

* Both with a slight Muslim majority.

Viceroy for his part was convinced that Jinnah had no notion of what it needed to establish a new state.

For a fleeting moment there did seem to be a chance of preserving Bengal as an independent unity. But when the Viceroy asked Bengal's Governor, Sir Frederick Burrows, what the outlook was, he was told that Bengal was like a barrel of gunpowder which might blow up at any moment.

Governor Jenkins of the Punjab was even more explicit; he would need, he said, sixty thousand men to prevent civil war. The Sikhs, under their bearded, loquacious leader, Master Tara Singh, were talking of a state of their own, *Sikhistan*; they had sworn to avenge the recent Muslim outrages and to fight to the last man were they left under Muslim domination. When warned by the Sikh Maharaja of Patiala that the Sikhs were likely to fight, the Viceroy replied sternly: 'If they do start a war, Maharajah Sahib, it will be against the entire might of India and will be ruthlessly put down.' The Maharaja appeared shaken. He might have been less so had he realized that, in the King-Emperor's own words, 'there were not enough troops to keep order'.

The North-West Frontier Province, too, was in ferment – 'the bastard situation', General Ismay, Mountbatten's chief of staff, called it: ninety-seven per cent Muslims with a Congress ministry. During a visit to Peshawar, the Viceroy found one hundred thousand excited demonstrators gathered in Cunningham Park, ready to march on Government House. He immediately forestalled the marchers and decided to march on them. From a nearby railway embankment, he and the Vicereine – both in bush-shirts – faced the gesticulating multitude. Instantly its ugly mood was transformed. Cries of '*Pakistan Zindabad*' changed to 'Mountbatten *Zindabad*' '(Long live Mountbatten!'). Alan Campbell-Johnson, the Viceroy's press-attaché, remarked of the viceregal couple: 'The impact of their friendly, confident personalities on that fanatical assembly had to be seen to be believed.'

Mountbatten was convinced that the only way to clear

the air of communal strife was to announce an acceptable plan for the transfer of power. In the meantime, he figured, Gandhi and Jinnah could help; he induced them, after the usual bickerings, to sign a joint appeal: 'We deeply deplore the recent acts ... that have brought the utmost disgrace on the fair name of India ... We denounce for all time the use of force to achieve political ends ... we call upon all communities of India ... to refrain from acts of violence.' The apostle of non-violence was as one crying in the wilderness.

Back in his sombre, teak-lined study in Delhi, the Viceroy patiently continued his talks with Indian leaders. In a brush with Patel, he told the Congress strong-man: 'They tell me you are a tough guy. Well, so am I.' Patel complained that the Muslim ministers of the coalition cabinet were saboteurs and should be sacked. Other leaders spoke their minds, if less forcibly. Finally Congress president Acharya Kripalani told the Viceroy: 'We shall let the Muslim League have their Pakistan.' He begged him, though, to temper logic with mercy in the partition of Bengal and the Punjab.

During the second half of April, Mountbatten's plan for the transfer of power took shape. Its first principle was that the provinces would have the right to determine their own future; the Viceroy was insistent that the decision on partition should rest on the shoulders of the Indian people, thus avoiding the accusation that the British had divided the country. On 2 May, General Ismay flew with the Plan to London, where the Cabinet set to, adding the finishing touches.

Meanwhile Viceroy Mountbatten, who had been averaging eighteen hours' work a day, had gone to Simla hoping – vainly as it turned out – for a rest. Pandit Nehru was invited as house-guest.

A few days later, the British Cabinet's redrafted, but essentially unaltered, version of the Mountbatten Plan was telegraphed from London. The Viceroy locked it up in his safe. The afternoon of Sunday the 10th found him and his house-party strolling in the hills. Nehru was in great form, playing with the children and demonstrating how to save energy by walking uphill backwards. Not a cloud darkened the political horizon.

That evening, after dinner, the Viceroy invited Nehru to his study for a night-cap. As they talked, Mountbatten had a sudden hunch – they had happened before to him as 'Supremo' and were always right. He got up, unlocked his safe, took out the Plan and said to Nehru: 'Take it up to bed with you and read it.' Next morning, Mountbatten received what he called a bombshell of the first order from Nehru. The Plan, wrote Nehru, had produced a devastating effect on him. The Cabinet's redraft would leave India in a state of fragmentation and conflict. And he accused His Majesty's Government of functioning 'in an ivory tower ... isolated from the realities of India.'

The Viceroy sent immediately for his Reforms Commissioner, V. P. Menon – 'little Menon' as Wavell had affectionately called him, but a man of formidable intellect and understanding. Menon, who had previously told the Viceroy 'I do not like your plan a bit,' had been working on one of his own, whereby power would be transferred to two separate Commonwealth dominions, India and Pakistan. This would greatly speed up the transfer. In deference to India's republican susceptibilities, Menon envisaged dropping the terms 'King-Emperor' and 'Empire' but using the scheme envisaged in the 1935 Government of India Act.

Menon found the Viceroy in a state of near panic. What should he do now? asked Mountbatten and Menon told him: 'The best hope of getting agreement would be to follow the lines of my plan.' Congress would be attracted by an early demission of power; Jinnah, it seemed, was resigned (if reluctantly) to the partition of Bengal and the Punjab. Nehru, however, was leaving Simla on the evening train; the only hope of putting things right, insisted the Viceroy, was to get his approval, before he left, of a revised draft. Could Menon make it in time?

Never in his life had 'V.P.' drunk a whisky and soda

before sundown. Back in his hotel, he poured himself a
stiff one. He had, as he wrote later, only two or three hours
to prepare a new draft plan – on which the fate of four
hundred million Indians would depend. By 6 pm he had
a splitting headache, but the plan was finished. It was
almost snatched from him and rushed to the Viceroy,
who handed a copy to Nehru. Menon took four aspirins
and went to bed.

That evening he dined at Viceregal Lodge. Lady
Mountbatten, all smiles, greeted him with an affectionate kiss and whispered: 'He accepted it, V.P.' The Viceroy, Menon noticed, was once again in cracking form.
Without that hunch, he had told his press-officer,
Campbell-Johnson, a few hours earlier, 'Dickie Mountbatten would have been finished and could have packed
his bag.' And Campbell-Johnson noted in his diary:
'Mountbatten has had a shattering day.'

On 18 May, as reports of increasing communal violence
came pouring in from the Punjab, Mountbatten flew from
Delhi to explain the new plan to the Cabinet in London.
Before leaving, he had sounded out the Indian leaders.
Nehru gave his general acceptance to the plan. Jinnah still
held out against partition of Bengal and the Punjab.
But to the Viceroy, as he read and re-read Jinnah's comments, it became clear that he could assume that Jinnah
would eventually accept. Liaquat Ali Khan's attitude was
that the Muslim League would never agree, but would
have to bow to the inevitable. For the Sikhs, Baldev Singh
neither accepted nor rejected; he only hoped that if there
was to be partition it would allow the East Punjab to embrace the largest possible percentage of the Sikh population.

In London, where he stayed with the King-Emperor at
Buckingham Palace, the Viceroy had no difficulty in
getting the Cabinet to agree to his plan, and with it the
dominion status of the two new states, which would
ensure the smooth and rapid transfer of power on the
basis of the 1935 India Act, once so much maligned by
Attlee and Nehru. He even managed to persuade Win-

ston Churchill to help speed up the necessary legislation, for his opposition could have imposed a fatal delay.

In India, meanwhile, events were not helping to improve the already critical situation. The Punjab was smouldering into flames; blood flowed freely in Lahore, Amritsar and the district of Gurgaon. Jinnah demanded a corridor between east and west Pakistan, which Nehru qualified as fantastic and absurd. Jinnah, moreover, told the press in trenchant terms of his views on 'the new clamour' for partition by caste Hindus in Bengal and Sikhs in the Punjab. Partition would have disastrous results, he said; it was dangerous and reckless and 'if His Majesty's Government favour it ... it will be a grave error, dangerous immediately and far more so in the future'. Jinnah was dead against partition of Bengal and the Punjab, though he was more insistent than ever at over-all partition of the sub-continent.

Gandhi, too, had his say. 'It is not for the British cabinet to give us liberty. They can only get off our back.' All Britain had to do was to withdraw. If, on the other hand, British power was weak enough to submit to India's 'mad career of violence ... it will only have left a bloody legacy for which not only India but the whole world will blame Great Britain'. Considering Gandhi's strange predilection for Indian blood-baths and his advice to Mountbatten 'to take the risk of leaving India to chaos and anarchy' – the one thing that the British were trying scrupulously to avoid – it might be thought that the Mahatma, now nearing seventy-eight, was either gaga or behaving, as Wavell used to say, like a unscrupulous old hypocrite.

Viceroy Mountbatten returned to Delhi late on 30 May. Ismay, who accompanied him, said: 'A long flight with Mountbatten was an experience which I was careful not to repeat.' No idea of comfort ever entered the Viceroy's head. Speed was all that mattered. On 2 June, the Viceroy met the principal Indian leaders: Nehru, Patel and Kripalani on the Congress side; Jinnah, Liaquat Ali Khan and Abdur Rab Nishtar, for the Muslim League.

Baldev Singh represented the Sikhs. Numbers were kept to a minimum to ensure a friendly atmosphere and Ismay noticed that they greeted each other with unusual *bon-homie*. Yet the atmosphere was at first very strained. But Mountbatten made the running; the less the leaders talked the better. He remained undisputed master of the situation, which soon became more relaxed. He told the Indian leaders that of all the momentous meetings he had attended during the war, none had such an importance in world history as this one. What impressed him most since his arrival in India was the terrific sense of urgency; the sooner power was transferred the better. The Viceroy regretted that the Indians had not accepted the Cabinet Mission plan for an Indian Union; especially as the partition of the Punjab would mean dividing the Sikh people. But their leaders had repeatedly insisted that the Sikhs would prefer to live in a partitioned Punjab rather than in a province of Pakistan. Mountbatten asked the leaders for a formal reply by midnight.

Meanwhile, a distinguished visitor was waiting to see the Viceroy: Mahatma Gandhi. The Mahatma had recently been preaching at his prayer meetings against partition. 'Let it not be said', he declared, 'that Gandhi was a party to India's vivisection.' The apostle of non-violence even wanted to use force to impose the Cabinet Mission plan. But, he thought to himself as he waited to see the Viceroy: 'I am come to Delhi to fight a losing battle.' This was certainly not what the Viceroy thought, any more than Congress, who were apprehensive about his seeing Gandhi. So, frankly, was Mountbatten. He feared, to use a well-worn viceregal cliché, that Gandhi would throw a spanner in the works. But he had overlooked a Gandhi custom. To the Viceroy's intense relief, Gandhi, as he entered the room, was holding his finger to his lips. It was Gandhi's day of silence. While he scribbled a few notes on the back of old envelopes, the Viceroy was at leisure to explain that to enforce the Cabinet Mission's plan was hardly the way of non-violence; the present plan was the best way of trusting to the will of the people. Gandhi, though apparently mollified, scribbled back: 'We must meet again.'

By midnight, Congress president Kripalani and Baldev Singh had sent word accepting the plan, though with reservations. Jinnah, never eager to commit himself to paper, called back at Viceroy's House at 11 pm. He was hesitant, telling the Viceroy that the whole issue must first be submitted to 'his masters, the people'. Mountbatten asked, would Jinnah at least agree to the Prime Minister's announcing the plan's acceptance next day? To this Jinnah agreed to assent with a nod of his head when asked for his acceptance.

When the conference gathered again the following morning, Mountbatten felt more afraid than ever to let the leaders speak, so he spoke for them. (How right Attlee had been to choose a Viceroy who could out-talk an Indian, let alone six.) All three parties, the Viceroy realized, had grave objections to the plan, but it represented almost unanimous agreement. The date of transfer, he proposed (and all agreed), would be 15 August – in less than three months. It would mean that the Indian leaders would have to work day and night. So also would the British government, to get the legislation rushed through Parliament. The leaders all accepted the plan, Jinnah with the agreed nod of his head.

In the House of Commons that afternoon of 3 June, Prime Minister Attlee made the momentous announcement; the House's 'overheated atmosphere' was charged, *The Times* said, with a sharp sense of expectancy, proper to a great parliamentary occasion. The Plan, declared Attlee, for the transfer of power on a dominion status basis, left it to Indians to decide for themselves whether or not there should be partition of Bengal and the Punjab. Churchill (restrained, for once, on the subject of India) stated that he would not oppose the Bill; the man who had seen the Empire through its finest hour thought, hopefully, that, after all, 'the many nations and states of India may find their unity within the mysterious circle of the British Crown'. He wondered whether any better plan might be found for saving India from 'the blood-bath which may stand so near', but hoped that the present settlement 'may offer to India some prospect of escape from one of the most hideous calamities which has ever ravaged the vast expanse of Asia'.

More prosaically, Prime Minister Attlee, in a broadcast that evening, told Britons that the Plan had a two-fold purpose: to involve, if Bengal and Punjab were partitioned, as little loss and suffering as possible; secondly, to allow the British to hand over in an orderly manner. Thus the two leading British statesmen expressed their hopes – uncrowned ones as it would turn out.

At about the same moment (allowing for the time difference) that Attlee was speaking in the Commons, the Viceroy went to the microphone in Delhi. 'For more than a hundred years', he told the people of India, 'four hundred million of you have lived together and this country has been administered as a single entity ... To my great regret, it has been impossible to obtain agreement ... on ... any plan that would preserve the unity of India.' The present plan, the Viceroy admitted 'may not be perfect ... its success will depend on the spirit of goodwill ... May your decisions ... be carried out in the peaceful and friendly spirit of the Gandhi–Jinnah appeal.' More uncrowned hopes.

The Indian leaders followed the Viceroy; none seemed overjoyed at the prospect of independence. 'It is with no joy in my heart', said Nehru, 'that I commend these proposals to you ...' and he reminded Indians: 'There has been violence, shameful, degrading and revolting violence ...' It must stop, he insisted. 'Political ends are not to be achieved by methods of violence.' Jinnah confessed: 'We cannot say or feel that we are satisfied ...' He appealed for 'peace and harmony: we must galvanize and concentrate all our energies to see that the transfer of power is effected in a peaceful and orderly manner'. Baldev Singh, the Sikh leader, was understandably gloomy. 'We have closed a dreary chapter ... Our common quest for freedom need never have ... torn us asunder. We have let ourselves be rent apart.' The British plan did not please the Sikh community, but 'it is certainly something worthwhile'. Baldev Singh believed 'with all his heart that the divisions which ... keep us apart will not last long'. Yet more uncrowned hopes.

Meanwhile, fires raged in Amritsar, holy city of the Sikhs.

4 June marked the royal Viceroy's crowning glory. For two and a quarter hours the King-Emperor's cousin faced a barrage of questions fired by three hundred journalists. Mountbatten admitted: 'I was under violent cross-fire.' His answers were punctuated by un-viceregal, let alone un-regal, remarks such as 'I am the mechanic who keeps the car running, but I do not actually sit in the driver's seat ...' The Indians themselves were steering their destiny. Again, to a question on dominion status, the Viceroy snapped back: 'Let no one say "Look at these British. They have trapped us into dominion status."' India desired it; she was perfectly free to quit the Commonwealth if and when she liked. When Congress journalists, headed by Devadas Gandhi, son of the Mahatma, demanded that, if Hindustan (the future India) decided to quit, Pakistan should be forced to do so also, because of the 'potentialities of mischief' in having a Commonwealth state as neighbour, Mountbatten answered witheringly: 'Why are you asking me to say that people cannot do what they like, but must do what the majority wants? Is all this talk of independence a hollow mockery?'

Mountbatten had accomplished a *tour de force*. The *Statesman* called it 'a remarkable performance ... an extraordinary achievement of intellect and personality'. And from the pen of America's most celebrated political writer, Walter Lippmann, came a compliment which supported the King-Emperor's thinking on Britain's future role: 'Attlee and Mountbatten have done a service to all mankind by showing what statesmen can do, not with force and money but with lucidity, resolution and sincerity.'

Mountbatten's intellect and personality triumphed once again that day when Gandhi came back to see him – this

time without his finger to his lips. Gandhi was very
upset; he complained that his life's work for a united
India had been destroyed by the Mountbatten plan –
forgetting that he himself had spiked the Cabinet Mission plan for union. Mountbatten was soothing; he understood the Mahatma's feelings, but the present plan did
follow Gandhi's precepts: leaving the choice to India,
avoiding coercion and ensuring a rapid transfer. In fact,
concluded the Viceroy disarmingly, it should really be
called the Gandhi plan. Nehru and Patel later helped
to console Gandhi; and so between them they managed
to prevent the unimaginable chaos which would have
followed had Gandhi denounced the plan. Gandhi was
convinced. He declared: 'The British government is not
responsible for partition ... but if both of us, Hindus
and Muslims, cannot agree, then the Viceroy is left with
no choice.'

On 9 June, the All-India Muslim League Council met
in the ballroom on the first floor of Delhi's Imperial
Hotel to decide their verdict on the plan. Suddenly their
deliberations were rudely interrupted when a group of
Khaksars* rushed through the hotel gardens, brandishing
belchas (sharpened spades), jostling peaceful residents at
tea yelling 'Get Jinnah'. They were half-way up the stairs
to the ballroom when stopped by police. It was not the
first time† – nor the last – that mortal danger would
threaten Jinnah. When the commotion had died down,
the Muslim League Council passed a resolution; while
disagreeing with the partition of Bengal and the Punjab,
it authorized Jinnah (happily still alive) to accept the
British plan as a compromise.

The All-India Congress Committee met on the 14th and
resolved to accept the Plan. 'Geography, the mountains
and the sea fashioned India as she is,' said the resolution;
'... the AICC earnestly trusts that when present passions have subsided ... the false doctrine of two nations

---

* A fanatical Muslim group – anti-Muslim League – led by an
ex-under-graduate of Cambridge University

† A Khaksar tried to murder Jinnah in 1943.

in India will be discredited.' President Kripalani explained with feeling why Congress had accepted partition: 'If we go on like this, retaliating and heaping indignation on each other, we shall progressively reduce ourselves to a state of cannibalism.'

Passions, meanwhile, rather than subsiding, were mounting. Muslims and Hindus were feverishly preparing for what everyone called 'the civil war'. The ranks of private armies were swelling fast. The Rashtriya Swayam Sewak Sangh (RSSS), assault force of the fanatical Hindu Mahasabha, and the Muslim League National Guards (MLNG), rival champions of violence, were busy training with *lathi*, dagger, sword and gun; the syllabus included knife- and acid-throwing for good measure. Less militant, but powerful and well organized, was the Congress Seva Dal. In the north-west, the pro-Congress Red Shirts were led by Abdul Ghaffar Khan, the 'frontier Gandhi'. The Sikh S. A. Dal made ready to wreak vengeance on the Muslims in the Punjab. India's greatest city (and the Empire's second), Calcutta, was under curfew – a city of the dead, a garbage-strewn desert. Police and military ceaselessly patrolled its streets. 'We kept our ammunition boot heavily down on the two contending factions,' wrote army commander General Tuker. Upstream of the Ganges there filtered into Bihar State bands of Khaksars, with their sharpened shovels, bent on avenging their Muslim brothers. Around Gurgaon, on the Punjab border, a stone's throw from Delhi, the Meos, a primitive Muslim tribe, had risen against the Hindus, determined to fight for survival – or extinction. In the United Provinces, violent Hindu hordes from over the Punjab border were ravaging Muslim villages. On the night of 15 June they did considerable slaughter – a dark and bloody presage for the future.

14

'Avenge our blood!'

There now came, almost out of the blue, the news that Ceylon was to get Dominion status. It was as easy as that – without the curse of communalism. Ceylon, said one observer, exemplified the political ideals evolved in Britain to transcend race and creed. Some time later, Ceylonese prime minister Senanayake said proudly: 'We glory in the fact that this transformation has been effected without shedding one drop of blood.'

Burma, too, appeared initially to accede peacefully to power. Spurning violence, Burma had been keeping pace with India and Palestine along the road to independence. On 19 May, at a momentous meeting of the AFPFL in Rangoon's Jubilee Hall – despite its imperial connection the symbol of Burma's struggle for freedom – Aung San declared that Burma must have complete independence; monarchy in any form was out. It was the AFPFL's firm and solemn resolve to proclaim Burma as an independent Sovereign Republic.

On 10 June, the day that the Khaksars tried to murder Jinnah as he and the Muslim League agreed on the creation of Pakistan, Aung San, the youthful creator of modern Burma, opened its new Constituent Assembly. It was the day of days in Burma's history, said U Thein Han, poet and writer, whose job it was to put the English draft of the new constitution into flowing Burmese. 'It was a brave day,' he wrote, 'brightened by the promise of coming freedom.' Bogyoke Aung San wore national costume – pink *gaungbaung* (head scarf), a jacket of white silk and a pink *longyi*, holding a corner of it in his right hand as, with firm step, he headed the procession of Assembly members into the quadrangle of the Secretariat. At that moment the Resistance flag, red with a white star, was broken from the masthead; to every Burmese it was the symbol of freedom. Aung San bowed to the flag, then passed into the Assembly chamber.

It was a solemn occasion. At 11 am, the Assembly first exercised its powers by electing Thakin Mya as Speaker – a post he would all too soon leave vacant. In his address Thakin Mya rejoiced that Burma had at last reached the threshold of freedom after years of 'foreign rule, full of suffering and sorrow, trials and tribulations'. On 16 June, while terror reigned in Palestine and India shuddered with the horror of mass slayings, Aung San, in the peaceful atmosphere of the Assembly, moved a resolution to establish the Union of Burma as a republic. The constitution would guarantee justice, liberty and equality of status. Burma would thus 'resume her place in the family of nations'. The Assembly approved the resolution; Burma, since the tyrannical King Thibaw and his scheming wife Supayalat had bowed before the majesty of Victoria, had come a long way in a short time – sixty years.

What a contrast with the Holy Land, where the Jewish freedom-fighters, despite the UN's appeal to desist, still pursued their career of violence. The terrorist campaign had until recently an intelligible if perverse aim: to force Britain to change her policy. But it was meaningless now that Britain had put the baby squarely on the lap of the UN.

The terrorists now carried their war to Britain. It was a remote and personal war, conducted by means of a fiendish weapon, the letter-bomb. Invented many years earlier by a gifted but crazy Swedish scientist, Eckenberg, it had only been employed by him to settle certain private scores. Jewish terrorists now used it for the first time as a weapon of war. The first one arrived in London on 3 June. Others soon followed. Among the terrorists' selected targets were Sir Stafford Cripps (whose girl secretary narrowly escaped being blown to pieces), Food Minister John Strachey, Anthony Eden MP, and, naturally, the Yishuv's *bête noire*, Ernest Bevin, who was saved by a vigilant secretary. Another natural for the terrorists was

General Barker, lately commanding in Palestine. It was Lady Barker who spotted the wires in the parcel. That was the last, for the time being, of the postal bombs. Another twenty-five years were to pass before the next one, sent by Palestinian terrorists, arrived in London. It killed an Israeli diplomat.

Unscop went to work on 16 June. One of the first witnesses it heard was Chief Secretary Sir Henry Gurney, a man of complete integrity and machine-like efficiency. He was under terrific pressure, having to take daily, sometimes hourly, decisions in a permanently dangerous and unstable situation. Yet he always remained completely unruffled. 'That,' said Golda Meyerson later, 'is why we hated him. No one in that position had any right to be unruffled. He ought to have been pacing the room day and night, trying to find a solution to the Jewish problem. It was our objective to ruffle people, but we could make no impression on him.' Small wonder that Gurney's report to Unscop referred to the Jews as 'a bustling, thrusting people'.

On 26 June, in dead secrecy, Unscop chairman Judge Sandstrom, with two colleagues, Dr Ralph Bunche and Dr Hoo, met Begin face to face. Begin told the Unscop men that Irgun had the support of the Jewish people. Irgun fighters, he claimed, were legal fighters; it was the British who were illegally in Palestine. Begin then stated flatly (according to Dr Bunche) 'that if the British execute Irgun men, Irgun will execute British men'.

Begin also had a secret meeting with two other members of Unscop, Dr Granados (Columbia) and Professor Fabregat (Uruguay), both freedom-fighters in their own right. When they parted, Fabregat hugged Begin, and the Irgun leader, almost sobbing, replied: 'All the world's fighters for freedom are one family.' With the exception, evidently, of the British.

Unscop heard Ben Gurion on 7 July. The UN, he said, must decide whether the case for a Jewish state was right or wrong; if given a state, the Jews would immediately try to come to terms with the Arabs. But if the Arabs used force, then the Jews would 'take care of themselves'.

Weizmann in a 'private capacity' addressed Unscop next day. The 1939 White Paper, he said, had released a phenomenon (terrorism) in Jewish life which was contrary to Jewish ethics and tradition. ' "Thou shalt not kill" has been ingrained in us since Mount Sinai ... I hang my head in shame when I have to speak of the fact ... I have never believed that the Messiah would come to the sound of high-explosives.' Only partition, said Weizmann, would give finality, equality and justice. The British in trying to be fair to both Arabs and Jews, had acted too slowly for the Jews. Despite this the Zionist leader felt 'eternally grateful' to Britain for inaugurating the policy of a Jewish National Home. It must have been hard for him to say, but, as Dr Bunche remarked of Weizmann: 'That's really a great man.'

That day, in Jerusalem, sentence of death was confirmed on three Irgun terrorists. So, said terrorist chief Begin, 'we pursued our efforts to capture Britons'. Two young sergeants, Mervyn Paice and Clifford Martin, as they walked back at 1 am on 12 July with a Jewish friend, were pounced on by Irgun men. The British sergeants were chloroformed and abducted. A terrible fate awaited them.

On 13 July, in Burma, Aung San addressed the Assembly. There seemed to be a farewell note in his speech. 'Let me leave word with you,' he kept repeating as he told members a few 'brutal truths'. Independence was coming, but it was not going to bring a heaven on earth. Years of toil lay ahead. Britain was an inspiring example, said Aung San. 'We may not like the British, because they have been our rulers', but they had fought backs to the wall and were still struggling to rebuild their economy. Then Aung San said, innocent of what was in store: 'Political tensions have eased ... there is a lot of nation-building to be done.' He ended: 'These words I leave with you.'

Two days later, U Saw – alias 'Galon', conqueror of

the mythical dragon, – U Saw, whose motto was 'he who dares must bear the consequences' and who boasted nine maternal uncles, all tried for murder (his paternal uncles were worse), was in conclave at his home, No. 4 Ady Road on the banks of Kokine Lake, near Rangoon, with two of his lieutenants, Maung Soe and Ba Nyunt. Men like them of the 'inner circle' had taken a solemn vow before the holy image in U Saw's family shrine and – just in case – signed a paper saying 'I died by my own hand'. U Saw kept the papers and – if the need arose – looked after the rest. That evening U Saw told Maung Soe and Ba Nyunt: 'For politics to continue, all the present leaders must be killed.' He possessed the necessary means, having cultivated the right friends – among them Major Young of the British army, who, for a consideration, had arranged for automatic weapons, rifles, pistols and ammunition to be 'stolen' from his armoury. Major Lance-Dane similarly obliged with a Springfield rifle and Tommy-guns, all of which were a mere trifle to what Captain Vivian, U Saw's Welsh arms-expert friend, came up with: two hundred Bren guns. There were plenty of British officials and businessmen who, far from being dishonest, had nevertheless little sympathy for Aung San. He was, after all, doing them out of their jobs. 'My guess', wrote Police-Commissioner Broughton-Smart at this time, 'is that we shall all be turfed out by the 30th September.'

U Saw had worked out his plans in great detail. One thing he had overlooked, however, was the presence of a fisherman on the banks of the lake near his home. The angler was a police detective.

Meanwhile, on the 17th, another of U Saw's henchmen, Khin Maung Yin, confirmed to 'Galon' that on Saturday 19th there was to be a meeting of the Executive Council. The following evening U Saw gave orders for the next morning's work to his executioners. Maung Soe, Maung Sein, Thet Hnin and Yan Gyi Aung were to kill Aung San and the other councillors; Ba Nyunt was to shoot Thakin Nu.

At about 10 am on the 19th Aung San, dressed in silk

jacket and golden-coloured *longyi*, kissed his wife and children and left for the Secretariat. He did not notice U Saw's man Khin Maung Yin loitering in the quadrangle. At that moment Khin Maung Yin could have changed the course of Burma's history. Had he not been so terrified of disobeying U Saw, he would probably have warned Aung San. Instead he went straight away and telephoned 'Galon'. 'The piston rings have been received,' he told him. Whereupon U Saw, in white shirt and dark blue shorts, came out of his house and waved away his murder gang: four, plus a driver, Thu Kha, wearing jungle green with 8th Army badges, in his private jeep; Ba Nyunt in a Fordson truck. The vehicles carried false number plates, freshly painted, and tags of red and white cloth – these were to propitiate the *Nats* (spirits) during the particularly hazardous journey.

Arrived at the Secretariat, Ba Nyunt walked over to Thakin Nu's office; through the window he saw a man wearing a black jacket. But it was not Thakin Nu. So Ba Nyunt returned to the Fordson, parked outside. On the way, he said, he stopped at a teashop and had a cup of tea.

The jeep meanwhile had driven into the quadrangle and stopped under the portico. While Thu Kha remained at the wheel, keeping the engine running, the other four, led by Maung Soe, entered the building and made for the Executive Council room. U Ohn Khin, an office superintendent, as he talked to a friend in the corridor, heard a sort of 'click, click' as the murderers climbed the stairs. Then he saw them, their automatic weapons at the ready. He saw Maung Soe kick open the door of the Council room, heard him shout: 'Don't run, don't stand up.' Aung San, at the head of the table, immediately rose and faced the killers. A second later he fell, riddled with thirteen bullets. All four killers were firing; one of them, Yan Gyi Aung, was sitting on the floor shooting at people under the table. The Council room had changed to a death chamber, filled with acrid gun-smoke; spent cartridge cases littered the floor and the blood-spattered walls were scarred by over forty bullets. Bogyoke Aung San lay dead beside his overturned chair; Thakin Mya, first elected Speaker of the Assembly, crouched lifeless beneath the table. Slumped dead in their chairs were four more councillors. The Sawbwa (ruler) Sao Sam Htum lay bleeding profusely from the mouth; he died that evening.

Unmolested, the killers sped off. Minutes later they turned their vehicles into U Saw's compound. As they climbed out, U Saw embraced them warmly and everyone burst into delirious cries of 'Aung-byi!' – 'Victory!' U Saw then led them into the house where he plied them with drinks from his liquor cabinet, so that all could toast the abominable carnage. 'Aung-byi!'

U Saw's victory was short-lived. The fisherman-detective, swiftly abandoning rod and line, had warned police headquarters. That afternoon U Saw was arrested along with his accomplices. Incriminating evidence was found in his house; nearby, sub-machine guns were fished out of Lake Kokine. As U Saw was led off to gaol, angry crowds yelled: 'Tear him to pieces, lynch him!' But justice took its proper course. The King's peace had been disturbed; His Majesty's Burmese prime-minister-designate had been brutally done to death. The case 'The King versus U Saw' and others lasted months. U Saw (who was defended by a leading London counsel) and his henchmen were found guilty of murder and hanged.

Burma and Britain were stunned by the death of Aung San and his colleagues. As the body of Burma's thirty-two-year-old hero began its month-long lying-in-state in Rangoon's Jubilee Hall, tributes came pouring in. The first was from the King-Emperor, against whom Aung San had once waged war, but who now 'remembered with pleasure' his recent meeting with him at Buckingham Palace and was deeply distressed at his death. Premier Attlee (who with Mrs Attlee had entertained both Aung San and U Saw in his home) deplored this 'brutal outrage' and called Aung San and his colleagues men of intelligence, courage and public spirit.

Nehru was particularly grieved. No foreign visitor to India, he said, had made a more profound or lasting impression. Aung San was one of Asia's bravest and most far-seeing men, Nehru thought, and his death was a reminder to Indians (and others) that 'violence and in-discipline were the enemies of freedom and their off-spring are chaos and misery'.

Thakin Nu, whom Providence had spared, immediately answered Governor Rance's call to form a new govern-ment. Closest confidant of Aung San since the start of the Thakin movement, Thakin Nu was his natural heir, the man to see things through – now that independence was coming, as Aung San had said just before his death.

Few people recalled that, exactly seven years before that tragic day, Britain, on 19 July 1940, had rejected Hitler's last summons to surrender. Because of that, the Japanese were no longer masters of Burma. It was Britain, at enor-mous sacrifice, who had restored independence to the Golden Land – a modern democracy in place of the cruel and autocratic regime of King Thibaw.

Burma's struggle for freedom had been consummated in carnage. Nor, as independence dawned over other parts of the British Empire, could the pleas of responsible leaders stem the spate of abuse and bloodshed. In Pales-tine, the diligent enquiries of Unscop had brought no peace. On the contrary, a counter-wave of Arab terror-ism was gathering pace. The Arab delegation told the Committee: 'a state established by violence must be op-posed by violence.'

Violence occurred, too, on the high seas. The *President Warfield* skippered by twenty-three-year-old Mike Arono-vitch, had hardly left Sete, France, when she found herself being shadowed by British destroyers. The little Chesa-peake Bay pleasure-boat was now renamed *Exodus 1947* and 1500 volunteers, armed with iron bars, nuts and bolts, canned-food tins and sacks of potatoes, were mustered on deck. On the night of 18 July, the *Exodus* was sandwiched between two British warships and after a two-hour battle with a naval boarding party she signalled Haganah HQ in Palestine: 'Have lost three dead, taken thirty prisoners.' The world was immediately informed that the Royal Navy had committed an act of piracy on the high seas.

By 22 July, the immigrants were on their way back to France in three British 'prison-ships'. When the ships anchored off Port-le-Bouc, near Marseille, on 29 July, the refugees sent a message ashore: 'We have sworn not to land in France. We appeal to the conscience of the French public.' Their morale was meanwhile boosted by a barrage of pep-talk and they hung out Union Jacks emblazoned with the Nazi swastika.

The only solution that Bevin could devise was to keep the refugees waiting under the scorching *Midi* sun for another three weeks, then have them escorted back to Hamburg. Happily, during the slow, terrible return voyage to Hamburg, the *Exodus* refugees discovered another side to the British Nazis. A genuine comradeship grew up between them and the Tommies of the ships' guards. At the German port, they fought a violent battle against troops and police who forced them out of the ships into waiting trains. Then, before the gaze of grinning Germans, they were borne away, back behind the barbed wire.

Bevin, in other spheres of international policy, had fully justified the King-Emperor's confidence in him as Foreign Secretary. His handling of Palestine, on the other hand, was for Britain a disaster, whose shame would long outlive him.

On 29 July, the day that the *Exodus* refugees anchored off Port-le-Bouc, the macabre carousel of Palestine terrorism took a dramatic turn when the three Irgun terrorists went to the gallows. All three sang, at the last, supreme moment of their young lives, *Hatikvah* ('The Hope', the Jewish Anthem). 'Avenge our blood' were their last words.

Since they were kidnapped on 12 July, no trace had been discovered of the two British sergeants Mervyn Paice and Clifford Martin. *Va'ad Leumi* begged the terrorists not to seek revenge. But next day, 30 July, a written message from Irgun stated: 'The two British sergeants have been executed.'

The search for their bodies continued until next day. One of the searching units was commanded by Captain Rogers. 'Tempers were running high among our men,' he said. But orders were never to fire until fired upon. It was frustrating, said Rogers, 'almost more than the average soldier could endure.'

At 7.45 am on 31 July the Mayor of Nathanya reported that the bodies of the two sergeants had been found. Begin had promised to repay in kind; he did more. The bodies of Mervyn Paice and Clifford Martin were hanging by eighteen inches of rope, each from a eucalyptus tree. They had been previously strangled. On the chest of each was pinned a notice signed by the Irgun. It said that the 'spies' Martin and Paice had been tried and found guilty of belonging to a terrorist organization called 'the British Military Occupational Force'. These two boys, barely twenty years old and NCOs with no executive responsibility, were found 'guilty' and sentenced to be hanged.

The ground around the hanging bodies had been mined. Sappers swept a path. The sapper officer then cut the first body down. As it fell there was a terrific explosion – the body had hit a mine which disintegrated it and severely wounded the officer. As Captain Rogers said, with striking understatement: 'It was a beastly thing to do, even for the terrorists,' and added, 'It spoke well for the discipline of our soldiers and airmen,' for such was the feeling that 'hundreds of civilian Jews could have been massacred'. As it happened seven were – Tommies, beyond themselves with rage and despair, avenged their comrades by murdering seven perfectly innocent Jews. In Britain too, after all these years of vilification and terror, there occurred a sudden but brief outbreak of anti-Jewish rioting in the north. As the entire nation gave voice to its anger none expressed himself better than an English Jew, Maurice Edelman, MP. (Sergeant Martin was one of his constituents.) With feeling Edelman told the Commons: 'The murder of the two sergeants cannot be considered in isolation. It is part of a vicious circle of blood and terror ... of reprisal and counter-reprisal.' As for the anti-Jewish riots in Britain, Edelman commented: 'When the Lord Mayor of Liverpool described them as un-British, he said all that was needed.'

Terrorist chief Begin later argued dementedly, 'Had we not retaliated, avenues of gallows would have been set up in Palestine and a foreign power would be ruling in our country today.' This when Britain, months before, had left to the United Nations the entire responsibility of deciding the fate of Palestine. The British had had enough of Palestine's squalid warfare. They longed to clear out.

But the agony – this particular chapter, anyway – was ending. As the dejected *Exodus* refugees headed back to the barbed-wire camps in Germany, Judge Sandstrom and his Unscop investigators had left Palestine for the peace and sanity of Geneva. By 31 August they had produced two plans for Palestine: a majority plan, signed by seven members, for partition; and a minority plan, signed by three, for a federal state. Partition was nothing new: the Peel Commission had advised it ten years earlier, but to its plan the Zionists had reacted with 'unacceptable', the Arabs with 'total refusal'; the British deemed it impracticable. The UN partition plan wanted the mandate to end at the earliest (sighs of relief in Britain); a Jewish and an Arab state would be set up without delay: Britain was asked to continue administering the country until then (the answer to Begin's charge of her 'illegal' presence there). Jerusalem would be assigned to UN trusteeship.

Partition was enthusiastically accepted by the Zionists; the Arabs, in the words of *Al Ahram*, swore to oppose it with a relentless war. The turning point had been reached in the Jews' struggle for statehood. While for tens of thousands of Arabs a long night was beginning, while Jews had many more dark hours to live, dawn was slowly breaking over the State of Israel.

15

Tryst with destiny

The sun was setting, a gory red, on Britain's Indian Empire. When, on 20 June, the Bengal Assembly opted for partition and, three days later, the Punjab Assembly followed suit, more blood was shed. In Calcutta, what Governor Sir Fred Burrows called the 'daily dose' of incidents increased. In a bomb attack on a Muslim funeral, thirteen were killed or injured. A few days later, hooligans took charge of the funeral of a murdered Muslim policeman, gathering a cortège of thousands who stoned and attacked Hindus as it proceeded. Not until evening did the police recover the corpse for decent burial. In the Punjab, Lahore and Amritsar were aflame. Indian mobs had discovered how easy it was to burn a city; hurling their fireballs through windows and skylights, they made off in the dark.

In Bharatpur State, villages of the Muslim Meo people were burnt to the ground by Hindus. At Kadirpur, an Indian corporal and six sepoys repulsed a mob of four thousand. While the dour and doughty Meos took to the hills to sharpen their spears for revenge, Jinnah was begging the Viceroy: 'Be ruthless in suppressing trouble. I don't care whether you shoot Muslims or not, it has got to be stopped.'

As bloodshed and burning spread in the provinces, Viceroy Mountbatten and his staff were working with the skill and the patience of surgeons to accomplish Jinnah's 'surgical operation' on India. On 27 June, the Partition Council (chaired by the Viceroy) named Sir Cyril Radcliffe as Chairman of the Boundary Commission. His terms of reference: to demarcate the boundaries of the new parts of Bengal and the Punjab. 'Otherwise,' an official told him breezily, 'you will have nothing to worry about.' Within a few weeks, Sir Cyril would be the most worried man in India.

Three days later the Partition Council agreed on the

procedure for division of the Indian army, or as C-in-C Auchinleck tactfully put it, its 'reconstitution'. Ismay, who, like Auchinleck, had joined the Indian army over forty years before, was more forthright; for him, it was 'the biggest crime and the biggest headache'. But both Congress and the Muslim League refused to accept the transfer of power until they each had an army of their own. So Ismay had to assist with the dissection of his beloved Indian army, 'a living entity! with one brain, one heart, one set of organs'.

The share-out taxed Mountbatten's wisdom more than Solomon's ever was. After the Indian army, he had to preside over the carve-up of the navy and the air force, while the two claimants quarrelled bitterly. The allocation of India's national debt, of her assets in real and personal property, were all hotly debated, as was the future of the numberless 'all-India' associations, including the Kennel Club.

Another problem which greatly exercised the Viceroy was the future governor-generalship of the two new Dominions. He believed that they should both have the same Governor-General, who would act as a mediator and bridge the gap between them. He was willing, if invited by both, to accept the post. Nehru agreed, but Jinnah differed. He wanted to be Governor-General of Pakistan himself. Mountbatten tried to argue him round: as prime minister, Jinnah would run Pakistan; as Governor-General his powers would depend on the advice of his ministers. Icily Jinnah replied: 'In my position, it is I who will give the advice.' Mountbatten tried another line: India possessed most of the assets; as joint Governor-General he would ensure that Pakistan received its fair share. At which Jinnah admitted sadly: 'It may cost Pakistan several crores of rupees, but I cannot accept any other arrangement.' However, he did beg Mountbatten to stay on as Governor-General of India.

'I am in a complete quandary,' Mountbatten now wrote to the Secretary of State. It was morally wrong, he thought, to stay on with only one of the two sides. 'My inclination was to go,' he said, but he asked for higher guidance. It was generously forthcoming, in the first place from the King-Emperor, who was convinced that he should stay on as Governor-General of India. Premier Attlee told him: 'I believe it to be essential if the transition is to go through smoothly.' Winston Churchill gave his blessing; exact symmetry and balance at the top, he said, was unimportant. What mattered was that under the British constitution, which, said Churchill, 'is much in vogue in India', Mountbatten, as Governor-General, could greatly help the Indian government in its dealings with his opposite number, Governor-General Jinnah. Mountbatten, still 'most uneasy and unhappy', accepted the post. India, which had asked specially for a British governor-general, was not made to feel 'as a lover, scorned'. Acute observers saw more than love or even prestige in the Indian request. It was a very astute move, for Mountbatten, with his resolute and royal influence, would be invaluable in rallying the princes to join India.

The princely states covered about two-fifths of India's surface; their eighty million inhabitants represented a quarter of her total population. The princes were independent rulers, acknowledging only the paramountcy of the King-Emperor. While the states were tied by treaty to their protector, Britain, their rulers were free to do as they liked; His Majesty's government only intervened in rare cases, where scandal or misrule might damage the Raj.

The six hundred-odd princes were a mixed lot, rich and poor, good and bad. The most powerful, the Muslim Nizam of Hyderabad, though a miser, was reputedly the richest man in the world. The Hindu Maharajah of Kashmir was wealthy enough to buy hundreds of dancing girls at over £20,000 apiece. Though ninety-five per cent of his people were Muslims, he ran his state on Hindu lines; cow slaughter was punished by a seven-years' gaol sentence. The wealthy, sadistic Nawab of Junagadh was crazy about dogs; he spent more on them than on state hospitals. His 150 kennels resembled private rooms, each with its own telephone, bed, bath and valet. One of the Nawab's pleasures was to shoot and wound deer or lions, then unleash his hounds and watch them tear their prey to pieces.

Another fabulously rich ruler was the Maharajah of Jodhpur, who had inherited his father's odd tastes. Old Jodhpur once gave a banquet for two hundred, who were served with pie. When the pie was opened – out hopped a little bird, which began to sing. Another perched casually on the tiara of the Vicereine, Lady Curzon. Young Jodhpur had a passion for drink, flying and dancing-girls. They were to be the death of him.

In contrast to the richissime playboy princes were some, like the princelings of the Deccan, who eked out a modest existence on £80 a year. Many also were the enlightened princes: the Maharajah of Mysore who ruled a model state; the Maharajah of Travancore, who opened Hindu Temples to Untouchables; the modern-minded Gaekwar of Baroda and responsible statesmen like the Sikh Maharajah of Patiala, the Nawab of Bhopal, and the Maharajah of Bikaner.

In the plan for Indian independence, Britain was to surrender her paramountcy. The princes would thus forgo British protection. Dark consequences were threatened by Nehru in an inflammatory speech: join the Constituent Assembly, he told the princes, or be treated as hostile. Nehru's ultimatum earned him a stern rebuke from the Viceroy. For, theoretically at least, the princes were at liberty to choose between independence or accession to one or other of the two new Dominions. Either way, it was the beginning of the end for them of the good life, whether as playboys or responsible rulers. All but half a dozen or so of the states faced accession to India, the remainder to Pakistan. But there were controversial cases: Hyderabad, whose Muslim Nizam ruled some fifteen million people, nearly all Hindus; Bhopal, whose Muslim Nawab ruled a Hindu majority; similarly Junagadh. On the other hand, the Hindu Maharajah of Kashmir's people were almost entirely Muslims. Some princes stood out vigorously for independence, preferably as a British dominion. In the forefront of these 'dissidents' were Hyderabad, Travancore, Dholpur, Indore, Jodhpur, and Bhopal. Bhopal, as Chancellor of the Chamber of Princes, hoped to unite the states as a Third Force, eighty million strong.

It was not surprising that the King-Emperor should be worried about the princes' future; they had been the most loyal of allies and, more, he felt a special sympathy for them as members of the 'Royal Trades Union'. While Mountbatten was staying at Buckingham Palace, during his flying visit to London, the King-Emperor urged him, between cousins, to help the princes all he could, to persuade them to accept the inevitable and come to terms with one or other of the new dominions. The new Viceroy had no idea, any more than did the King-Emperor, of the gravity and magnitude of the problem. Nor did Whitehall give him the slightest hint that it might be the hardest of all to solve.

Pressure of work prevented the Viceroy from giving much thought to the states before he had evolved a plan for British India – a fact which infuriated Sir Conrad Corfield, head of the Political Department responsible to the Viceroy for relations with the states. Corfield was an old friend of the Viceroy's, having met him twenty-five years earlier in Delhi as a young naval lieutenant, ADC to the Prince of Wales. The meeting over the Indian princes was to cause that friendship to cool. Exasperated, Corfield remarked: 'It proved impossible to distract his attention from British Indian problems.'

If Bhopal was their front man, the princes regarded Corfield as the real power behind their six hundred-odd thrones. His aim, like Bhopal's, was to get them organized into a united front to resist the Indian politicians. He was counting on Mountbatten, for old times' sake and because of his royal personage, to back his plan for the states to settle with India or Pakistan *after* independence; this would give them better bargaining power. Corfield was dismayed to find that Mountbatten thought exactly the opposite: the princes, he maintained, must settle *before* independence, while he was still Viceroy and could help them – as the King-Emperor had charged him to do.

On 2 June, Mountbatten, lunching with the Maharajah of Bikaner and the Nawab of Bhopal, had given them the gist of the Plan for independence (to be announced on the morrow). Bikaner was delighted at the prospect of India and Pakistan becoming Dominions. It would ease the pain caused by the ending of paramountcy; accession to one of the Dominions would preserve the link with the Crown. Bhopal, less euphoric and further-sighted, exclaimed bitterly: 'Once more His Majesty's Government have left us in the lurch. Whichever Dominion we join, it will utterly destroy us.' This royal son of the Prophet had accurately forecast the dire truth.

Mountbatten himself foresaw a series of 'difficult meetings'. He presided over the first one on 13 June. Nehru, always highly emotional about the states (especially his own state, Kashmir), pushed the Congress line that paramountcy ought to pass to the successors of the British Raj; the states had no right to remain independent. When Corfield demurred, Nehru's anger rose; the Political Adviser, he said, should be tried for misfeasance. About his friend Nehru, Mountbatten commented drily: 'As usual, he lost control of himself.' Jinnah, with obvious delight, took the opposite line to Nehru; the states, he said, were independent and could negotiate as they pleased. After an acrimonious discussion, it was decided to create a States Department for each new Dominion. How glad Mountbatten was that Sardar Patel, not the nervy Nehru, was named head of the Indian one. The formidable 'little Menon' was made secretary. Menon told journalist Durga Das: 'Mountbatten is doing business with Sardar and has Nehru in his pocket. Sardar in turn is flattering Mountbatten and using him to net the princes. We must have them all in the bag before 15 August.'

Mountbatten's *Instrument of Accession*, inspired as usual by Menon, envisaged that all the princes should accede to India (and in a few cases to Pakistan) on the basis of three subjects: defence, external affairs, and communications. An entertaining exchange occurred between the Viceroy and Patel, who said: 'I will accept your offer if you will give me a full basket of apples ... I'll buy a basket of 565' – the number of states that Congress hoped to get – 'but if there are even two or three apples missing the deal is off.' 'I will do my best', replied the Viceroy, 'but a basket of, say, 560 apples – will you buy it?' 'Well, I might,' agreed Patel.

On 5 July, Patel came out with a statement which was enticing, almost, compared to Nehru's 'ultimatum'. Appealing to the princes to accede on the three subjects, it was better, he said, 'to make laws as friends than treaties as aliens'. The Congress were no enemies of the princely order, he went on, nor would his policy savour of the 'domination of one over the other'. If there was to be any domination, it would be that of 'our mutual relations and welfare'. Patel's policy of friendship with the princes ended with his early death. In time the princely order would cease to exist and most of the princes would be relegated to the level of aristocratic nonentities.

It remained for Mountbatten to set the wheels in motion. Frankly, he thought the princes were 'a bunch of nit-wits' for not having democratized their states and for refusing to join the Indian Federation conceived by the 1935 India Act. Now he was about to use all his charm and persuade them to accept the consequences. On 25 July, the royal Viceroy, in full regalia to match the bejewelled finery of his audience, addressed – for the first and last time – the Chamber of Princes. As he strode up the red carpet he was greeted by the giant, bearded Maharajah of Patiala, the new Chancellor of the Chamber, with little Menon dwarfed at his side. Inside, the heat was stifling – the only fan was monopolized by the portly Jam Sahib of Nawanagar. As the Viceroy rose to address the august and gorgeously attired assembly, the activities of the press photographers, running half-bent up and down the aisles and letting off their flash-bulbs, reminded

Press Attaché Campbell-Johnson of 'one of the more zany episodes in a Marx Brothers film'.

Mountbatten's speech was, as V. P. Menon described it, 'the apogee of persuasion'. The states, he explained, were theoretically free to join whichever dominion they chose, but there were certain 'geographical compulsions' which left the vast majority irretrievably linked with India. Accession on three subjects only – defence, external affairs, and communications – 'leaves you', said the Viceroy, 'with all the practical independence you can possibly use and makes you free of all those subjects you cannot possibly manage on your own'.

The *Instrument of Accession*, the Viceroy thought, was an offer that Congress was unlikely to repeat. Moreover – a detail, but he knew it meant a lot to the princes – they would continue to receive honours and awards from the King.* To this carrot he added a genial touch of comedy. During the discussion that followed, a Dewan (prime minister) admitted: 'I do not know my ruler's mind. He is on board a ship returning to India.' Mountbatten immediately picked up a large glass paper-weight from the rostrum and gazing at it intently he said: 'I will look into my crystal.' After a few seconds of tense silence he continued: 'His Highness is sitting at the Captain's table and wishes you to sign the Instrument of Accession.' In the storm of laughter and applause that followed, it was clear that the British prince had carried the Indian princes with him.

In the days that followed, the princes, headed by the Maharajah of Bikaner, queued up to sign for accession. But there were still a few sluggards, as Mountbatten called them. First, Travancore. The Dewan, Sir C. P. Ramaswami ('Sir C. P.' for short) called on the Viceroy and showed him press cuttings which, he claimed, proved that Gandhi was a sex-maniac; he was the most dangerous influence in India and his backing of the unstable

---

* The Maharajahs of Jaipur and Bikaner both received the Grand Cross of the Star of India many months after the transfer of power.

Nehru would soon cause a split in Congress. Sir C. P. certainly did not intend to ally Travancore with so dangerous an ally as India. Back in Travancore, the Congress-run States Peoples Organization turned the heat full on (as Mountbatten put it). Gandhi's unfaithful disciples of non-violence staged riots during which Sir C. P. was nearly killed with a bill-hook. The Maharajah of Travancore hesitated no longer; he telephoned his acceptance to the Viceroy.

The Maharajah of Indore, who had cut the Viceroy's meeting with the princes, was summoned to Delhi where the Viceroy let him have it: he would inform the King-Emperor and the Prime Minister of the Maharajah's lamentable lack of responsibility. Indore's signed copy of the *Instrument of Accession* duly arrived in a very plain envelope, a day after the date limit.

The young playboy Maharajah of Jodhpur, who had recently succeeded his father, a Hindu ruler of a largely Hindu state, first agreed to accede to India. Then, after Jinnah had told him 'write your own terms', he changed his mind. Jodhpur, too, received a summons from the Viceroy. He flew himself to Delhi, where he succumbed to Mountbatten's arguments. Left alone with V. P. Menon to sign the *Instrument of Accession*, the Maharajah took out a very large pen. This, at the touch of a button, he transformed into a pistol which he pointed at the unfortunate Menon, shouting: 'You've tricked me, I'm going to kill you.' Coolly Menon told him: 'Stop these juvenile theatricals' – and produced a proper pen, with which Jodhpur meekly signed.

Mountbatten's second-best friend (after Nehru) in India, the Nawab of Bhopal, proved very difficult. He had resigned as Chancellor of the Chamber of Princes and refused to attend the Viceroy's meeting. Like Pethwick-Lawrence at the Simla conference, Bhopal saw an *Alice in Wonderland* touch about the whole thing, 'as if we were being invited like the Oysters to the tea-party of the Walrus and the Carpenter'. Bhopal threatened to abdicate in favour of his daughter, but Mountbatten told him that it would be cowardly – and unfair on the girl. Mount-batten admired Bhopal for his high principles and spent more time on his case than on all the others. His efforts succeeded and Bhopal remained true to his principles. To Patel he wrote: 'I used every means in my power to preserve the independence ... of my state. Now that I have conceded defeat ... you will find that I can be as staunch an ally as I have been an inveterate opponent.'

Bhopal's moving story was only surpassed by the pathos of that of the Maharajah Rana of Dholpur, another old friend of the Viceroy's. Dholpur was a convinced believer in the divine right of kings – the indignity of acceding to a future republic was too much for him. Finally, though, the Maharajah Rana gave in. When he bid good-bye to the Viceroy there were tears in his eyes. 'This ends an alliance', he said, 'between my ancestors and yours, which has lasted since 1765.'

A last-minute hitch occurred with the Hindu Gaekwar of Baroda, who had originally asked for the honour of being the first to accede. When he failed to sign the *Instrument*, Mountbatten sent for him and listened while he explained that it was the astrologers who were holding things up, waiting for an auspicious day. Only later did the Viceroy discover that the Gaekwar was in the throes of marrying his second wife, whose own divorce revealed an unusual aspect of the communal problem. A Hindu, she converted to Islam; her husband naturally refused to do likewise, so she divorced him. She then switched back to Hinduism and married the Gaekwar, who now felt free to accede, as promised.

Finally there was the Khan of Kalat, whose prede-cessor the Empress Victoria had so spoiled, showering him with presents (including an elephant) at her acclama-tion seventy years earlier. Now the Khan was again given favoured treatment. Kalat was recognized as an inde-pendent sovereign state in treaty relations with Victoria's great-grandson, King George VI.

By 15 August, Independence Day, all the wanted states, with the exception of Hyderabad, Kashmir and Junagadh, were, as V. P. Menon had foreseen, 'in the bag'. The Nawab of Junagadh, after declaring for India, changed his mind; Kashmir's Maharajah was unable to make up his. The Nizam of Hyderabad held out for independence as a Dominion – His Exalted Highness had, after all, been accorded the title of 'Faithful Ally'. But during the months that followed, these three apples which Patel so coveted were culled, not without great difficulty, into the Indian basket.

The tear-off calendars indicating the number of days left until the transfer of power, installed, on Mountbatten's orders, in all the viceregal offices, were a daily reminder of the rapid approach of Independence Day. Never had the Viceroy's staff functioned under such pressure or so smoothly. Beyond Delhi, however, the picture was sadly different. As the days to independence shortened, the toll of murder and arson mounted.

Bengal and the Punjab were obviously the critical provinces. Originally, Bengal had looked like being the danger area, but now it was all too clear that the full force of the holocaust would break in the Punjab. The tiny village of Khanpur Dhadah (where Kanda, the boy with the bicycle nicknamed 'Chalo', lived) became a Sikh stronghold bent on wreaking vegeance on the local Muslim community. Five miles away, the Muslims, concentrated in the village of Kangana, were determined to smash Khanpur Dhadah and lay waste the country before decamping to Pakistan. The Khanpur Dhadah Sikhs were poorly armed with spears, knives and axes. But the village blacksmith's shop became an arsenal, turning out pistols, swords and bazookas. 'Those bazookas, what a marvellous achievement!' Kanda recalled later. They made a terrible noise but were not highly lethal.

It was a tragic situation. 'People who lived and worked together', said Kanda, 'became foes.' There was no police protection. Business and agriculture were at a standstill. The women and children hid all day in the surrounding crops, while the able-bodied men fought furiously to defend Khanpur Dhadah. 'At last,' said Kanda, 'came their finest hour', as they faced the Muslim attackers on the opposite side of a stream. The bazookas worked wonders, keeping the enemy at bay. Then the Muslims fled and a hideous slaughter began. 'There were killings, looting, burnings,' Kanda said, adding cynically: 'This was the independence everyone was aspiring for.'

On 1 August, the Punjab Boundary Force went into action. At its inception a week earlier by the Partition Council, Mountbatten had declared his determination to establish peaceful conditions for the transfer of power. Violence would not be tolerated, the Viceroy affirmed, not for the first time. Major General 'Pete' Rees, commanding the PBF, told reporters: 'We will do our utmost to defend law and order.' The PBF did its utmost. The discipline of its Indian troops, under British officers, never failed. But the belief expressed, from the Viceroy downwards, in its ability to arrest the slaughter was entirely illusory. It was there to aid the civil power, but the civil power had broken down; there was practically none left to aid.

The PBF numbered 55,000 men – 5,000 short of what Punjab Governor Jenkins deemed necessary to prevent civil war. But not even 155,000 men could have kept the peace among the Punjab's maddened and terrified population of 14,500,000, distributed over nearly 18,000 villages like Khanpur Dhadah, or densely packed in great cities like Amritsar and Lahore. Killings ran into hundreds, then into thousands and tens of thousands as Sikh and Muslim refugees fled to that half of the Punjab which provided sanctuary – east for the Sikhs and Hindus, west for the Muslims.

An Englishman, J. H. Lench, of the RAF, happened to be changing trains at Lahore station when he saw an unbelievable sight: a 'suffocating mass' of refugees was moving very slowly towards the platforms. So dense was the crush that the front of the crowd was forced slowly but relentlessly over the edge of the platform on to the track like ice-blocks 'calving-off' from the snout of a glacier. As the train came in, the flow of humanity, picking up speed, was compressed into it, through doors and windows, while others swarmed on to the carriage roofs, or packed on to the buffers. The train, as it slid out of the station, looked like a serpent covered with lice.

At Peshawar, where he was stationed, Lench reported that when 'things got dicey' the 'natives' simply climbed over the airfield fence and squatted near the aircraft 'on the well-founded assumption that if they were near our blokes they would be safe'.

The most hideous atrocities occurred in Alwar State, bordering on the Punjab. Its profligate Maharajah had once poured petrol on one of his obstinate polo ponies and set it alight. He had been deposed by the Viceroy but his successor looked on as his Hindu subjects set fire to villages of the Muslim Meos. They did a more efficient job than their sadistic, pyromaniacal former ruler, unimpeded and sometimes treacherously aided by His Highness's state troops. Eight out of ten Meo villages were burnt down. At Mandawar, on 7 August, 150 Muslims were massacred; another orgy of blood-letting took place at Tijara; at Silgaon, a mob of 10,000 Hindus butchered all but a few of the villagers. Some of the survivors, including wounded, crept out after dark to make for safety. They were intercepted and cut down – to the last man, the last woman, the last child.

As the blood-red stain of slaughter spread across the Punjab, Gandhi arrived in Calcutta at the Viceroy's urgent request. On 10 August he told his prayer-meeting: 'My head hangs in shame at this recital of man's barbarism.' Though admitting the bankruptcy of his non-violent methods, the Mahatma still believed in himself. So did the Muslim Shaheed Suhrawardy, Chief Minister of Bengal at the time of the Great Calcutta Killing. As Independence Day approached, he begged Gandhi to stay in the city. Gandhi agreed; he informed the surprised Patel: 'Suhrawardy and I are going to stay together in a Muslim quarter' – Belliaghatta, which Patel describes as 'a veritable shambles and a notorious den of gangsters and hooligans'. Patel added sardonically: 'And in what choice company, too!'

Hydari Mansion, a ramshackle old dwelling, was the chosen abode for this ill-assorted couple, one a saintly Hindu, the other a Muslim politician and playboy, known in all Calcutta's night-clubs. The Mansion's single lavatory being quite inadequate for the hundreds of visitors, the overflow excreted, urinated, and spat red gobs of betel nut in the corridors. It was only after Gandhi had walked barefoot through the repulsive slough that his faithful flock showed more consideration for him. Some of them, at least. Others, young toughs of the extremist Hindu Mahasabah, angrily heckled the Mahatma. 'Why have you come here', they cried, 'to save the Muslims? You never came to protect the Hindus during the Great Killing.' They greeted the arrival of Suhrawardy, in white shirt and tartan shorts, with yells of 'Muslim pig – let's hang the cow-killing degenerate.' Shaheed Suhrawardy was hustled inside, almost fainting from the stink, as the windows were closed against the hecklers. Bricks then came hurtling in and flying splinters narrowly missed Gandhi, who invited the furious young Hindus to come and talk. 'Go back, Gandhi,' they told him. 'We don't want you here.' Gandhi replied: 'I have come to serve Hindus and Muslims alike. I have nearly reached the end of my life's journey. If you again go mad I will not be a living witness to it.' He was prepared to start a fast unto death. After Gandhi had reasoned for hours with the demonstrators, they left quietly. Next day they were again in session with Gandhi, while cries went up outside for Suhrawardy. Gandhi, his arm on Suhrawardy's shoulder, led him to the window, where the Muslim playboy-politician declared firmly: 'It is Bengal's great fortune that Mahatmaji is in our midst. Will Bengal realize it and stop the fratricide?' Bengal's answer was immediate. Hindus and Muslims paraded in their thousands through Calcutta shouting *'Hindu Muslim Bhai Bhai'* ('Hindus and Muslims are brothers'). Thousands more attended Gandhi's prayer meetings. West Bengal's governor-elect Rajagopalachari, acclaimed Gandhi as 'the magician who performed the Calcutta miracle'. The Viceroy called him 'the one-man Boundary Force, not forgetting his second-in-command, Mr Suhrawardy'. Gandhi himself was as usual philosophical. 'It is not the work of one or two men. We are toys in the house of God; He makes us dance to His tune.'

Jinnah had bidden farewell to India on 7 August, when Mountbatten had seen him off from Delhi in the silver viceregal Dakota. A few hours later, as he looked down on the white-clad multitude awaiting him at Karachi airfield, Jinnah, according to one of his ADC's, suddenly became 'buoyant and quite young'. Feelingly he murmured: 'I never expected to see Pakistan in my life-time.'

When on 13 August the Viceroy, with the Vicereine, flew to Karachi to wish godspeed to Pakistan, Jinnah was not at the airport to meet them – the first of a series of contretemps which were to mark the viceregal visit. The next came when the Viceroy was informed of a plot to throw a bomb at Jinnah during the state procession next day. Jinnah, however, was prepared to go through with the drive if the Viceroy was. 'Of course,' agreed Mountbatten, unruffled.

A banquet followed; originally it was intended as a luncheon, only Jinnah, never too careful about religious matters, had forgotten that the day-time fast of Ramazan was on. Mountbatten had a sticky time, seated next to Miss Jinnah and the Begum Liaquat Ali Khan, between whom no great love was lost. The order was 'no speeches', but Jinnah sprang to his feet and delivered one – very pro-British in tone, as it happened – which he rounded off by proposing the toast: 'His Majesty the King!' Never again, while Governor-General, would he repeat it.

Next morning, when the Viceroy was to address the Pakistan Assembly, Jinnah, despite his recent effusions of loyalty, tried to bag the principal seat. At which Mountbatten put his foot down; Quaid-i-Azam, 'the great leader', Jinnah might be, but he, Mountbatten, was still, after all, Viceroy. Before the Assembly, he read a message from the

King who was still, with a day to spare, Emperor. On this great occasion, said the royal message, when Pakistan was about to join the British Commonwealth of Nations, 'their support will not fail you in upholding democratic principles' – support which, in time, would be direly needed. Then the Viceroy congratulated Jinnah. 'The birth of Pakistan is an event in history.' And history, he metaphorized (most refreshingly, considering the torrid heat of Karachi) 'seems to move with the infinite slowness of a glacier ... Just now our united efforts have melted the ice.' It was a parting between friends 'who have learned to honour and respect one another, even in disagreement'.

The state drive, which might have ended fatally for both future governors-general, was in open cars, but any apprehension that Mountbatten might have felt of a bomb being lobbed into theirs was allayed by the enthusiasm of the crowds as they cried: *'Pakistan Zindabad!'* *'Mountbatten Zindabad!'* Only when the car turned into the gates of Government House did Jinnah give way to his own feelings. 'Thank God I have brought you back alive!' he murmured. Mountbatten noticed that Jinnah was still deeply affected when, with surprising warmth, he bade him good-bye. Flying over the Punjab on the way back to Delhi, Mountbatten could see fires everywhere – no beacons of joy to light up the Day of Independence, but signs of the approaching holocaust.

That night, as midnight struck, the last Viceroy, surrounded by despatch boxes, was at his desk in Delhi. Helped by his press attaché, Alan Campbell-Johnson, he began to tidy the room and stow away those outward and visible signs of viceregal authority. At that moment India's prime minister was addressing the Assembly. In a solemn voice he said: 'Long years ago we made a tryst with destiny and now the time comes when we shall redeem that pledge ... At the stroke of the midnight hour, when all the world sleeps, India will awake to life and freedom!'

Then, with the eagerness of a man freed from captivity,

Nehru – whom it had cost nine years in gaol to achieve this crowning moment – went with President Rajendra Prasad to call on the ex-Viceroy. The Assembly, they informed him, had taken over power from His Majesty's Government. It had also endorsed Mountbatten's appointment as India's first governor-general. Nehru, with a ceremonious bow, said gravely: 'May I submit to Your Excellency the portfolios of the Cabinet'; and handed over a large official envelope. Then he and the President were gone. Mountbatten, alone again, slit open the envelope. It was empty.

The oversight did not disturb His Excellency; he well knew all the names of the ministers he was to meet later that day, 15 August – 'the most remarkable and inspiring day of my life' he called it. After only a few hours of sleep, the first governor-general, at 8.30 am, was sworn in in the Durbar Hall. None of the traditional pomp of trumpets and scarlet and gold was lacking. Then, with the Vicereine, he drove to the Council Chamber. Never had there been such crowds – from the roof tops down to the surging mass which practically engulfed his carriage. To the Assembly the Governor-General spoke first for his cousin, the King. The royal message was a near-copy of that addressed to Pakistan, without any hint at the support available from the rest of the Commonwealth for 'upholding democratic principles' – presumably thought superfluous in India's case. As with Pakistan, the King sent sincere good wishes. 'Be assured of my sympathy.' But it was hard to believe that such a sincere man could honestly feel that it was 'inspiring to think that all this has been achieved by means of peaceful change' when so many thousands of his subjects had been butchered, burnt and mutilated in the most bestial manner during the past months and when, at that very moment, the stench of smoke and blood rose high into the Punjab sky.

On to lunch. The crowds swarmed so thickly round the Council Chamber that the athletic Nehru had to scramble on to the roof of the porch and wave them back, while they yelled back: 'Pandit Nehru, *ki jai! Pandit Mount-*

batten, *ki jai!'*

In the evening came the great event of the day, the salute to the Indian flag. It was originally planned to lower the Union Jack first, but this, Nehru felt, might offend the British. His psychology was faultless. At Lucknow, on the other hand, the British had had to take their own precautions; of all the flags run up and down during those momentous days, none was more sacred to the British than the Union Jack which flew proudly above the old Lucknow Residency, revered memorial to the two million British dead in India. Since the Indian Mutiny exactly ninety years earlier, it was the only flag in the British Empire which had never been lowered (except for renewals – over two hundred of them). The Residency flag, as General Tuker said, was 'the very core of our prestige'. That day, as Delhi prepared to hoist the national flag, Indians in Lucknow marched to the Residency for their own hoisting ceremony. They were shocked to find no British flag, no flagstaff even. The famous Union Jack had been secretly hauled down by British officers, to be saved for posterity. The mast had then been severed at its base.

Comedy, rather than drama, was the note at the Delhi ceremony. Pages of orders, hours of rehearsal, had preceded the great parade. Grandstands had been raised. But few of the VIPs or the parade itself were ever seen among the crowd of freedom-crazy Indians. The Governor-General's magnificent bodyguard on their patient horses breasted a way for his carriage on to the parade ground. There it became completely stranded. Of the grandstands there was nothing to be seen. A few bright *pugrees* bobbing on the human tide showed where the guard of honour was engulfed; they were the sole trace of the military parade. Nehru, striking out with his fists, was seen battling his way towards the carriage, aboard which he was hauled like a survivor from a shipwreck. Governor-General and Prime Minister then stood unsteadily on the swaying carriage to salute the flag as it was run up. At that instant the Almighty, who had been so involved between the rival factions in the Indian story, added a gracious touch. Light rain began to fall and a rainbow, its green, white and saffron matching the Indian flag, arched across the sky.

The carriage now moved forward with Nehru, like a look-out, perched on the hood. Mountbatten seemed to forget that he had ever been Viceroy or that he was now Governor-General. It was as if he were reliving those heroic moments on the bridge of his sinking ship, the *Kelly*, as he now shouted orders to pick up survivors and several fainting women with their terrified children were dragged aboard the carriage. Gradually it moved clear of the crowd and the Admiral, looking back over the stern, watched thousands of people running in its wake. 'A most impressive sight,' he found it – as he did the three thousand glittering guests who gathered that night at Government House.

As the sun finally set on the Indian Empire, the King-Emperor's erstwhile subjects went mad with joy. At Calcutta the delirious crowd invaded Government House, breaking furniture, slashing pictures (especially Empress Victoria's) and making off with most of the silver. As Leonard Mosley observed, Governor Rajagopalachari was left with only a few teaspoons. More restraint but no less joy was shown by the employees of Nimtollah Steamer Ghat, on the banks of the Hooghli, who had asked their Superintendent, Erroll P. Lumsden, to perform the flag-raising ceremony.

Hundreds of miles away, at Bellary, in peaceful Sandur State (adjoining Madras), District Judge W. W. George-son, on the night of the 14th/15th, listened in the club to the broadcast from Delhi. The only European, he felt touched by the courtesy shown by the Indian members. Later, above his court-room, the national flag was hoisted – upside down. E. A. Payne, of the RAF, was the only white in a train going to Cawnpore that day. 'The natives', he said, 'were very friendly.' He watched speech-less as they ripped the fittings off the carriage, explaining gleefully: 'They are ours now.'

Across the subcontinent, celebrations were in full swing. But many people, Nehru and Jinnah included, were deeply troubled. As J. H. Lench, the Englishman who had watched, stupefied, the refugees at Lahore station, so naïvely put it: 'Harmless natives were being butchered while the politicians were toasting their independence.' Indeed, as the cream of Indian society regaled themselves into the small hours of the morning at Delhi's Government House, not far away, at Connaught Circus, mass murder was being done; 'harmless natives', horses and dogs even, were being pitilessly slaughtered. 'It was akin to a battlefield of fury,' said an English witness, T. H. B. Burkitt-Tower. As refugees flocked on to an aircraft at Delhi's airport, men in a jeep dashed up and opened fire. Plane and passengers were carbonized. In their holy city of Amritsar, Sikhs celebrated Independence Day by rounding up a group of Muslim maidens, raping the loveliest, then hacking them and most of the others to pieces with *kirpans*. Muslims of Lahore, not to be outdone, set fire to a Sikh *gurdwara* (temple) in which scores of Sikhs had taken refuge, while Muslim police stood by, inert, listening to the screams of the trapped victims.

The greatest mass slaughter in history was now well launched. During the next nine months, fourteen million people – Hindus, Sikhs, and Muslims, would be driven from their homes; well over a quarter of a million would be atrociously massacred. Mountbatten later admitted that his threats to the Sikh leaders may have been empty ones. But what else could he have done? The King-Emperor himself had deplored that 'there are not enough troops to keep order'. 'Nor', added Punjab Governor Evan Jenkins, the man who best knew, 'could all the King's horses and all the King's men prevent communal violence in villages so widely scattered across the country.' In any case, it was too late. The men were off to Blighty. To the lilt of haunting barrack-room airs, they were seen off by the ex-Viceroy at Bombay, Gateway of India, where, over the years, so many thousands of them had arrived.

The British Raj had seen its last day. For a century and

a half it had held India's four hundred millions together
as a united people, at peace with themselves. Behind the
Raj's power had stood the prestige of the Emperor, backed
by the unswerving loyalty of the sepoy. It was natural
that their British officers should drink, as a last sun-
downer, 'to the King-Emperor and the Sepoy'.

The sun had gone down on Britain's Indian Empire.
While for the first time Pakistan's own flag flew in
Karachi, India's in Delhi, there took place a quiet little
ceremony at Balmoral Castle, Scotland, as the last Secre-
tary of State for India, Lord Listowell, delivered up his
seal of office to the last Emperor. In return the Emperor
made a simple request: that the famous flag from the
Lucknow Residency be handed to him for safe keeping.
It would be forever the cherished souvenir of his Indian
Empire.

'Dear Balmoral' as the first Empress, Victoria, had
called it and which the last Emperor loved as much. 'My
heart is fixed in this clear Paradise,' his great-grandmother
had written, and her thoughts about the place – 'all
seemed to breathe freedom and peace' – were the same
as his.

It was in this relaxed atmosphere, so different from that
of his freedom-crazy, hatred-ridden Indian Empire, that
the demise of the last Emperor, Emperor of India, took
place. There was no battle for his imperial crown, no
flight from hostile armies. The day that the Emperor lost
his empire was for him like any other. The little ceremony of the seal over, the ex-Emperor went off 'to the
hill' kilted in the Balmoral tartan – black, red and
lavender on a grey background, designed for Victoria by
her beloved Albert, whose name she had consented to
give to the infant who was to be the last of her imperial
dynasty. To the hill, there to indulge in his favourite
pastime, shooting. The hill, with its gentle curves and
jagged peaks embedded in the sky's soft, misty, purple-
blue, its honeyed scent of heather, with the sound of
voices carried on the warm, uneven breeze and the swift,

swerving flight of grouse. 'The hill' had more meaning for him that day than the loss of his Indian Empire.

'What Parliament can make, Parliament can unmake' had been the comment seventy years before when Disraeli had made Victoria empress by Act of Parliament, and so it had proved, for now Parliament 'unmade' the fifth heir of Victoria's imperial line, the shy, stammering, dutiful young man who, quite accidentally, had inherited the brunt and the burden of the Imperial Crown, only to be divested of it.

Apart from India, Burma was about to quit the British Empire, the first colony to do so since the American colonies showed the way in 1776. Palestine had just shaken off the British Mandate, too. Ireland was a friendly but faint-hearted Dominion who flatly rejected the King's authority. The end of the British Empire was beginning; the beginning of a new Commonwealth was in sight.

From 15 August 1947, King George was no longer entitled to sign George RI, *Rex et Imperator*. From then on *Imperator* was for the birds. A few days later the King wrote to his mother, Queen Mary. She noted: 'The first time Bertie wrote me a letter with the I for Emperor of India left out, very sad.'

It was an understandable, but entirely personal, point of view.

Epilogue

King George VI, according to his prime minister, Attlee, made not the slightest objection to the imperial crown being removed from his head. He was a king, Attlee said, who was never static but moved forward with the times.

There was in fact no time for the King to brood nostalgically on the past splendours and the vanished wealth of his truncated empire across the seas. Things were far too serious at home. As the British Empire began to break up, Britain herself had never had it so bad. Bankruptcy and economic ruin stared her in the face. Of the five thousand million dollars borrowed from the United States and Canada (and supposed to last for another two years), only four hundred million remained. The British, instead of dominating the globe as, half a century ago, they seemed destined to do, were poor, tired and hungry. And now Premier Attlee was demanding further sacrifices, attempting to rally the people with brave words to which their ears were dead. 'We are engaged in another Battle of Britain ... it demands a united effort by the whole nation.' But the spirit of 1940 was no longer there.

At the beginning of 1947 the King had noted anxiously in his diary: 'I have asked Mr Attlee three times now if he is worried ... I know I am ...' Now, nine months later, he seemed even more depressed. 'I do wish one could see a glimmer of a bright spot anywhere in world affairs. Never in the whole history of mankind have things looked gloomier ... and one feels so powerless to do anything to help.'

The next step in the break-up of his Empire came when, three months after the birth of India and Pakistan, the British Government recognized Burma as a republic. The mutual friendship of the two countries was sealed by a treaty of alliance; as Premier U Nu signed it, he complimented the 'great wisdom and vision of the British

Labour Government'. They were at pains, he said, 'to win our goodwill rather than our treasure'. Astrologers fixed Burma's Independence Day for 4 January 1948 – that day British troops were waved away by delirious, but friendly, Burmese crowds to the strains of 'Auld Lang Syne'.

On the 30th of that month, Gandhi was in Delhi. That morning he wrote to a bereaved co-worker: 'Death is a true friend. It is only our ignorance that makes us to grieve.' He spent the afternoon persuading Sardar Patel to end his long-standing feud with Nehru. 'A breach between you would be disastrous,' he said, and promised to speak to Nehru, who was coming in after the evening prayer-meeting – 'If I am alive,' joked Gandhi, who was in his seventy-ninth year. Gandhi died shortly afterwards, shot by a young Hindu extremist. He fell murmuring 'He Rama! Rama!' ('Oh God! God!') In the name of India, Nehru mourned the Master: 'A light has gone out of our lives.' Obeying his orders, Nehru and Sardar Patel ruled India as a duumvirate until, in 1950, the Sardar died.

Long before Gandhi was assassinated, a lung disease, aggravated by exhaustion, had begun slowly to kill Jinnah. When his faithful lieutenant, Liaquat Ali, now Pakistan's premier, visited him two months before his death, Jinnah characteristically ordered his doctor: 'Tell him nothing. I, as head of the State, will tell the nation about my illness when I think proper.' Though very ill, Jinnah's coquetry did not desert him. Waiting to be transported to Karachi on a stretcher, he objected 'I will not travel in pyjamas' and insisted on being properly dressed, monocle and all. When, on 11 September 1948, his doctor tried to rally him with 'God willing, you are going to live', the *Quaid-i-Azam* replied faintly 'No I am not'. He died a few minutes later. Liaquat Ali took over the *Quaid*'s task of building a nation. Then, exactly three years later, he too died – by the hand of an assassin.

It fell to Lord Alexander, one of the men who had helped India and Pakistan to freedom, to announce on 14 May 1948, that 10,000 square miles of Palestine were no longer part of the British Empire. That day, for which the Jewish race had waited two thousand years, Ben Gurion proclaimed the area, a tiny island in an Arab sea, as the State of Israel. The following day, Israel was recognized by the United States, and shortly after by Russia – not that the latter's magnanimity was to be of any lasting comfort to Israel. That same day Arab armies invaded the new state and Tel Aviv was bombed. Israel's War of Independence had begun. So also had the flight of Palestinian Arabs from their homeland. It began as a trickle, but as the months passed grew into a massive exodus – nearly a million Arabs, once the 'protected people' of the British King-Emperor, but now destitute refugees.

Chaim Weizmann was voted first President of Israel. One of his government's first acts was to amnesty the Irgun and Stern terrorists. It drew a harsh comment from one of Israel's most prominent supporters in Britain, Lady Violet Bonham-Carter. Israel, she said, 'has lost the hearts of all its truest friends in Britain'. Sternly President Weizmann reminded her that 'this evil thing was the result of a holocaust such as the world has not seen and of the heartless policy of those who bolted the doors of Palestine to the victims'.

Menachem Begin's Irgun men were now fighting with their habitual fanaticism and courage against the Arabs. But when Begin defied Ben Gurion's order to place the Irgun under the Israeli high command, Ben Gurion warned: 'We shall regard as a traitor anyone attempting to break the discipline of the state.' In July, as Israel accepted a temporary truce with her foes, she was herself on the brink of civil war. But in a few tense, dramatic days, Ben Gurion succeeded in smashing Begin's revolt – where the British for years had failed.

The War of Independence ended in January 1949 when Israeli forces pushed the Egyptians back beyond their own frontiers. It was then that Britain decided to recognize Israel. But when Bevin rose in the Commons to announce the decision, he made a passionate defence of the Arab cause. Churchill, who, since Lord Moyne's death, had refused to see Weizmann, describing Palestine as a 'hell-disaster for Britain', now spoke up once more for Zion. 'A Jewish state in Palestine is an event in history to be viewed in the perspective not of a generation or a century but ... of a thousand, two thousand or even three thousand years.'

Britain was quick to make it up with Israel. When Weizmann's seventy-fifth birthday was celebrated in London, the Empire's senior statesman, Smuts, said: 'The unconquerable reserve of man is his will to victory – it was proved in the Battle of Britain and repeated in the resurrection of Israel. I bracket them together as among the human highlights of our epoch.' The tragedy was that these two protagonists of human liberty should ever have quarrelled and between them deprived a million Arabs of theirs.

The King of Great Britain had seen two republics, Burma and Israel, carved out of his Empire. Now came a third, Eire. Although a republic (created in 1937) and a neutral during the Second World War, Eire had remained in the Commonwealth-Empire on the basis of 'external association', the formula invented by de Valera in 1921. The British king had no power in Eire, but de Valera, fervent republican though he might be, realized the convenience of His Britannic Majesty's patronage in certain of Eire's affairs abroad. Eire's External Relations Act defined this bizarre relationship.

In 1948 Eamon de Valera was succeeded as *Taoiseach* by John Costello, whose thinking, if less characteristically Irish, was decidedly more *avant-garde*. 'Friendship with Britain,' he declared, 'did not depend on archaic forms, but on principles of association unrelated to outworn formulae.' The External Relations Act was repealed, and on Easter Monday 1949 the sovereign Republic of Ireland was proclaimed at the General Post Office, Dublin, where, on the same day in 1916, the rebel Patrick Pearse had launched it on its first, brief career.

With Ireland out of the Commonwealth, King George asked her new Foreign Minister: 'What does this new legislation make *me* in Ireland, an undesirable alien?' His anxieties were allayed by yet another masterpiece of Anglo-Irish understanding. It was agreed that British and Irish citizens were not to be regarded as foreigners in each others' country.

Barely ten days later, the King dealt with another political conundrum. Nehru, for all his fulminations in the past, now wanted India to be a republic within the Commonwealth. But as George VI was king of the Commonwealth, how could a republic have a king? This was the problem that confronted the King and his Commonwealth prime ministers, at that moment in conference in London. All were enthusiastic to keep India 'in', and the King, disregarding his majesty, suggested that he might become President of the Indian Republic. So did that inveterate monarchist, Churchill. But Attlee and the prime ministers hit on a better title: Head of the Commonwealth.

On 27 April 1949, the King received his prime ministers in the White Drawing Room at Buckingham Palace. It was a historic meeting from which emerged a new concept of the British Commonwealth, a new meaning to the Crown. The King told his prime ministers that their solution was 'a striking example of the elasticity of our system. So far', he went on, 'it has stood tests such as no association of nations in history has ever survived.' The Commonwealth, he believed, possessed 'immense powers of good for humanity'.

So, a few days after the Republic of Ireland, rejecting de Valera's idea of external association, had quit the Commonwealth, the Republic of India adopted it and became a member. India had understood that the Commonwealth meant independence plus not independence minus. Ireland and Burma apparently had not. As decolonization went ahead, the external association idea caught on, and the British sovereign became head of many new republics.

The day of that historic meeting, the King was still con-

valescing from a serious operation. The war years had
exhausted him, the South African Tour had claimed 17
of the 140-odd lbs of his spare, lithe frame. A few months
after his return, he began to suffer from cramp in both
legs. In July 1948, during his customary visit to Holyrood
Palace, Edinburgh, I walked with him one evening as he
climbed the hill called Arthur's Seat, behind the palace.
Ordinarily, the King had, for his height and build, an
amazingly long, steady stride. Once I asked him how he
acquired it. He replied that he had developed it 'when
I was a small boy. It was the only way of keeping up with
my father.' But that evening the King made heavy going
of the climb; again and again he exploded angrily:
'What's the matter with my legs? They won't work
properly.'

Despite the discomfort, he went through with his heavy
programme of engagements until, in late October, he sent
for his doctors. So alarmed were they by his condition
that they believed the amputation of his right leg un-
avoidable. Meanwhile, treatment and complete rest were
prescribed. A bulletin told the King's anxious subjects
that there was an acute obstruction in the arteries of the
legs and added: 'There is no doubt that the strain of the
last twelve years has appreciably affected his resistance to
physical fatigue.'

The treatment saved the right leg, but to improve the
circulation the doctors decided on a lumbar-sympath-
ectomy operation. It was performed by Professor James
Learmonth, of Edinburgh University. The news of its
success spread fast, as London newsvendors scrawled on
their placards: 'He's all right.'

The King, however, was told that the operation, though
successful, was only a palliative, not a cure. It could not
be repeated. A second thrombosis might be fatal. Further
than this warning his doctors did not go, though it is
likely that they had discovered that the King's arteries
were already hardening prematurely and that another
thrombosis – the one that would within three years end
his life – was inevitable.

Professor Learmonth cautioned his patient: he must in future take things easier and adapt himself to a régime which would take less out of him.

The professor, a quiet-spoken Scot with a pleasant twinkle in his eye and an almost boyish shyness, was the last person one would suspect of being Regius Professor of Clinical Surgery at Edinburgh University, one-time member of the staff of the Mayo Clinic and one of the world's leading practitioners in vascular surgery. Always ready for a joke, there was none he ever enjoyed more than when the King, at the end of a routine examination, said to him gravely 'You have used a knife on me, now I am going to use one on you.' The astonished professor was ordered to kneel while the King, taking his sword, bestowed on him the accolade of knighthood.

The King's flair for discovery had made him deeply interested in his own case and he willingly adjusted himself to his go-slow régime. He had no intention, however, of depriving himself of his favourite sport, shooting. But to reduce the strain on his legs while walking the Balmoral grouse moors he invented a special harness by means of which he attached himself behind a pony; the pony did all the work while the King merely moved his legs. One vital detail the royal inventor incorporated in the harness: a parachute 'quick-release box' – in case the pony bolted.

By August 1949 the King was writing to his mother, Queen Mary, from Balmoral 'I am feeling ever so well in this good fresh air & I am trying to worry less about matters political.'

But for the convalescent King there was no escape from the cares of state. As the gloom and tension of the cold war persisted, Britain sank deeper and deeper into an economic morass. The pound was drastically devalued; the meat ration was cut to 1s (14 cents) a week, and sugar to 8 ozs (200 grammes). Only the imagination and sympathy of the United States, as the King said in his Christmas 1949 broadcast, saw Britain through. But by the end of the following year, the US and Britain had fallen out

bitterly over the conduct of the Korean war. 'I have been
very worried lately,' the King told Premier Attlee as the
latter hastened to Washington to straighten things out
with Truman. When he only partially succeeded, the
King felt more depressed. He wrote to a friend: 'The
incessant worries and crises through which we have to
live got me down properly.'

Although the King's programme had been curtailed
and he himself, fully aware of the danger of another
attack of thrombosis, was conscientiously observing the
go-slow régime, people began to notice how tired he was
looking. In May 1951 he and the Queen took a week's
break at Balmoral. It was perhaps the most peaceful, if the
shortest, holiday of their reign. The arrangements were
kept to a minimum; only a lady-in-waiting and myself
accompanied them. During that week in the highlands
they enjoyed utter, untrammelled peace, walking, fishing
or just lazing, as the spirit moved them. The sun shone
from a cloudless sky and the warm air was full of the
smell of pines. For once the King could get out and away
from it all (as he had once put it), where the only sounds
were the rustle of spring, the murmur of the River Dee
and the crackle of fircones as they burst open in the heat.

These blissful conditions relaxed the King. But he
needed not a week, but a month or two or three to help
him over the let-down after years of nervous and physical
stress. For him, however, there was no release; pressing
duties awaited him in London.

By the end of May 1951 people noticed that he was
looking thoroughly ill. His doctors treated him for an
inflammation on the left lung, but he recovered slowly:
though only fifty-five, weariness of mind and body had
laid him low. Before leaving for Balmoral in August,
however, he was able to write: 'I feel I am getting
stronger.' Yet to those who were with him it was obvious
that he was far from his usual form. He no longer strode
on the hill with his light, long gait. Instead he laboured,
coughing, and halted frequently to lean on his crummock
(long walking-stick). In the evening he left his guests early

and retired, but not always to a peaceful sleep.

The King's doctors were summoned; they advised him to return immediately to London. It was mid-September when he left his Scottish home – for the last time. After an examination in London on 18 September the King was told that his left lung would have to be removed. The medical bulletin of that day mentioned that 'structural changes had developed in the lung', but the King was not told, neither did he apparently suspect, that the lung was affected by cancer. He broke the news of the operation to his wife and his mother and that evening he confided to Prime Minister Attlee – not, he explained, as King, but as the father of Princess Elizabeth, that the critical operation that he was about to undergo might not, even if he survived it, leave him long to live.

The operation was performed on 23 September 1951 by Mr Price Thomas, Surgeon to the Brompton Hospital for Diseases of the Chest. Only three days later, state papers requiring his assent were laid before the King. Though still very weak, he signed them in his round, slightly sloping hand. Less than three weeks later he was writing with his habitual impulsiveness 'I must now start to get up and do more to get stronger.'

It was at about this time that I met him in the corridor outside his room at Buckingham Palace. Clad in a blue dressing-gown, he looked frail and thin. But he smiled warmly, almost apologetically – for when he spoke it was not in his firm, deep voice, but in a thin whisper.

The King now knew that the two operations for his arterial and lung complaints had put him under a double sentence of death whose execution might not for long be stayed. When someone suggested that Princess Elizabeth might read his Christmas 1951 message, he replied 'my daughter may have her opportunity next Christmas'. His own six-minutes' broadcast which, to save him the strain, had been recorded bit by bit, alarmed, by the harsh quality of his voice, his millions of listeners. It included a phrase typical of him: 'It is in bad times that we value most highly the support and sympathy of our friends.' And he thanked 'the people in these islands and the British Commonwealth ... from all my heart'.

With the knowledge that he was condemned, King George's courage faced the supreme test. It had never failed him in the past; while still in his 'teens it was said of him that 'he shows grit and a "never say I'm beaten" spirit'. A friend said of him 'he has tremendous guts' – the quiet sort of guts which does not show but is the highest form of courage. It had seen him through his shyness and the humiliation of his stammer, through the torment of the abdication and the blackest periods of the war, when all seemed lost; it never deserted him throughout the post-war gloom as his Empire broke up and his kingdom retrogressed into poverty and economic ruin.

King George was deeply religious; he was of the stuff of John Bunyan's Pilgrim:

> He who would valiant be 'gainst all disaster
> Let him in constancy follow the Master.

His valour stemmed from deep wells of religious conviction – as it does with most devoted and purposeful men, be they kings or kamikaze crews. His religious convictions, added to his belief in the mystique of monarchy, gave him a material detachment from events which might have shattered the lives of ordinary men. But they did not exonerate him from spiritual and moral involvement, which he felt very deeply. It the divine right of kings was a doctrine of the past, King George believed sincerely in the divine duty of kings and its thorough, selfless execution. He above all, and his family with him, impersonated the British nation, Commonwealth and Empire. There was no question for him, then, of giving way before adversity, in whatever guise it might appear.

Immense as was the King's intrinsic courage, it was profoundly inspired by the love he bore for his family. He was first and foremost a family man. He described his wife Queen Elizabeth as 'the most marvellous person in the world in my eyes'. Of his daughter and heiress

Princess Elizabeth he thus divulged his thoughts as he led her to the altar: 'I was so proud of you and thrilled at having you so close to me on our long walk in Westminster Abbey, but when I handed your hand to the Archbishop I felt I had lost something very precious.' Though little is recorded of what he felt for his younger daughter Margaret, anyone could tell by his expression that he was enchanted by her. Summing up his family he wrote 'Our family, us four, the Royal Family, must remain together.'

Beyond his own family, his next most uplifting inspiration came from the great family of nations of which he was Head. He had never deviated from his resolution, made the day of his accession, 'to work before all else for the welfare of the British Commonwealth of Nations'. His subjects responded warm-heartedly; at his Silver Wedding in 1948 he noted with typical modesty 'We are both dumbfounded ... we have received so many nice letters during these years.' Then, as he was struck down by his first illness he spoke gratefully of 'the wave of sympathy and concern which flowed back to me from friends known and unknown in this old country and in every one of the great brotherhood of nations to which we all belong'. The 'brotherhood' was now no hollow expression, for it still included the five hundred million inhabitants of India and Pakistan.

Recovering with surprising speed from his latest ordeal, he was again greatly cheered by 'the wonderful messages from all and sundry' as he described the thousands of letters which poured in from all parts of the Commonwealth – and the world beyond. Among them was one from Dr François Malan, now prime minister of South Africa, the anti-monarchist who had snubbed the King during his visit there. Malan was big enough to put sentiment before politics; he offered his official residence in Natal for the King's convalescence. The King sent me to look at the house. I reported on it to him at Sandringham at the end of January 1952. He seemed well and cheerful. His doctors were pleased with him and he was looking forward to a holiday in the sun.

On 30th January the King was in London for a family reunion on the eve of Princess Elizabeth's and Prince Philip's departure to Africa, Australia and New Zealand. That evening he took his family to Drury Lane theatre to see *South Pacific*. He was obviously enjoying himself and delighted at hearing Mary Martin and the company singing the hit tunes that he often hummed himself.

Next day at London airport he waved his daughter away on her long journey. His face showed signs of all he had been through, but standing there hatless in a cutting wind it was as if he meant to defy the gloomy prognostications about his health and thereby reassure his daughter. Some years ago I had watched his touching leave-taking of the Queen, in his eyes 'the most marvellous person in the world', when he flew off to see his fighting men. Now it was his turn to say farewell to one whose parting left him with the feeling of losing 'something very precious'. Both father and daughter knew that they might be parted for ever. If that was to be she would always remember this last sight of him – upright, fearless, his face turned squarely towards the future which, sooner than either imagined, would pass from his hands to hers. Never could he have felt more the meaning of those words he had quoted to his people at another moment of truth (see page 135): 'Go out into the darkness and put your hand into the Hand of God. That shall be better to you than light and safer than a known way.'

The King returned to Sandringham, there to throw himself once more into his work and his favourite sport. Tuesday the 5th of January was, as Mr Churchill described it, 'a happy day of sunshine and sport'. At the end of the day the King told his shooting guests, 'I shall expect you back at 9 o'clock on Thursday.'

On the morning of 6 February, I was in my office in London when a colleague walked in. 'I suppose you have heard?' he said. 'Heard what?' I asked. He hesitated a moment, then said, 'The King is dead.'

Bibliography

The Royal Family
Bolitho, Hector, *George VI* (1937)
Brown, Ivor, *Balmoral* (1955)
Buxton, Aubrey, *The King in his Country* (1955)
Darbyshire, Taylor, *King George VI* (1937)
Darbyshire, Taylor, *In the Words of the King* (1938)
Donaldson, Frances, *Edward VIII* (1974)
Fjellman, Margit, *Louise Mountbatten, Queen of Sweden* (1968)
Frère, James, *The British Monarchy at Home* (1963)
His Majesty King George VI, *Speeches* (1958)
Inglis, Brian, *Abdication* (1966)
John Murray (publishers), *King George VI to his Peoples, 1936–51* (1952)
Mathams, H. H., *Crowns over England* (1937)
Marie-Louise, Princess, *My Memories of Six Reigns* (1956)
Michie, Alan, *The Crown and the People* (1952)
Morrah, Dermot, *The Royal Family in South Africa* (1947)
Nicolson, Sir Harold, *King George V* (1952)
Shew, B. P., *Queen Elizabeth the Queen Mother* (1955)
South African Railways, *Royal Visit to South Africa* (1947)
Thompson, G. M., *The Life and Times of King George VI* (1953)
Wheeler-Bennett, Sir John, *King George VI* (1965)
Windsor, Duke of, *A King's Story* (1951)
Windsor, Duke of, *The Crown and the People* (1953)

India
Ali, Chaudhri Muhammed, *The Emergence of Pakistan* (1967)
Ambedkar, B. R., *Pakistan or Partition of India* (1945)
Azad, A. K., *India Wins Freedom* (1959)
Birla, G. D., *In the Shadow of the Mahatma* (1952)

Bolitho, Hector, *Jinnah, Creator of Pakistan* (1954)

Brecher, M., *Nehru, a political biography* (1959)

Brittain, Vera, *Pethwick Lawrence, a Portrait* (1963)

Cameron, James, *An Indian Summer* (1973)

Campbell-Johnson, Alan, *Mission with Mountbatten* (1951)

Casey, R. G., *An Australian in India* (1967)

Chaudhuri, N. C., *An Autobiography of an Unknown Indian* (1951)

Connell, J., *Auchinleck* (1952)

Das, Durga, *India, from Curzon to Nehru and after* (1969)

Duncan, R. (Ed.) *Selected Writings of Mahatma Gandhi* (1951)

Fischer, Louis, *The Life of Mahatma Gandhi* (1951)

Gandhi, M. K., *Delhi Diary* (1948)

Gandhi, M. K., *An Autobiography, or the Story of my experiments with Truth* (1927)

Ghosh, Sudhir, *Gandhi's Emissary* (1967)

Glendevon, John, *The Viceroy at Bay* (1971)

Griffiths, Sir Percival, *The British in India* (1946)

Griffiths, Sir Percival, *Modern India* (1957)

Halifax, Earl of, *Fulness of Days* (1957)

Hodson, H. V., *The Great Divide* (1969)

Iqbal, Muhammad, *Stray Reflections* (1961)

Ismay, Lord, *Memoirs* (1960)

Kaliquzzaman, C., *Pathway to Pakistan* (1961)

Mayo, Katherine, *Mother India* (1927)

Menon, V. P., *The Transfer of Power in India* (1957)

Moon, Penderel, *Divide and Quit* (1961)

Mosley, Leonard, *The Last Days of the British Raj* (1961)

Mountbatten, Earl, *Time only to look forward* (1949)

Murphy, Ray, *The Last Viceroy* (1948)

Nehru, Jawaharlal, *An Autobiography* (Reprinted with additional chapter, 1942)

Nehru, Jawaharlal, *Discovery of India* (1945)

Norman, D., (Ed.) *Nehru, The First Sixty Years*, 2 vols (1965)

Philips, C. H. and Wainwright, M. D., *The Partition of India* (1970)

Pyarelal, *Mahatma Gandhi, The Last Phase*, 2 vols (1956–8)

Russell, W. W., *Indian Summer* (1952)

Segal, R., *The Crisis of India* (1965)

Tagore, Rabindranath, *Collected Poems and Plays* (1955)

Tendulkar, D. G., *Mahatma*, Vol. V of VIII vols (1952)

Tuker, Sir Francis, *While Memory Serves* (1950)

Wavell, Earl, *The Viceroy's Journal* (1973)

Woodcock, George, *Gandhi* (1972)

Woodruff, Philip, *The Men who Ruled India*, Vol I *The Founders* (1953) and Vol II *The Guardians* (1954)

Burma

Collis, M., *Last and First in Burma* (1956)

Donnison, F. S. V., *Public Administration in Burma* (1953)

Donnison, F. S. V., *Burma* (1970)

Maung Maung, *Aung San of Burma* (1962)

Maung Maung, *A Trial in Burma* (1962)

Tinker, Hugh, *The Union of Burma* (1967)

Trager, Frank, *Burma; a historical and political analysis* (1966)

Woodman, Dorothy, *The Making of Burma* (1962)

Ireland

Bromage, Mary, *De Valera and the March of a Nation* (1965)

Longford, Earl of, *Eamon de Valera* (1970)

MacManus, M. J., *Eamon de Valera* (1957)

Palestine

Alem, Jean-Pierre, *Juifs et Arabes, 3000 ans d'histoire* (1968)

Bar Zohar, Michael, *The Armed Prophet* (1967)

Begin, Menachem, *The Revolt* (1964)

Ben Gurion, David, *Recollections* (1970)

Ben Gurion, David, *Israel: Years of Challenge* (1963)

Berlin, Isaiah, *Chaim Weizmann* (1958)

Cohen, Geula, *Woman of Violence* (1966)

Collins, Larry and Lapierre, Dominique, *O Jerusalem* (1972)

Derogy, Jacques, *La Loi de Retour* (1969)

Edelman, Maurice, *The Story of Ben Gurion* (1965)

Farran, Roy, *Winged Dagger* (1948)

Furlonge, Geoffrey, *Palestine is my country: the story of Musa Alami* (1969)

Glubb, Sir John, *Britain and the Arabs* (1959)

Hadawi, Sami, *Bitter Harvest* (1967)

Hecht, Ben, *A Child of the Century*, Book Six *The Committee* (1954)

Hyamson, H. M., *Palestine under the Mandate* (1950)

Kessel, Joseph, *Terre d'Amour et de Feu* (1965)

Kimche, Jon, *Seven Fallen Pillars* (1953)

Latour, Anny, *The Resurrection of Israel* (1968)

Litvinoff, Barnet, *Ben Gurion of Israel* (1954)

Longrigg, S. H., *Oil in the Middle East* (1954)

Rose, N. A., (Ed.), *Baffy: The Diaries of Blanche Dugdale, 1936–47* (1973)

Roth, Cecil, *History of the Jews* (1954)

Samuel, Viscount, *Memoirs* (1945)

Samuel, Maurice, *Light on Israel* (1968)

Soustelle, Jacques, *La Longue Marche d'Israel* (1968)

Stein, Leonard, *The Balfour Declaration* (1961)

Survey of Palestine [For the Anglo-American Committee of Enquiry] (1945–6)

Supplement to Survey of Palestine [for the United Nations Special Committee on Palestine] (1947)

Sykes, Christopher, *Cross-roads to Israel* (1965)

Trevor, Daphne, *Under the White Paper* (1948)

Uris, Léon, *Exodus* (1959)

Vester, Bertha, *Our Jerusalem* (1950)

Weisgal, M., and Carmichael, J., *Chaim Weizmann* (1963)

Weizmann, Chaim, *Trial and Error* (1949)

Weizmann, Vera, *The Impossible Takes Longer* (1967)

General

Agar, Herbert, *Britain Alone* (1972)

Attlee, C. R., *As it Happened* (1954)

Bagehot, Walter, *The English Constitution* (1920; first published 1867)

Barnett, Correlli, *The Collapse of British Power* (1972)

Bullock, Alan, *Hitler, a study in tyranny* (1952)

Bullock, Alan, *The Life and Times of Ernest Bevin* (1960)

Churchill, Sir Winston, *The Second World War*, 6 vols (1948–54)

Cross, Colin, *The Fall of the British Empire* (1968)

Fieldhouse, D. K., *The Colonial Empire* (1965)

Grierson, Edward, *The Imperial Dream* (1972)

Kipling, Rudyard, *Sixty Poems* (1939)

Mansergh, Nicholas, *Survey of British Commonwealth Affairs, 1939–1952* (1958)

Mansergh, Nicholas, *The Commonwealth and the Nations* (1968)

Mockford, Julian, *Here are South Africans* (1944)

Millis, W. (Ed.), *The Forrestal Diaries* (1951)

Morris, James, *Pax Britannica* (1968)

Morrison, Herbert, *Government and Parliament* (1954)

Nasser, Gamal Abdul, *Egypt's Liberation* (1955)

Roosevelt, Eleanor, *This I Remember* (1947)

Roosevelt, Elliott, *As he saw it* (1946)

Shirer, William, *The Rise and Fall of the Third Reich* (1960)

Smuts, J. C., *Jan Christian Smuts* (1952)

Stark, Freya, *Dust in the Lion's Paw* (1961)

Sykes, Christopher, *Orde Wingate* (1959)

Truman, Harry S., *Year of Decisions* (1955)

Truman, Harry S., *Years of Trial and Hope* (1956)

Williams, Francis, *Ernest Bevin* (1952)

Williams, Francis, *A Prime Minister Remembers* (1961)

Young, Desmond, *Try Anything Twice* (1963)

Newspapers and Periodicals

British
The Daily Express

The Daily Mirror
The Daily Telegraph
The Manchester Guardian
The Times

American
The New York Times
The United Palestine Yearbook

Irish
The Irish Independent
The Irish Press

Jewish
The Jewish Clarion
The Jewish Struggle
Miroir de l'Histoire – Les Combats d'Israël

Indian
Amrita Bazar Patrika
Calcutta Municipal Gazette
Dawn
The Hindu
Hindusthan Standard
Illustrated Weekly of India
Morning News
Star of India
The Statesman
Times of India

Other references
The Annual Register
Encyclopaedia Britannica
Hansard
The Round Table
Whitaker's Almanack

Author's Acknowledgements

I am grateful to Sir Martin Charteris, the Queen's Private Secretary and Keeper of the Royal Archives, and to Sir John Wheeler-Bennett, King George VI's biographer, for clearing up certain points.

Admiral of the Fleet Lord Mountbatten helped me generously. I consulted him at length about the events during his time as 'Supremo' and as the last Viceroy. I am greatly indebted to him for reading the relevant passages and for his invaluable suggestions.

I was particularly touched by the kindness of Sir Hubert Rance, last Governor of Burma, in receiving me. It was over twenty-five years since we had met, when he came to see the King on taking up his appointment. Though now in poor health Sir Hubert was keen to help. He died before he could do so, but during our pleasant meeting I was able to understand why Aung San, Burma's youthful leader, found him such a good friend. I am grateful to Lady Rance and to Philip Nash, the Governor's Chief Secretary, for arranging this meeting.

Lord Hartwell, Chairman of the Daily Telegraph, most hospitably offered me a spacious office in which I was able to relive the past day by day from hundreds of back numbers of his newspaper. The BBC kindly provided me with a similar experience, allowing me access to their Sound Archives and a number of scripts. I acknowledge, too, the courtesy and help of the London Library, the India Office Library and the Colindale Library.

Despite my expressed feelings about the terrorism in Palestine, I thank its chief practioner, Menachem Begin, for receiving me in his home in Tel Aviv. Happily he has mellowed with the years and even conceded that the British were second after the Persians as benefactors to exiled Jewry. One of his men, David Niv (now Irgun's historian), helped me to understand the mentality of the Jewish freedom-fighters.

During more than two years of research I was fortunate enough to have the expert help of Ann Meo and Deborah Sutherland, of Jeff Goldman in the United States, and of Nicole Gaudfroy who classified the mass of information. Marjorie Gerson tracked down scores of out-of-print books; her knowledge in this specialized market was indispensable to me. I am also very grateful to my friends Dominique Lapierre and Larry Collins for the loan of several books on Palestine.

Finally I express my profound thanks to the very large number of people who, in response to my appeal, sent me written reports, diaries and photos. Some of their names appear in the text. Lack of space forbids me to thank them all by name but I should like to assure them that every one of their eye-witness accounts and every photo and document had its place in helping me to understand what the British lived through in India, Burma and Palestine during those troubled times when the dismantling of the Empire began.

Index